FROM BANKING
TO THE THORNY
WORLD OF
POLITICS

FROM
BANKING
TO THE THORNY
WORLD OF
POLITICS

SHAUKAT
AZIZ WITH ANNA MIKHAILOVA

QUARTET

First published in 2016 by Quartet Books Limited
A member of the Namara Group
27 Goodge Street, London W1T 2LD
Copyright © Shaukat Aziz 2016
The right of Shaukat Aziz to be identified
as the author of this work has been asserted
by him in accordance with the
Copyright Designs and Patents Act, 1988
A catalogue record for this book
is available from the British Library
ISBN 978 070 437 399 0
Typeset by Josh Bryson
Printed and bound in Great Britain by
T J International Ltd, Padstow, Cornwall

To the people of Pakistan,
my parents,
my wife Rukhsana
and my children, Lubna, Abid and Maha

CONTENTS

INTRODUCTION
THE PHONE CALL

News of the coup came at half past five on a crisp October day. I was sitting in my executive office in 399 Park Avenue, with New York bustling fifteen floors below me. As the head of global wealth management for Citigroup, I was part of the inner sanctum of one of the biggest banks in the world. But, that afternoon, all my attention was focused on the television screen in front of me.

A man in a camouflage commando uniform with red lapels appeared on CNN. He sat behind a plain wooden desk with a portrait of Pakistan's founder, Quaid-i-Azam Mohammad Ali Jinnah, behind him and the national flag to his right. General Musharraf's eyes flickered behind rimless glasses as he read out his speech. It was short and to the point – his plane had not been allowed to land after three fire trucks had blocked the runway in Karachi. Nearby airports had also been shut. As his PK805 started running dangerously low on fuel, its options for a safe descent narrowed. The army stepped in, cleared the runway and seized the control tower at Karachi airport. There was just seven minutes-worth of fuel to spare when the plane finally landed.

By 2 a.m., the coup was a done deal and General Pervez Musharraf made his announcement on air, ousting Nawaz Sharif, the elected prime minister, from power. The general declared martial law in a loud, clear voice, his punchy and brief sentences ringing out on television screens across the

1

world. He vowed the military would 'preserve the country's integrity to the last drop of our blood.'

My first thought was whether there would be any violence. Concern for my homeland and the family I had back in Pakistan put me on edge. At the same time, I could not help feeling disappointed: in more than five decades since independence, Pakistan had still not managed to find a way to constitutionally replace governments. Its short history already included three periods of military rule and no democratically elected government had ever completed a full term. I also wondered what would happen to Nawaz Sharif – I had known the deposed prime minister since my early days in Citibank. When I was head of its Lahore branch, he and his brother Shahbaz Sharif would come in to negotiate credit facilities for their steel business.

But, after watching the television report, I got on with my life. It was 1999 and only a year after Citibank had gone through the biggest merger in history, with Travelers Group. The face of Wall Street was rapidly changing, and we were leading the way. The Glass-Steagall Act was repealed that year, paving the way for banking 'supermarkets' that provided everything from loans to insurance. I was the head of Citigroup's global private bank, in charge of managing ultra-high net worth business. My corner office – Wall Street shorthand for having made it – used to belong to Walt Wriston, the bank's legendary chairman who had built its reputation in the 1970s and 1980s. It was here that, two days after General Musharraf's television announcement, my life completely changed. I was halfway through a meeting when my secretary Pamela rushed in and said: 'I've got a general on the line. The one on the news the other day.'

I was taken aback. The army is the most powerful institution in Pakistan – the reputation of its reach and effectiveness precedes it. But, until then, I had lived my life without coming into contact with it. I had never met General Musharraf or any of the serving generals who made up his corps command. I had not set foot inside army headquarters or any other military buildings in Pakistan. As I walked over to my desk, I wondered what the army chief might want. Drawing a blank, I tentatively picked up the phone.

I listened patiently while General Musharraf launched into a monologue about his vision for Pakistan and the myriad of problems it faced.

'I want to get the country on the right track,' he said, adding that the economy was a major part of this. He was building his team and wanted to meet me. Could I come to Pakistan for a chat?

Surprised, I asked for time to think about it.

I went to see my Citigroup bosses, the two co-CEOs of the bank, John Reed and Sandy Weill. John encouraged me to hear what the army chief had to say. Sandy was excited for me and exuberantly suggested I take the bank's plane. Thinking this would draw too much attention – Musharraf had told me to keep the purpose of my visit quiet – I boarded a commercial flight to Islamabad.

A suit among uniforms

And that is how I found myself on a mild day in Rawalpindi, sitting in front of half a dozen generals in khaki-coloured uniforms. After getting a night's sleep in my hotel, I had been promptly driven to the army's General Headquarters and led into the Chief of General Staff's office for this meeting. My unfamiliarity with the military meant they all looked the same to me – a panel of upright figures with closely-cut black hair. The one face I would have recognised from the news – General Musharraf – was distinctly absent. It was the first of several surprises during my initial encounter with Pakistan's new leadership.

As I sat drinking their sweet, hand-stirred coffee, the generals began to ask me questions. Among them were General Aziz Khan, Chief of General Staff, and his deputy, General Orakzai, as well as General Ehsan ul Haq, head of military intelligence. My jetlag quickly disappeared.

General Aziz led the discussion. He asked me: 'What do you think about Pakistan's economy and how quickly can it be fixed?'

Thinking on my feet, I replied: 'Pakistan has tremendous potential, good human capital and a wealth of natural resources – but because of frequent changes of government and the absence of a reform agenda, it has struggled.' They asked what could be done and I told them there were no instant solutions and some tough decisions would undoubtedly have to be made.

However, the meeting soon became dominated by questions about me. It felt like a job interview for a government position I had not applied for. There are always people who lobby for government posts – regardless of who is in power. I was suddenly conscious of looking like this was the purpose of my visit. 'I came under the impression that General Musharraf wanted to see me for my advice,' I said, feeling increasingly uneasy about his continued absence.

'General Musharraf will receive you at his private residence for dinner tonight,' one of the commanders said. I politely explained I could not stay the night – I had a plane to catch back to New York. We agreed to have a quick discussion before my flight instead and General Aziz accompanied me to Army House.

I was not sure what to expect. The last I'd seen of Musharraf was at the end of his television announcement, when he climbed into the back of a black Mercedes and sped away with his security detail in tow. On entering Army House, I sat down on a sofa in the traditional-looking waiting room. The army chief's principal secretary, Tariq Aziz, was there, along with General Mahmud, the head of the ISI, Pakistan's intelligence service. Finally, General Musharraf walked in, dressed in a casual shirt and trousers. Gone were the uniform and dark army cap.

'Welcome! I am just in the middle of writing my speech to the nation,' he said. Perhaps it was the contrast with seeing him in uniform, but my first impression was that he was quite humble and down to earth. He gave me a warm reception and asked what I thought of Pakistan's economy. I repeated the points I had made to the generals – the country's foreign exchange reserves were at an all-time low and, to make matters worse, markets would not react well to his military coup. But it could be improved if the government was willing to create an enabling environment for growth and reform.

General Musharraf listened patiently. After a long pause, he asked: 'If we decide to take you, can you start next week?' He had not yet chosen which position to offer, but it was between finance minister and a few other possible roles. He also made it clear that I was not the only candidate.

Realising that this was all more serious than previously anticipated, I felt a rush of excitement and anxiety at the prospect of having to take charge of a troubled economy of nearly 140 million people.[1]

I drove to the airport in a half-daze, consumed by thoughts of the day's events. During a brief transit stop in Karachi, while rushing to get from one gate to another, I almost collided with

5

a tall figure coming quickly towards me. We both stopped in our tracks and, to my surprise, he called out: 'Shaukat!' It was Imran Khan, the cricket legend turned politician – I knew him from attending fundraisers for his cancer hospital in Lahore.

'What are you doing here? Don't tell me you're meeting Musharraf!' he exclaimed. I just smiled. I knew my body language could not lie, so I quickly told him I had to catch a flight and rushed along. But news of my trip was already starting to get out.

Back in New York, I told John Reed and Sandy Weill about my meeting with General Musharraf and asked them to prepare a contingency plan, in case I was offered the position. But there was no word from the new chief in Islamabad, so I went back to business as usual. I travelled to Evian in France for our annual budgetary review of the European private bank division and hosted twenty-five executives who ran our European, Middle East and Africa wealth management businesses. Looking out on the peaceful shores of Lake Geneva from the Hotel Royal, I had time to reflect. I had a number of concerns about joining a military government. The international community was bound to frown upon a coup, and there was the question of how the courts would look at the takeover, namely whether it would be deemed constitutional. Even if it was, could I uproot my family and leave a thirty-year career in a respected global institution like Citibank for an uncertain future?

The journey back from Evian involved a brief stop in London for a day of meetings. To my surprise, General Aziz called me in my hotel room.

'How did you know I was here?' was one of the first things I said.

'We have ways of finding out,' he laughed before quickly getting to the point. 'We want you in the new cabinet, as minister of finance and commerce.'

I asked when he would need me to start.

'Immediately,' he replied. I told him I required at least two weeks – I had about 3,000 people working for me in Citibank and leaving abruptly was not exactly simple.

'OK, give us a date as soon as you can,' he said and hung up.

How do you pack up your life in two weeks? By taking that call in October, I had pressed the reset button for my family and myself. I discussed General Musharraf's offer with my wife, Rukhsana, and we weighed up the pros and cons of making the move. Citigroup, in particular John Reed, was fully supportive.

I met with Bob Rubin, the former US Secretary of the Treasury and then a senior executive of Citigroup, to ask for his thoughts on the task ahead. We talked through the main issues facing Pakistan and he gave me valuable advice on how to deal with deficits, build the country's credibility and raise money. I also consulted several friends, including Paul Collins and Richard Huber, my former bosses in the bank, as well as Shuaib Ahmed and Shahzad Husain, former Citibank executives I had worked with in Pakistan. I had no illusions about the challenges ahead. Pakistan's economy faced slow growth, low reserves, a mountain of debt and an absence of any clear strategy. I also knew that, as a technocrat parachuted in by the new leader, I would be seen as an outsider by many others in government and the country.

But the decision itself was easy. Even though I had been living outside Pakistan for more than twenty years, I welcomed the opportunity to serve my country. I always had a strong sense of being a Pakistani and I was proud of my identity and heritage. I had fond memories of going to the Republic Day military parades with my father, invited as the chief engineer of Radio Pakistan. I remember the excitement I felt as a boy watching the soldiers march past and the air force fly overhead, filling me with national pride.

I was also more than an observer of the country's economy. Both Nawaz Sharif and Benazir Bhutto had asked me to advise them in the past. It started with Nawaz Sharif – the first time he was prime minister, in the early 1990s, he came to New York and asked the embassy to arrange a meeting with a group of prominent Pakistanis working on Wall Street. We were not academics but we understood how markets and the real economy worked, we had experience of dealing with the finances of nations across the world. The prime minister invited us to fly to Islamabad and give presentations to him and his main economic advisers. The government suggested paying our airfare and hotel costs but I insisted on covering my own expenses. On each trip, the prime minister gave several hours of his time and we provided him with a game plan for reform. However, I felt that there was not enough buy-in from his team, so our proposals were not completely taken up.

I also knew Benazir Bhutto from my Citibank days, and always found her good-humoured and disarmingly warm. I remember one occasion in Singapore during her first term as prime minister. I was heading the bank's corporate and investment banking business in Asia-Pacific at the time and she had come on an official visit. Over a dinner hosted by Pakistan's ambassador, one of her entourage, who had previously been a guest in my Citibank residence there, turned to Benazir Bhutto and asked:

'Have you been to Shaukat's house?'

Benazir jokingly said: 'He hasn't invited me.'

I replied: 'Prime minister, you are always welcome.'

The next day, I was at home having dinner with my family. We lived in a colonial black and white villa on Swiss Club Road. As we were finishing off, a call came from the chief of protocol in Singapore. He told me Prime Minister Benazir Bhutto would be at my home in seven minutes, adding: 'The police will be coming before that, so don't panic when you see them.' Everybody rushed around, trying to make themselves presentable. Meanwhile, the advance Singapore police team arrived in its usual prompt manner.

Dressed in a bright yellow silk shirt, Benazir Bhutto arrived with her husband, Asif Ali Zardari. She wanted to spend some time in a relaxed environment after a long day, and told the Pakistan ambassador and most of her staff to go, leaving her military secretary, one security officer and an aide with her. They sat in my study while she and her husband were in the living room with us. We chatted over a light second dinner and ice cream.

About a year later I saw her again, this time while she was visiting New York. Her brother, Murtaza Bhutto, had just been killed in Karachi and she was in mourning. I made my way to her room at the Waldorf Towers, after our consul-general called me and said the prime minister wished to see me. Benazir was there with her mother and sister and I paid my condolences. But she wanted to talk about our country. It was living precariously, with low reserves, modest growth and a heavy debt burden.

'The IMF are coming to see me later today,' she said. 'Give me your advice on how to handle them.' I gave her my views about what should be done to get the economy back on track and how the IMF could help with this objective. Despite Benazir's good intentions, her two terms in government were steeped with numerous challenges that prevented her from being able to implement the necessary changes. While she was highly educated, with degrees from Oxford and Harvard, and had much of the political insight and judgment associated with her father, her lack of experience of governance when she first came to power set her back.

After years of observing Pakistan and sharing my views with Nawaz Sharif and Benazir Bhutto, I felt it was time to do more than advise and welcomed an opportunity to convert my ideas into practice. The country's many complexities and centres of power could impede potential progress. I was putting my reputation on the line, acutely aware the probability of failure was high, but welcomed the challenge nonetheless. I was still in New York when the announcement was made: I would be joining Pakistan's new government as its finance minister.

And so I said goodbye to friends and colleagues and prepared for the big move. 'Pakistan's gain is Citibank's loss,' John Reed said in his farewell speech. One of the last things I did in New York was stock up on CDs in the usual place, a shop called Naghma House on Lexington Avenue. I have always loved music and find it therapeutic – something I suspected I would need, considering the task ahead.

Needless to say, I had to say goodbye to my corporate lifestyle and my executive corner office at 399 Park Avenue. For many, power is perceived as being a means to enrichment; I was proud that in my time in government my earnings substantially went down and I had no time to look after my personal finances. I went from a senior banker's compensation package to earning a very modest government salary, and my lunches in the Citibank executive dining room gave way to a perfunctory KFC Zinger at my desk.

Perhaps naively, I thought that I could get the economy on the right track in three years and move on. I soon realised there was a mountain of work to do to get Pakistan back on its feet. At times it seemed daunting. My hours shot up from twelve to sixteen a day and I had to forget about the concept of weekends and holidays. In my eight years in government, I do not recall taking a day off – from the moment I touched down in Islamabad, it was non-stop all the way. But I refused to let the huge task we faced demoralise me – in fact I felt energised.

1
A TALE OF TWO COUPS

Inside the arrivals hall at Rawalpindi airport, two fresh-faced students hurried to reach the gate, craning their necks to catch a glimpse of the crowd coming through. It was the summer of 1966 and I had read in the newspaper that Zulfikar Ali Bhutto would be visiting Rawalpindi. He had been on a trip to Europe, after resigning as foreign minister months before. Intrigued at the prospect of seeing Bhutto, my friend Fahim Saddiqui and I decided to go and watch him land. But we were moments too late.

'He's gone. You just missed him,' a security guard told us.

'Do you know where he is staying?' I asked, undeterred.

'Try Flashman's.'

The legendary hotel's reputation preceded it. It was one of the last vestiges of the Raj, with a clientele that had predominantly consisted of British army officers and other dignitaries.

When we got there, the doorman directed us to suite number 106A on the ground floor. Bhutto's private secretary opened the door and cordially invited us in. We stepped inside and were pleasantly surprised to see Bhutto himself walk in from the bedroom and greet us. He looked dapper in a cream silk shirt and tie and a smart dark brown suit.

'You are the first to call on me,' he said – he had not even had a chance to unpack.

Bhutto was there with his wife, Nusrat, and we had a rare chance to speak to him in such a private setting. He instantly put us at ease with his charm, motioning us to sit down on the sofa in the suite's living area.

'Why don't you have an iced coffee?' he suggested, asking his private secretary to order us two tall glasses. He sat with us, drinking an orange juice, and asked questions like: 'What are you studying? What do you plan to do with your future?' We told him we were enrolled in Gordon College in Rawalpindi, in the middle of our bachelor degrees. He urged us to focus on our studies.

Fahim and I were mostly short for words, overwhelmed by the glamour of being in a five-star hotel for the first time, not to mention the private audience with Bhutto. By then he already had a great deal of resonance with the youth of Pakistan. Referred to as Quaid-i-Awam, 'People's Leader', Bhutto was a brilliant orator, an effective foreign minister and someone who had represented Pakistan well around the world. He was much admired for his intellect and gutsy style, and had left President Ayub Khan's government after publicly criticising the Tashkent Declaration – signed by the president after the 1965 war with India.

A few weeks after we met him, Bhutto began to travel up and down Pakistan, gathering support. He drew crowds of tens of thousands as people gravitated towards him in every city he visited. When I read that he was coming to Rawalpindi again, Fahim and I wasted no time before going back to the hotel. Luckily, he was staying in the same suite. We felt we were as welcome as before, although this time the room was packed with his supporters. You could feel the air crackle with excitement and anticipation. The foundations of the Pakistan Peoples Party were being laid.

Bhutto founded the party in 1967 and led it in the general election three years later. He became president while

13

the country was recovering from the trauma caused by the breakup of East and West Pakistan in 1971. He skilfully negotiated the return of Pakistani prisoners of war and astutely handled the diplomatic recognition of Bangladesh.[1] Bhutto restored the pride and morale of the defeated nation, gradually rebuilding its prestige. He strengthened Pakistan's relationship with the Middle East and China and became regarded as a truly global figure. I remember the euphoria we felt when he hosted the Islamic summit in Lahore in 1974. The roads were packed as thousands came to greet the delegates, including Anwar Sadat of Egypt, King Faisal of Saudi Arabia and Yasser Arafat, chairman of the Palestine Liberation Organisation.

However, when it came to domestic policy, Bhutto's handling of the economy left a lot to be desired. He nationalised all the banks, the biggest steel producers and major private sector industries. When he visited Beijing in 1972, even the Chinese premier, Chou En-lai, tried to dissuade him from taking these steps. As Bhutto spoke eloquently of the people's revolution in Pakistan and his plans for nationalisation, Chou En-lai recalled the difficulties faced after the 1949 Chinese revolution when the Chinese government had to appeal to former owners to run the nationalised industries.[2]

Bhutto's most fateful decision was his appointment of General Muhammad Zia-ul-Haq as head of the army. The four-star general eventually overthrew him, seizing power in a military coup in 1977 and declaring martial law. Amid the upheaval, Bhutto was charged with authorising the murder of a political opponent in 1974. The world watched as the court delivered a guilty verdict in the high-profile trial and sentenced Zulfikar Ali Bhutto to death. Government leaders and supporters across the world appealed to Zia-ul-Haq to pardon Bhutto. His lawyers set up an office in Flashman's Hotel – from which his family and supporters worked tirelessly to rebut the charges.[3] Still, the sentence was carried out. Before dawn on 4 April 1979, Bhutto was hanged in a Rawalpindi jail. I was in Jordan at the time, having been posted there by Citibank. I felt deeply saddened to lose a national leader, one I had a great amount of respect for. I remember many Pakistanis, Palestinians and Jordanians in Amman mourned Bhutto's death, once again reflecting his global stature.

This high-profile execution is just one example of the political turmoil and absence of smooth transitions of power in Pakistan's history. Few of Pakistan's leaders have emerged out of this system without recrimination. Prime Minister Liaquat Ali Khan was assassinated in broad daylight while addressing a crowd in 1951. General Zia-ul-Haq eventually perished in a plane crash. Bhutto's daughter, Benazir, was killed on the campaign trail in 2007.

Kofi Annan told me this pattern is one of the things that worries him about Pakistan's prospects. When we met in his office in Geneva in 2014, the former UN Secretary General said: 'I have a feeling serious citizens who want to help the country may be held back, because the way people treat politicians and political leaders after their term – the people who offer to serve their nation come in for such abuse and disrespect. It is not an invitation for people to enter public life.'

Not only is it domestically damaging but Pakistan's history of political turnover followed by recrimination can also affect its standing abroad. I witnessed this first hand within a few months of joining the military government in 1999. Our membership of the Commonwealth was suspended and we struggled to obtain access to certain countries. Many doors were closed to us overnight and memories of General Zia's coup and Bhutto's fateful end hung over the new government and Pakistan's deposed leader, Nawaz Sharif.

Clinton and the Saudis step up for Nawaz Sharif

Although the military coup had been bloodless, many viewed the new government with trepidation. Months after it had taken place, the fate of the former prime minister was still up in the air. Nawaz Sharif had been detained in the aftermath of the military takeover, as was his brother, Shahbaz Sharif. The deposed prime minister was charged with terrorism, hijacking and conspiracy to murder – offences which carry the death penalty in Pakistan – and fears he would meet the same fate as Bhutto mounted.

Once more, the international community rallied, with the United States and Saudi Arabia leading the way. Shortly before the court was expected to deliver its verdict, we got news that President Bill Clinton was coming to personally urge General Musharraf to spare Nawaz Sharif's life.

Clinton arrived in Islamabad on 25 March 2000. His executive jet was preceded by Air Force One, which served as a decoy, and accompanied by several other planes. His motorcade sped through the streets of Islamabad, cleared in advance for the visit. The American president came for just six hours while on his way from India and gave us a checklist of preconditions for the trip. He would not be photographed shaking hands with General Musharraf and he would not spend the night in Pakistan. Most humiliatingly for the new government, he made an extraordinary request to address the Pakistani people directly on television. During this he declared that: 'the answer to flawed democracy is not to end democracy, but to improve it' – a clear sign that the United States was not happy with the change of government in Pakistan. The brevity of Clinton's visit was further highlighted by his lengthy and much-publicised trip to India.

After he landed, President Clinton travelled to the presidential estate, where he was formally received by President Muhammad Rafiq Tarar. After this Clinton was brought to a room in the adjacent cabinet block where a meeting was held with General Musharraf. The American president was accompanied by Madeleine Albright, the Secretary of State, and the National Security Advisor Sandy Berger, among others. The Pakistani side included Musharraf's chief of staff and the ministers for foreign affairs, finance, information and the Foreign Secretary.

During our meetings, President Clinton expressed concern over Pakistan's history of leaders meeting a tragic end. 'Be very careful something like this doesn't happen. You must be able to look people in the eye,' he said, urging a spirit of compassion and reconciliation.

General Musharraf responded: 'I am not a vindictive man and I hear what you are saying. Nawaz Sharif's life will not be in danger.'

Despite the complex nature of his visit, Clinton was impressive, charming and well-spoken. I sat opposite him during an official lunch in the ballroom of the presidential residence, among sixty guests. At one point he turned to General Musharraf and said: 'I see you brought a banker over to run the finance ministry. I did the same with Bob Rubin, and he served me well as Treasury secretary.'

But even with the friendly demeanour, the official message of his trip was clear – he wanted Sharif spared and permitted to leave the country.

Less than a fortnight after President Clinton's visit, Nawaz Sharif was found guilty of terrorism and hijacking and sentenced to life imprisonment. Crucially, he was spared the death penalty.

While the United States applied its efforts to save Nawaz Sharif, Saudi Arabia also worked to help him leave Pakistan and come live in the Kingdom. During Musharraf's visit to Riyadh that year, Crown Prince Abdullah, who was actively involved in the day-to-day running of the government, raised this matter with him several times.

Even though Nawaz Sharif's life was now not in danger, months passed and he remained incarcerated. International frustration mounted at the lack of movement on the matter. At one point I had invited Rafic Hariri, the former prime minister of Lebanon who was living and working in Saudi Arabia, to come and consider some investments in Pakistan. I had got to know him while I was working in the Kingdom for Citibank and always considered him a man of integrity. Hariri accepted the invitation but later apologised and said he could not come due to the issues in the Pakistan-Saudi relationship regarding Nawaz Sharif. I briefed President Musharraf about this; soon a process of negotiations about Nawaz Sharif's release began.

Crown Prince Abdullah asked Hariri to get the process moving. His son, Saad Hariri, travelled to Pakistan to be the interlocutor with Nawaz Sharif and sign an agreement between him and Islamabad's government. The idea was to organise a discreet visit, ostensibly to explore investment opportunities in Pakistan. As finance minister, I became involved. I would meet Saad at the airport, where he would fly in on his private Boeing 777 before travelling to Attock jail to see Nawaz Sharif. His father's former pilot, Shujaat Azeem – who went on to become Pakistan's adviser on aviation – would accompany him to meet with the deposed prime minister.

Between them, Saudi Arabia and the United States were instrumental in saving Nawaz Sharif's life and helping him leave Pakistan. It was eventually agreed that the former prime minister would live in Saudi Arabia for ten years, with restrictions on travel, after signing a pardon deal with Pakistan's government. With the help of Saudi Arabia, Nawaz Sharif was finally set free at the end of 2000. He travelled to Jeddah, where he was personally received at the airport by Crown Prince Abdullah and several cabinet ministers, and given the red carpet treatment. He continued to live in a comfortable villa in Jeddah with his family until his return to Pakistan in 2007.

Shortly after Nawaz Sharif had left Pakistan, General Musharraf was a guest of the Saudi government for the Hajj pilgrimage. He invited me and Abdul Sattar, the foreign minister, to join him and stay in the royal protocol apartments in Mina. As I strolled through the royal compound with Abdul Sattar, I heard a familiar voice shout out my name. It was Nawaz Sharif, taking a walk with his grandchildren. As I later entered the lobby of our apartment block, I saw General Musharraf and his wife Sehba. I told him: 'We just met Nawaz Sharif outside. He is staying in a royal protocol building, in the same compound as us.' To his credit, Musharraf took it in his stride.

Governing Pakistan

By the time I joined the government, Pakistan's political system had been interrupted on four occasions by military coups in its relatively short history – orchestrated by Ayub Khan in 1958, Yahya Khan in 1969, General Zia in 1977 and General Musharraf in 1999. Several other attempts had been unsuccessful, while elected politicians struggled with poor governance, accusations of wrongdoing and an inability to improve the country's prospects. Until 2007, no civilian government had completed a full term in office.

We must ask ourselves why Pakistan has not been able to achieve political stability in the years since its independence. Moreover, what has prevented it from being able to successfully calibrate the relationship between its political and military establishments?

One of the major challenges in Pakistan, and the source of both its historical political instability and poor policy-making, is the weakness of its political institutions. In part, the explanation for this can be traced back to Partition in 1947, when Pakistan was created to give Muslims a home.

The British Empire had been distinguished by its decentralised system of governance, with its colonies running their own agendas. This helped those countries inherit the culture of democratic institutions, when they eventually became independent. In contrast, the Spanish style of managing its colonies from Madrid arguably made it harder for South American countries to establish democracy.[4]

However, the institutions of government set up by the British in the Raj were largely concentrated in the Indian part of the subcontinent – as was the bulk of the infrastructure and development efforts. Moreover, Muslims had not been well represented in the Raj's civil bureaucracies. This meant that the newly-formed Pakistan did not inherit the same foundations of democracy and established institutions. It also did not have the same long-term political and cultural movements that could create the social basis of a centralised state, while inheriting its own complex tribal structures, which had their own traditions, customs and processes.

Pakistan's founder, Mohammad Ali Jinnah, had rallied the nation with his vision and energy and he led the Muslim

League to advocate giving Muslims their own country. His death after only one year in office, however, and the assassination of the first prime minister, Liaquat Ali Khan, made it hard for the Muslim League to develop a strong political culture. The party splintered within just a decade of Pakistan's creation.[5]

Since then, frequent changes of government have made it harder for democratic institutions to mature and develop. As Pakistan's former Foreign Secretary, Riaz Mohammad Khan, states in his book, *Afghanistan and Pakistan: Conflict, Extremism and Resistance to Modernity*: 'Every change of government would bring about a change of administrative and police officials and new, politically-motivated recruitment. The deterioration was across the board.'[6]

Unlike previous military leaders who had seized power in a coup, General Musharraf did not surround himself with men in uniform and there was a distinct lack of serving members of the military in the new cabinet. It undoubtedly boosted Musharraf's brand to recruit technocrats and helped the new government to be accepted by the international community.

The constitution was amended to allow General Musharraf to hold the offices of both president and army chief. It also provided for the restitution of the president's power to dismiss Parliament.[7] His new empowered role as chief executive essentially combined the powers of the president and the prime minister into one entity. He chaired cabinet meetings and had the political authority to push through the substantial structural reform Pakistan needed. Although the country's democratic process had been interrupted, the new government functioned in an efficient and expedient way in those early years.

I had a constructive working relationship with General Musharraf and he provided me with sufficient space to operate without interference. When it came to tough decisions regarding the economy, I did not need to struggle to get him on board. Occasionally certain interests overlapped and I had to argue my case for the more difficult measures, so I would come to him and say: 'We've got to bite the bullet.'

One day he asked me: 'How many more bullets do you want me to bite?'

He later tried to legitimise and extend his rule – in 2002 President Musharraf held a general election as part of a gradual return to democracy. In order to do this, he had to make compromises to get the right majority in Parliament. A coalition of parties came to power, headed by PMLQ, which supported Musharraf. Having several parties in government inevitably involved serving the interests of several different stakeholders. The decision-making process noticeably slowed.

In 2004, the president called me and said: 'I'm sending Tariq Aziz to see you and discuss an important matter.' Tariq was the national security adviser; he came and told me that Zafarullah Khan Jamali would soon resign as prime minister. He also said: 'The president believes you would be a good prime minister, should you be interested in doing it.'

'I'm honoured but I'm not sure it is for me,' I told him, feeling hesitant. I asked for time to think it over and consult with my wife.

After an initial lull, word came that Jamali had submitted his resignation. The PMLQ party chairman Chaudhry Shujaat Hussain was appointed by Musharraf to serve as the interim prime minister for about two months, in accordance with provisions in our constitution. I went to the party's headquarters, where my candidacy was announced.

I was a senator by then, a member of the upper house. To serve as prime minister, I had to become an MP and join the lower house. Chaudhry Shujaat Hussain selected two constituencies for me to run in – Attock, a district near Islamabad where his niece, Eman Wasim, offered to give up her seat for me, and Tharparkar, a desert district in Sindh province. This seat was vacated by Arbab Zakaullah, the cousin of Arbab Ghulam Rahim, the chief minister of Sindh.

The PPP, Benazir Bhutto's party, put up opposing candidates in both constituencies and I began campaigning.

2
UNDER ATTACK

The silver-grey Toyota had been trailing us for about half an hour, as far as I could tell. I first noticed it as we pulled over to open a new campaign office in Attock. Across the road, four young men were carefully watching us from the car. They had small, untrimmed beards and fair skin. As we drove off, they followed.

As soon as my candidacy had been announced, a group of militants met in Swat and decided to eliminate me before the election. While I travelled around my prospective constituencies, their men followed closely behind on reconnaissance missions. On this occasion, they caught my eye.

Our intelligence services were quick to recommend I wear a bulletproof vest and use a Level Seven armoured car. Musharraf had already survived three assassination attempts and they said I was vulnerable on the campaign trail. They brought me a car from the president's fleet. However, I felt it would not give a good impression to drive around in an armoured S-Class Mercedes in an underdeveloped rural area, so I kept it in the garage and used a Jeep.

As the by-election approached, General Ehsan ul Haq, the head of the ISI, and Brigadier Ijaz Shah, the head of the intelligence bureau, came to see me at my residence.

'Why did you choose this place to campaign in?' General Ehsan ul Haq asked, referring to Attock. 'It is frequented by extremists.'

24

Attock was a conservative area with a history of hosting young fighters who had fought the Soviets in Afghanistan. The intelligence chiefs took out a map and showed me suspected militant hideouts.

'This could be a serious security risk during the campaign,' they warned, pointing out that my candidacy was opposed by extremist groups.

Days after their visit, I started using the armoured car. On 30 July, I made my way to a large public gathering in a marquee in the constituency, near the town of Fateh Jang. My intelligence briefing prior to the event said adequate security measures had been taken. Everyone who came in the 5,000-strong crowd was physically checked by security with electronic gates and metal detectors.

The mood that day was euphoric. As I looked out from the stage, I saw a sea of decorations, banners with my photograph, billboards and press crews. After the rally, all the organisers, local leaders and party officials gathered around me. I shook hands with a few people in the crowd before my security officer ushered me into the car.

A mud track through a field had been watered down and levelled for our vehicles and the heavy police escort to pass. I could see the shrubs and debris on either side as I sat behind the driver. One of the provincial ministers, Colonel Anwar, was in the front and the district mayor of Attock, Tahir Sadiq, was with me in the back. The armoured car moved slowly, impeded by its weight. There was a moment's delay as the security staff, who were meant to be running alongside us, regrouped into the correct formation. With two men now on each side, we proceeded down the track. While this was happening, a tall young man wearing a beige *shalwar-kameez* lifted his hand.

A fireball engulfed the car. I felt the thud of an explosion on my side and the whole vehicle shook, shoving me forward. My head was pounding. I looked out and saw we were surrounded by smoke and dust and debris. Body parts covered the blood-stained windshield. I could see people running and screaming around us, but the armoured car muffled their screams. Dozens had been wounded by shrapnel, others were panicking. Amid the turmoil, the policemen and security officers rapidly tried to regroup.

My driver slumped in his seat. I thought he was unconscious so I shook him, but got no reaction. That's when I noticed a trickle of blood coming out of his ear. The terrorists had used armour-piercing pellets in the bomb, making a small hole in his window. The explosive was designed to hit my door but, because the car had slowed as a result of the brief delay, I was spared. The driver died instantly, killed by a shockwave that came through the tiny hole, bursting his eardrums. I could see no other physical injuries but his collar and sleeve soon became drenched in blood.

Captain Zafar, the chief of the local police and part of my security detail, opened the door and quickly covered me. I said I wanted to see what had happened to my personal staff. 'Sir, we must evacuate you immediately,' he said. 'I have enough people here to look after them.' He grabbed hold of my arm and escorted me to a backup vehicle, surrounding me with policemen with automatic rifles. Omar Ayub Khan, the minister of state who accompanied me to the rally, brought his Jeep to a pre-determined escape point and we sped away, along with my security detail in separate cars. Some of them were injured so I instructed one of the cars to go to the nearest hospital before re-joining us.

My wife was in shock after seeing an initial news report of a bomb explosion, which claimed I was injured. I called her as soon as I got within telephone range and said I was safe and unharmed. By the time I reached home, news crews had already assembled, along with concerned friends and colleagues. I addressed the crowd of reporters, paying tribute to the victims who had tragically lost their lives. I added that this event merely strengthened my resolve to contest the election and redouble our efforts in fighting terrorism. Shortly afterwards, President Musharraf called me and said: 'God wants you to serve the country and he has saved your life for this.'

The next day, I attended the funeral for Rehman Khan, my driver. It was held at Prime Minister's House and all the staff came to pay their respects. Security was ramped up tenfold. Rehman was one of eight people who had died in the explosion, including the suicide bomber. Had the car moved a second faster, the ninth victim would have been me.

I received support from different corners of the world. Soon after the attack, Rafic Hariri, the prime minister of Lebanon, called me to express his commiserations. He said: 'You have lost an armoured car, I will send you one of mine.' Two days later, the car was airlifted to Islamabad and added to the prime minister's motor fleet. Tragically, a year later Hariri was himself killed by a bomb that detonated as his motorcade drove through Beirut.

A videotape of the Attock event showed that there had been a second bomber who did not – or could not – explode his suicide belt as planned. He was positioned so that, if the first explosion did not get me, the second would as I tried to escape. The reason I am still here is that the second bomber lost his nerve.

There was a considerable effort by the police and security services to find the perpetrators. They discovered that, after my

27

candidacy had been announced, the militants Matiur Rehman and Amjad Farooqi held a planning session in Matta, a town in Swat. Apparently they believed I was sent to Pakistan to promote an American agenda. Nothing was further from the truth.

The chief investigating officer and his team then tried to locate where the bomber had had his staging post, as well as who the facilitators were. Over a hundred eyewitnesses came forward. After analysing the crime scene, police discovered the shirt collar of the suicide bomber in the remnants of the explosion. The label read: 'Arif Tailors Attock.' They found the tailor and asked whether he remembered the relevant customer. He didn't, so they pursued other leads.

It then dawned on them that tailors usually keep the clippings from the suits to sell as stuffing for pillows. The police returned to the store and asked for the bags full of cloth remnants. They painstakingly went through each one, until they found a perfect match. After intense questioning, the tailor eventually remembered that two young people had come in with a person who lived in a nearby village, who had left his address. The police raided his home and found the suicide belt of the second bomber, as well as other evidence which confirmed the property was a staging post. Several suspects were arrested before four were sentenced to death and three were imprisoned for life.

A few days after the attack, a note arrived through the post. The handwritten Urdu scrawl read: 'This time you have escaped. We have fifty more suicide bombers ready for you. You will not get away.'

Letters like this would continue to arrive daily in an effort to intimidate me. There was speculation that I would pack up and return to the comfort of New York. On the contrary, the incident only reinforced my resolve to serve my country. Even during the attack, I had not panicked – at the critical moment a renewed strength coursed through my body. In some respects, coming so close to losing my life empowered me. I thought: 'God has given me another chance to serve my country.' It strengthened my conviction in fate and faith – the combination of destiny, embodied by events which we may not be able to control, and the divine presence which shapes our lives.

Becoming prime minister

Riding on a wave of popular support following the attack, I felt a new lease of life as I took office as prime minister. My circumstances changed dramatically – for one, my security detail alone now numbered hundreds of people. The Toyota I had as finance minister was replaced with a fleet of bullet-proof Mercedes and a high security convoy, which included ambulances, helicopters, a fire engine and a bomb disposal squad.

I knew there had been other aspirants for the job. I was also aware that a number of them were in my cabinet, either actively or discreetly engaged in pushing their case forward and biding their time. I could feel the politics, particularly in the early days, but I did not let it bother me. Musharraf needed out-of-the box reforms and so he backed me, as did Chaudhry Shujaat Hussain, the party chairman. In many ways, not being an insider was an advantage and allowed me to take a fresher view, without being hampered by political baggage.

Meanwhile, the security situation in the country only deteriorated. The spill-over of weapons and influx of refugees from Afghanistan into the porous border areas between the two countries created a breeding ground for extremism. This was only exasperated by a rapidly growing population, which between 1999 and 2004 had increased from 137 million to 153 million.[1] The local infrastructure was not equipped to meet its needs and disaffection subsequently mounted. In time, the Federally Administered Tribal Areas (FATA) became host to many different terrorist groups, some of which had links to agendas beyond Afghanistan.[2] The nature of FATA, and the way the area was created, made it harder for the government in Islamabad to control the situation. During Partition, Pakistan's tribal areas were given their own autonomy and the central government did not interfere with them much for years, broadly continuing the British approach. Mark Lyall Grant, then Britain's permanent representative to the United Nations and former high commissioner to Pakistan, told me in 2013: 'The British created these tribal areas as a buffer between British India and Afghanistan, which was under Russian influence. We deliberately left them as sort of lawless, partly because it would have been quite difficult to control them, but also because it was in our interests to have this quasi-lawless area.'[3]

That is not to say the tribal system is inherently prone to extremism. The border regions between Afghanistan and Pakistan were once peaceful and thriving. I have fond memories of spending my honeymoon in the Swat Valley – Rukhsana and I stayed at one of the hotels on the majestic river, watching it coming down with force. We took a driver and explored the vibrant green valleys and the Buddhist sites. It was very peaceful, and an altogether different Pakistan. Tourists came in large numbers, filling the hotels and buying local handicrafts. I could never have imagined that this idyllic place would become the focal point of global outrage when, in 2012, a Taliban fighter shot 15 year-old Malala Yousafzai as she took the bus to school. How did we get to such a state?

Everything changed as a result of the first Afghan war, when the tribal zones started to be used as sanctuaries and a launching ground for the mujaheddin, the fighters who engaged in jihad against the invading Soviet forces. Pakistan's government, which had trained and funded these fighters, did not do enough to retrain them and bring them back to normal life. There was no strategy to repatriate those who had come from the Middle East, Chechnya and other countries. After the Soviets left Afghanistan, international focus shifted. The mujaheddin, many of whom had not known any other life after a decade of fighting, turned their attention to new enemies – first, the West, then eventually the state of Pakistan.

Resources assigned to the tribal areas were insufficient and inadequately spent. Promises of help from Pakistan's allies did not materialise – most notably the Reconstruction Opportunity Zones (ROZs) which we thought we could agree with the United States. These would have provided duty-free entry into the United States for goods made in the tribal areas and would have given them a significant boost, creating employment, income and a reserve of goodwill. That said, the Taliban was so driven that even increasing development may not have halted its progress. Soon it effectively controlled large swathes of the tribal areas.

The challenges were not limited to FATA. Over time, provincial grievances assumed particular gravity in Balochistan.[4] These have been in turn exploited by outside powers that wish to destabilise Pakistan and encourage terrorism.

In 2005 and 2006 the government became preoccupied with the deteriorating situation in Waziristan. Since the hostile elements were mingled with the local population, major military operations against towns and villages were ruled out to try and avoid collateral damage, primarily civilian

31

casualties.[5] The controversial North Waziristan agreement with tribal elders, religious leaders and local Taliban was negotiated over several months and concluded in late August 2006. Some viewed it as emboldening the militant tribesmen and raising their stature in the eyes of the locals. Despite the agreement, the tribal insurgents never abandoned violence, which increased towards 2007 when Baitullah Mehsud formally launched the Tehrik-e-Taliban Pakistan (TTP).

The TTP then began to attack military sites and burn aircraft on the ground across the country. In 2012, Kamra Base near Islamabad and before that Faisal Base in Karachi were notably both targeted in terrorist attacks. The Taliban have since spread from the tribal areas to the cities of Pakistan including Karachi, Peshawar and Quetta. After taking control over a vast part of the country, the Taliban began imposing its tough regime: shutting down schools; terrorising the local population and making the threat of terrorism from within Pakistan more real than ever. This culminated in the atrocities of 16 December 2014, when gunmen disguised in paramilitary uniforms stormed the Army Public School in Peshawar, killing 132 children and nine members of staff. It was the deadliest attack ever seen in Pakistan and it horrified the world.

In 2015 I sat down with a former senior intelligence officer from Pakistan to try and understand what had been happening in recent years, with the spread of the new 'Pakistan Taliban'. He pointed out that it is hard to talk about one Taliban, or one TTP: there are sub-groups in several areas which are not even under the control of their own leaders. The officer told me the TTP is broadly comprised of people with conviction, some who see Pakistan as partnered with the US, as well as those who have been encouraged by foreign powers and some criminal elements.

These groups are clearly well-funded, well-armed and highly motivated. We must ask ourselves how they are encouraged and trained. There have been suggestions that elements within RAW, India's intelligence agency, have been active in promoting the TTP and influencing its members to attack the establishment of Pakistan. The full picture, however, is more complicated. Speaking about the growth of the TTP, the officer said:

'Some sources are pumping money into the TTP for sectarian reasons. But is that money fungible? Perhaps it comes from various religious sects or foreign donors, but then that money is diverted to destabilise Pakistan. The terrorists do not know the full picture of who is funding them. They may be acting out of conviction but they are being manoeuvred by some outside sponsor wanting to destabilise Pakistan. These external forces are suited to the idea of a weak, "defanged" Pakistan.'[6]

How did the TTP manage to grow its reach? For years, Pakistan's establishment distinguished between terror groups that attack the state, and those that have their focus away from it. The former intelligence officer told me: 'Partly, we are to blame. It was too late before Pakistan started to attack them with its full might. We did not act fast enough to nip the TTP in the bud.'

There was a lack of resources set aside to combat the 'Pakistan Taliban', as the army had traditionally focused on the most immediate security threat to the country – India. Some arrangements were made with certain terrorist groups which were less hostile to Pakistan. In addition, many Pakistanis supported the cause of the Kashmiri people, and therefore distinguished between Kashmiri freedom fighters and other non-state actors.

The former intelligence officer explained Pakistan's reasoning at the time: 'We were helping all those who helped us fight the Taliban and the Northern Alliance. The Haqqani group, for example, worked with us in Afghanistan against the Soviets, then against the Northern Alliance.'

The idea that we should cut all ties, after supporting them against common foes, was not realistic. The officer continued: 'We were conscious that an unmanaged free force of fighters cannot be left on their own as they will be vulnerable to forces hostile to Pakistan and used against the state of Pakistan. Where do the terrorist groups go? What do they do? It is their way of life.' Some attempts were made to rehabilitate the fighters. Unfortunately, the approach failed in the long run. 'We should go after all groups of terrorists,' he said. 'However, we must recognise that disengagement takes time.'

With the arrival of General Raheel Sharif as head of the army in 2013, momentum substantially picked up against the TTP and the military has been effectively targeting these non-state actors. However, the army cannot be the only method of defeating them. The police, paramilitary forces, civilian government and judiciary have an important role to play in the cities where the TTP has been spreading. A wide-ranging economic effort is needed, and the government should seize opportunities provided by foreign investment, most recently from China, to develop the regions most vulnerable to extremists.

Although some progress has been made in addressing Pakistan's security threats, more funds and training should be set aside to tackle extremism. As General Petraeus, the former commander of United States Central Command and later director of the CIA, told me in 2014: 'What Pakistan needs badly now is a comprehensive counterinsurgency campaign. Without that, the threats by internal extremist groups like TTP will shake the very foundations of the country. In fact, the most significant existential threat to Pakistan is not India, it is Pakistan's internal extremists.'[7]

The root causes of terrorism

Terrorism and extremism are both often caused by deprivation, which can manifest itself in many forms: be it lack of justice, lack of human rights, lack of income, lack of resolution of disputes or a denial of what people feel society owes them. The suicide bomber who tried to kill me was from a poor family, the son of a tailor. He dropped out of school and worked as a part-time telephone operator in his twenties at one of the local hotels. He had been spotted regularly praying at a mosque in Lahore. His recruiters engaged with him and encouraged him to follow them to the tribal areas of Pakistan, where preachers and trainers influenced his thinking.

When young men like him are indoctrinated to commit heinous acts, they are not necessarily acting against the individual they target. Professional motivators know how to get these young people charged up, ready to give up their lives for their faith. Sometimes they send money to the recruits' families, or let them send it directly to give them a sense that they are helping. That is how they can be brainwashed, even though terrorism is fundamentally against the principles of Islam.

The problem in Pakistan and elsewhere in the world today is that parts of the population have reached a high level of frustration and disempowerment and are expressing their anger through militancy. The gradual spread of arms across the country has contributed to the problem. We must look who is training and recruiting them, and redouble our efforts to tackle extremism on a local, regional and global level.

There are two main facets in fighting terrorism – a security side and a hearts and minds side. I believe we have collectively failed when it comes to hearts and minds. On too many occasions, terrorism has been viewed predominantly as a security or military matter. While this is necessary, it will not solve the problem and a more holistic approach is needed.

Inside a madrassa

More than 50% of Pakistan's population is under the age of 24, while only 55% of people over 15 can read and write.[8] A quarter of children aged between 7 and 16 have never been to school and Pakistan has the second-highest number of out-of-school children in the world.[9] Only 5% make it as far as higher education. Much more needs to be done to provide quality education and skills training for this burgeoning youth and both the public and private sectors should be encouraged to invest in schools and vocational colleges. At present, much of the gap is filled by madrassas and their number has grown to an estimated 35,000 from about 3,000 in the late 1980s.[10] While these religious seminaries provide much-needed free schooling for children across the country, they do not offer the well-rounded education and skills that are typically needed to get jobs. Moreover, some may even encourage extremism.

A former Pakistani senior intelligence officer told me in 2015: 'Madrassas opened across Pakistan, ostensibly for religious training but, in some, people got trained to fight. We did not do enough to tackle them. Madrassas should have been brought into the mainstream education system.'

In 2007, a team of psychiatrists conducted a study of a cross-section of madrassa students and their views and out-looks. They aimed to address the general lack of understanding surrounding the mentality of young people who turned to extremism. The researchers assessed more than 130 students, predominantly aged between ten and twenty.

Nearly all the students came from poor backgrounds and large families. The psychiatrists' report said socio-economic deprivation was an important reason for why they were in the madrassa system, which gave them free boarding and lodging, as well as a means for parents to educate their children. Some were there to further their religious education. Their material needs were being well-looked after, but their 'intelligence and potential had not developed due to the limitation[s] of their environment,' it said.

Moreover, 'misinformation had been fed to them that the government was un-Islamic. They had a lack of information about the outside world, as there was no access to the media or Internet facilities there. They found it difficult to absorb the changes happening in our society in terms of modernisation.'

The psychiatrists detected a 'lack of sense of civic responsibility' among the students they assessed. While most denied affiliation with extremist elements, they had a 'myopic view of the world and had little tolerance for the view of others.' The report continued: 'They seem to have an allegiance to their religious teachers because of the closed system in which they were groomed and the fact that all their basic needs were being provided by the madrassa system.' Moreover, 'the madrassa represented a cult of which they were part.'

On a positive note, most of the students were interested in furthering their education, both Islamic and other. They were 'flexible in their views, however it is likely that within a few years of remaining in the same system this could change.'

The psychiatrists concluded: 'What we are seeing is just the tip of the iceberg. Cult culture should be discouraged by reducing the influence of one single person over the whole student community in an institution. The key to this problem is assimilating this population into mainstream life rather than letting them remain marginalised.'

In terms of improvements, the report recommended the following: the madrassas need to be brought in under the auspices of the government's education department, with regular inspections carried out. There is clearly a strong need for free schooling in Pakistan, ideally combining religious and formal education.

Schools, whether religious or secular, should provide access to the Internet and other means to achieve a broader perspective. Any suspected extremist elements should be neutralised and not allowed to influence young minds. The teachers themselves must be educated and should have a balanced and tolerant view of the world. The students should be periodically assessed and those with potential should be offered scholarships at the top universities in the country.

Moreover, madrassa pupils should follow a more balanced and tolerant lifestyle. If possible, the government should house them in general accommodation, where they can mix with other students from different educational institutions. Other activities, such as sport, should be encouraged. The total years they spend in the madrassa should be limited to a certain number to improve their outlook, the psychologists concluded.

I agree with these recommendations, and would add that skills training is needed for both boys and girls in order to unlock opportunities for them in later life and give them a means of earning a living. While for many faiths religious education can play a positive force, it should not be used to promote extremism and potential terrorism. I believe it is time for the government to start a dialogue with the madrassas to try and eventually bring them into a formal structure. Wafaq ul Madaris, the self-regulating body which oversees madrassas in Pakistan, should be brought into the mainstream, strengthened and provided with more resources to improve standards and transparency.

Meanwhile, more of the government's budget should be set aside for building new schools and vocational training institutions. In the short term, the private sector can play an active role and bring tangible improvements. We should encourage the development of more private institutions such as Beacon House, a chain of schools run by Mona Kasuri, and non-governmental organisations such as the Citizens Foundation and Developments in Literacy to provide valuable access to education for our rapidly growing population of young people. As the number of Pakistan's 15-24 year-olds is expected to grow by 20% by 2020, the shortfall between their needs and what the education system can provide requires urgent attention.

3
BIN LADEN: WHO KNEW WHAT?

It was as early as June 2010 that CIA analysts zoned in on the one-acre compound in Abbottabad, Pakistan, which had been home to the most wanted man in the world for years.[1] The information was a closely guarded secret even at the highest levels in the United States. General James Jones, national security adviser at the time, was one of the select few in President Barack Obama's administration who knew what was happening. He told me: 'When we found the house, there were probably no more than four or five people in our government who knew about it. It was so preliminary that we didn't advertise it to anyone. There were other targets as well that were possibilities, but this was one that stuck out.' How did they decide to focus on the Abbottabad house? 'There were enough anomalies to say: "This is of interest"'.[2]

They found it by tracking the movements of Abu Ahmed al-Kuwaiti, Osama Bin Laden's courier. Al-Kuwaiti drove an unremarkable white SUV and would come and go from the compound, which had several outhouses and one main three-storey house with barbed-wire-covered walls. Al-Kuwaiti lived there with his brother, Abrar. The house had no phone or Internet connection, and its inhabitants burned their trash. There was a man living on the third floor, who never left. It was enough to draw the Americans' attention.

Even when it came to planning the raid nearly one year later, when a team of Navy SEALs from the Naval Special

Warfare Development Group (DEVGRU) carried out practice runs in the Nevada desert, few in the United States knew
about the upcoming mission. General David Petraeus, who
was at the time commander of the US forces in Afghanistan,
told me he was only told about the raid in the week before it
took place.[3]

Crucially, America did not inform Pakistan's leadership of
its plans. Trust levels had fallen to a critically low point between
the two allies by this stage. For example, the United States
command felt that in certain cases where Pakistan had been
made aware of planned attacks, the targets would somehow
disperse. Pakistan's point of view was different. Events such
as the Raymond Davis affair in January 2011, when a CIA
operative killed two Pakistani civilians in the middle of Lahore,
caused outrage in Pakistan.[4] The incident and Washington's
handling of it gave rise to already existing anti-Americanism
in Pakistan and fuelled suspicions that a wide network of US
intelligence agents operated on its soil.

There had been efforts to smooth over tension between the
two countries, General Jones told me: 'In January 2009, when
the president asked me to be his national security advisor,
we had a big meeting in Washington and invited the Pakistanis, both civilian and military, to come and recalibrate the
relationship.[5] We did the same with the Afghans. I thought
that was a very successful start, and it triggered a number of
trips back and forth to Pakistan and a close relationship with
General Kayani, the army chief. We worked quite actively on
it, but I don't think we ever really achieved the level of trust
and confidence that allowed the military in Pakistan to take a
longer range view of the strategic relationship.'

'Coupled in all of this were on-going discussions for our
search for Osama Bin Laden,' Jones said. 'I had very direct

conversations with Pakistani officials, who assured me on several occasions – just one on one – that they were very sure that he was not in Pakistan at all. In my own calibration, I felt that I was dealt with in a not very truthful way.'

In the end, Bin Laden was killed in the poorly-guarded one-acre compound in Bilal Town, Abbottabad, a quiet city 70 miles north of the capital, less than a mile from the Pakistan Military Academy of Kakul and a short distance from the local ISI office.[6]

I knew Abbottabad well – I spent a year in the 1960s attending a boarding school about fifteen minutes away from where Bin Laden was found. It was a picturesque, well-to-do city, which developed a reputation for having two well-known boys' boarding schools: Burn Hall School and Abbottabad Public School.

When I heard about the raid, I remembered a meeting I had with President Hamid Karzai in Afghanistan in 2006. We were sitting in the Presidential Palace in Kabul when the subject of Bin Laden came up. Karzai said: 'Prime Minister, we suspect he is in Pakistan. He is probably in an urban area.'

Other more vague warnings that Bin Laden was in Pakistan were also passed on, as reported by the Abbottabad commission, which was established to investigate how the world's most wanted man could have been undetected for so long. It concluded: 'Neither accusations by foreign leaders and intelligence officials were taken seriously, nor were their possible military implications ever seriously considered. This was unprofessional behaviour.'[7]

It was in 2005 that a clean-shaven Bin Laden slipped into the Abbottabad house wearing a cowboy hat to avoid detection from above. He would keep a low profile there, sharing ten small rooms with his three wives and twelve children.[8]

Ahmed and Abrar al-Kuwaiti moved into the outbuildings on the compound with their families. Khalid Sheikh Mohammed, the mastermind of the World Trade Center attacks, had introduced the brothers to Bin Laden. Working as his guards and couriers, they provided cover by being the official owners of the compound. They referred to him as the 'Sheikh' and were paid 9,000 rupees a month for their service.[9] Locals, when they were interviewed after the raid, said they thought the house belonged to Pashtuns laying low after a family feud – not an unusual scenario.[10]

The Abbottabad commission asked how the Al Qaeda chief could have lived undetected for six years in the compound, and, before that, for two years in Haripur, a city south of Abbottabad. It listed local, regional and national failures, and said that either police or intelligence officials should have noticed a few anomalies about the compound, such as the lack of phone lines or television cable and the fact that the children did not go to school. The report included statements from police and security officials saying they had never heard any mention of Bin Laden's possible presence in the area. No one took responsibility in what was explained as a 'collective failure' by all the relevant institutions.

The commission's report also said local and national intelligence should have been more focussed on Abbottabad since a number of 'high value targets' had been caught in and around the town. The home of terrorist Abu Faraj al-Libbi had been previously raided only a kilometre away from the Bin Laden compound.[11] The Bali bomber Umar Patek was seized in Abbottabad in January 2011, making it clear that Al Qaeda had a presence and support network in the city.

These intelligence failings, and the compound's proximity to the military academy, led to much speculation that Bin

Laden was being protected by Pakistan's government or security forces. This was not the case. When I later met with General Petraeus in New York, I asked him what he thought. The four-star general told me that it was generally believed that that neither Pakistan's government nor the ISI knew of Bin Laden's whereabouts.[12]

My view is that there was a disconnect of objectives between the two countries. Pakistan was not protecting or hiding Bin Laden – there was too much at stake. But finding him was not as high a priority for Pakistan as it was for the United States. While President George W. Bush asked his staff daily for progress on tracking the Al Qaeda chief, in Pakistan he was considered no longer actively involved. The real Al Qaeda leadership was already perceived to be moving elsewhere – towards Yemen and Africa. The United States had also identified Al Qaeda's geographical shift at around this time. General Jones told me in December 2013: 'Four years ago, we plotted where Al Qaeda would go. We said they'll jump over the Red Sea, they'll get into Somalia after Yemen. Then they'll go across to North Africa, to Mali – they'll try Algeria but it's too tough – then Mauritania, then down to Nigeria. Because they [Nigeria] have money, they have oil, they have everything.'

The Americans were looking at the relationship through their own objectives, which were different to ours. Pakistan had to be primarily concerned with its own national interests, and had other priorities. It could not shift its focus away from India, which had historically been Pakistan's greatest security threat. And while the United States wanted to have 'hot pursuit' of terrorists, Pakistan could not allow that at the expense of its sovereignty. As a result, the trust deficit between the two nations grew.

Nevertheless, finding Bin Laden was a crucial task in the War on Terror and the military action in Afghanistan. The inability to track him down after so many years was a significant failure. Pakistan was legally bound by several United Nations resolutions to actively look for Bin Laden, and gave frequent assurances to the United States that it was doing so.[13] In reality, Pakistan could not come up with credible intelligence to build on.

It did not help that Pakistan's focus was diverted – not only by India, but by the growing threat of terrorism within its own borders.[14] The TTP had already begun to attack the institutions of the state and its military bases. Meanwhile, Al Qaeda had continued to focus on the jihad against America, without being an immediate threat to Pakistan. A former Pakistani senior intelligence officer told me: 'The TTP started to go against the state of Pakistan. The United States and Pakistan's objectives diverged. We felt we were on our own.'[15] This is not the same as saying that Pakistan sheltered, protected or turned a blind eye on Bin Laden, as many have speculated.

The United States was slow to recognise this. Steve Hadley, the former national security advisor, told me: 'There were two problems in the counter terrorism cooperation. One is that Al Qaeda was more of a threat to us, but, as time went on, the Pakistan Taliban became more of a threat to Islamabad. We were not balanced to being directed at both Al Qaeda and enemies of the United States and other terrorist enemies of Pakistan. If it is going to be a joint effort against terrorists, then it has to be a joint effort whether they threaten the United States or threaten Pakistan. We were slow to get that.'

With hindsight, it emerges that both countries were not singing from the same hymn sheet and, despite being partners in the War on Terror, each focused on their own priorities – without much consideration for the other side's aims.

'We got him'

On 1 May 2011, two MH-60 Black Hawk stealth helicopters set out into the night from eastern Afghanistan. Built to mask heat, noise and movement, they were covered with radar-dampening 'skin'.[16] Just before midnight, they entered Pakistan's airspace between Ghursal and Shilman in the Khyber Agency – shortly followed by two Chinooks.[17]

It was a still, moonless night, chosen because the lunar cycle had reached its darkest phase. The compound was silent and in the middle of a blackout as the electricity in the surrounding area was down until 0035 hours.[18] The SEALs relied on night vision goggles to navigate their way through the darkness and up the stairs of the house in their hunt for the target, codenamed 'Crankshaft'.[19]

The helicopters penetrated deep into the gut of Pakistan's territory by 150 kilometres in an operation that lasted over three hours and resulted in the deaths of three Pakistani citizens. One Black Hawk helicopter crashed and was then blown up by the SEALs.

Pakistan's sovereignty was violated. A foreign power had covertly crossed its borders and carried out a military attack on its soil without prior warning. The fact that the helicopters flew in undetected by Pakistan's radars led to criticism of its establishment and raised serious security concerns.

It was an added embarrassment that Bin Laden had lived so close to the military academy. In reality, its proximity is largely irrelevant. Years later, while speaking at a panel organised by the Atlantic Council in Washington DC in the presence of former US national security advisers Brent Scowcroft and Steve Hadley, I was asked: 'If Bin Laden was so close to the military academy, how could they not have known he was there?' I responded: 'The military academy does not monitor who is living in the nearby area. In the same way that anyone could go and rent a house near West Point in the United States. It is the job of the local intelligence and police to keep an eye on those who could pose a threat – not of the commandant.'

Still, the fact that he was in the Pakistan establishment's backyard was embarrassing. The local head of the ISI offered to resign after the incident, but in the end no one ostensibly lost their jobs over the multitude of failings.[20]

In some ways, the nature of the raid helped Pakistan domestically. Overnight, Pakistan's government and establishment became the victims, rather than the collaborators. Politically it was a much better position to be in and countered the domestic criticism we had faced for being perceived as too close to the Americans. It was also important for Pakistan to realise that it is not trusted on this issue as a nation.

Donald Rumsfeld heard the news directly from the US army chief of staff, Martin Dempsey. Once the raid was over, Dempsey came home and called the former US Secretary of Defense, who had launched the War on Terror.

'We got him,' Dempsey said.

Rumsfeld later recalled to me: 'My immediate reaction was – number one, it was good that he was off the scene, second that there was a risk people would think that therefore the problem with radical Islamism was over. In fact we found that, every time we took out an Al Qaeda leader in Iraq or Afghanistan, they were replaced within thirty days by someone else – and the only question was: "Would the replacements be as effective?"'

The atrocities carried out by the Islamic State in Iraq and Syria and by Boko Haram in Nigeria, among others, vividly illustrate that terrorism is a growing global problem, which requires more international cooperation than ever. Building trust between strategic partners is essential in combating such militants. The discovery of Bin Laden's home was a significant setback for the Pakistan-US relationship, one that still requires time and effort to overcome. Christina Rocca, the Assistant Secretary of State for South and Central Asia in 2001-2006, put it to me this way: 'Finding Bin Laden where we found him was the single worst event that happened in our bilateral relations, from the American perspective. It created distrust at the highest levels.'[21]

America's most sanctioned ally

There have always been challenges within Pakistan-US relations. It is a friendship of transactional necessity, which burns stronger in moments of need. Pakistan relies on its alliance with America, which has been a source of military and financial aid since its independence. Crucially, the United States dominates the Bretton Woods institutions, such as the World Bank and the IMF, which Pakistan often depends on. In turn, the United States has used Pakistan's strategic position in South Asia – particularly during the two wars in Afghanistan. The link between the two countries is thus primarily driven by geopolitical events rather than long-lasting ties. As a result of the help provided in moments of need, the Americans have included Pakistan in many of their alliances – I have often said Pakistan is 'the most allied ally of the United States, and its most sanctioned ally'. It was a member of SEATO and CENTO from the 1960s, now it is a non-NATO ally and has signed several agreements since then. However, if provoked and during periods when the strategic relationship is less important, the superpower's attitude can become adversarial. The United States has imposed sanctions and withdrawn its support of

48

Pakistan. This fundamental contradiction in the relationship has proved challenging for both sides. It has fuelled distrust from Pakistan, and pushed the allies further away from one another, only leading to breakdowns in communications. No two countries' national interests will align 100% of the time. But when there is distrust, normal diplomacy can falter and differences in approaches are then not properly communicated. Both the United States and Pakistan should have been upfront with each others' objectives, and acknowledged that they differed. Instead, they pursued their own paths, thereby contributing to the growing gap between them.

This is not the first time the two countries hit a rocky patch. I sat down with Brent Scowcroft, who had been national security advisor to Presidents Gerald Ford and George H. W. Bush, in order to get a wider perspective. I was struck by the candour of his analysis when he described the Pakistan-US relationship as 'a tragic one'.[22] He said: 'When Pakistan first became independent, we were sort of your security blanket, and you were at the centre of our strategic needs. After the second Indo-Pakistan war, we put an embargo on arms sales on both sides. It didn't matter to the Indians, because they got all their equipment from the Russians.' Pakistan, however, was seriously hampered by the sanctions.

Scrowcroft added: 'My perception is that Pakistan then moved to get nuclear weapons, because it didn't have [the conventional weapons] we had been providing. Then came the Russian invasion of Afghanistan and we got back together again, because the Pakistanis were fighting our fight for us.'

Even during times of friendship, the United States has not always been consistently reliable. 'One of the most graphic examples is – once we sold Pakistan some F-16 airplanes, took the money and didn't deliver,' Scowcroft said. 'We should be close friends and allies, but it has never really turned out that way. So it is really very tragic and in a way it is India-centric.' Attempts to recalibrate the relationship – most recently the one spearheaded by Richard Holbrooke, the special envoy for Pakistan and Afghanistan, in 2009 – have failed.

The Bin Laden raid and the Raymond Davis affair, among other issues, chipped away at the already delicate relationship. Instead of trying to repair the ties between the two countries, the United States has pursued a more unilateral approach. The Americans were not happy with the security services in Pakistan, so they developed their own security network within it. Pakistan's government of the time allowed this, providing them with the necessary visas. Officially these were for guards and embassy staff, but actually they were given to CIA employees or contractors. In 2011, reports of hundreds of such visas increased tension.[23]

By developing its own security network within Pakistan, the United States took the fight against terrorism into its own hands. The Americans were able to gather the necessary intelligence to carry out controversial drone strikes in Pakistan, for example. As with the Bin Laden raid, the Americans continuously bypassed Pakistan's government and intelligence services. Pakistan, in turn, did not like the idea of what was effectively a foreign police force pursuing its own agenda. The presence of such a security network makes the host country look like a client state and only turns the public sentiment against cooperation. As a result, the gulf between the two allies grew.

4

AMERICA'S TRANSACTIONAL RELATIONSHIP

When I joined the government, Pakistan was one of only three countries which officially recognised Taliban rule in Afghanistan, alongside the UAE and Saudi Arabia. All other major powers refused to deal with the new government, in part because of its human rights record, in part because the Taliban struggled with diplomacy and building the necessary relationships with the outside world. Even years after the Taliban had seized control, the United Nations continued to recognise the ousted post-Soviet government instead.

During his few months in government, General Musharraf would bring up the Taliban in his meetings with other heads of state, in an attempt to drum up support for the new Afghan government. His pitch was usually to encourage other powers to give resources to the Taliban, so that it could strengthen its hold on Afghanistan.

I was present on one such occasion, while serving as finance minister. Musharraf and I were at the court of Sheikh Zayed bin Sultan al Nahyan, the founder and president of the UAE and ruler of Abu Dhabi. At the time, Sheikh Zayed was still in good health, and my impression of him at that meeting was that he was wisdom personified. His remarks were weighted with experience, maturity and sincerity. He had an affinity for Pakistan – the Sheikh had palaces in Rahim Yar Khan, Lahore

51

and Karachi, and every year he would come falcon hunting for houbara bustard in the Cholistan desert.

It was one of General Musharraf's first official visits abroad as leader of Pakistan. We arrived at the royal palace in Abu Dhabi and Musharraf updated Sheikh Zayed on the Taliban government and hinted that it needed more funds and support. Sheikh Zayed was a man of few words. He listened patiently then said:

'General, I have a lot of love for Pakistan, and I appreciate what you have been doing for this cause. May I suggest that you coordinate closely with the Americans, whose input could be valuable.' This was sound advice from an experienced statesman – to engage with all stakeholders. But it took the tragic events of 9/11 to change Pakistan's approach to the Taliban.

The United States had been demanding the extradition of Bin Laden from the Taliban and a crackdown on Al Qaeda since the mid 1990s – particularly following the attacks on the American embassies in Kenya and Tanzania. These requests were in vain – the tribal culture of the Taliban dictated that, since the Al Qaeda members were their guests, it should treat them hospitably. The only solution Mullah Omar, the Taliban's leader, suggested was to arrange a trial for Bin Laden in a religious court, at which the Americans could provide evidence through Saudi Arabia.[1] The United States did not find it a satisfactory offer.

The West asked Pakistan to put pressure on the Taliban government to hand over Bin Laden, but Islamabad stuck by the Afghan leadership. This was largely because of Pakistan's historical links with the mujaheddin and its plight against foreign occupiers. The ties with the Taliban also partly served as a counterweight to Indian influence exerted through the Northern Alliance.

Not that Pakistan would necessarily have been able to fulfil the Americans' request. In early 2001, General Musharraf pleaded with Mullah Omar not to destroy two sacred sixth-century Buddhas in Bamiyan, but he had no success. Prime Minister Shinawatra of Thailand had also called me and asked our government to intervene over the Buddhas. We sent our interior minister to Kabul in an attempt to reason with the Taliban. Thailand wanted, at the very least, to have the remains of the Buddhas sent to them. However, Mullah Omar rejected all our requests and the Taliban blew up the Buddhas.

After the mass devastation of the World Trade Center attacks, however, the dynamic between Pakistan, the Taliban and the United States changed overnight.

9/11

My wife saw the plane hit the second tower from our New York bedroom window. As she looked out from the thirty-fourth floor apartment, she watched the iconic World Trade Center collapse into dust before her eyes. The smoke and ash would hang in the sky for days, blocking out the sun.

Being in Islamabad and not able to get hold of my family once I had heard the news was agonising. My son Abid worked in midtown, Manhattan, and had just left home after the first plane hit the tower. Like many at the time, he thought it was an accident, nothing major, and went into the office. As mobile phones had stopped working in the aftermath of the attack, there was a period of panic while we could not reach Abid. I cannot describe my sense of relief when Rukhsana finally called to say he came home safe that afternoon.

Then, like millions of others, I realised the world would never be the same again. This was the biggest assault on a free society that we had ever seen. Terrorism was now a global problem and the focus would soon turn sharply on our part of the world.

The Bush administration acted fast. Within hours of the Twin Towers collapsing, United States Secretary of State Colin Powell picked up the phone and called General Musharraf. He did not mince words, saying: 'You are either with us or against us.' Powell and Rich Armitage put together a list of seven demands for Pakistan. They did not wait for input from the Department of Defense – time was of the essence.[2] A day after the attacks, Armitage welcomed General Mahmud Ahmed, the head of the ISI, into his office. The general had happened to be in Washington at the time, visiting as a guest of CIA director George Tenet.[3]

In a pivotal meeting, Rich Armitage told the general: 'Yesterday you came to one country. This is a different country today. You have got to understand that – and Pakistan is going to be in this, one way or the other.'

Armitage presented General Mahmud with the seven demands, which included cutting off support for the Taliban and providing territorial access to the United States and its allies as needed. These were the general principles of what was required in cooperating – the finer points would be ironed out later. Armitage said General Mahmud 'had already talked on the phone to General Musharraf, and told me he would accept these.'

Overall, 9/11 was a game changer for Pakistan's relationship with the United States. President Bush announced he would take decisive action against any country that harboured terrorists. Once again, Afghanistan became a battle ground and Pakistan's strategic value became clear. The United States needed a route to reach Afghanistan, and Pakistan could provide an air corridor, as well as bases for troops and drones.

The Port of Karachi was the easiest way to bring supplies into Afghanistan, which is land locked. The shortest distance from the Arabian Sea to Afghanistan is through Pakistan. Alternatively the troops would have to go through Russia and Iran – neither of which have warm relationships with the United States.

Overnight, we moved from being a pariah military state to a much-needed strategic partner for the West. Until then, most world leaders would not publicly recognise or deal with our new government. After the coup, Pakistan's membership of the Commonwealth was suspended. America enforced sanctions, adding to those that existed since we had tested our nuclear weapon in 1998. The financial help provided by the international Aid to Pakistan Consortium, which had been formed in 1960 to help our country, had cut down to barely more than a trickle. The War on Terror not only gave legitimacy to the new leadership in Islamabad – after 9/11, doors that had been closed for decades suddenly opened wide.

General Musharraf realised all this and the valuable position it would give Pakistan on the world stage. He was also personally opposed to terrorism, having been a victim of several attempted attacks, so he had no trouble condemning Al Qaeda. He knew that support of the Taliban was now impossible. In his memoir, he wrote: 'I made a dispassionate, military-style analysis of our options, weighing the pros and cons.'

Musharraf changed the phrasing of some of Powell and Armitage's demands, regarding the nature of access the United States would have to Pakistan's territory and military and naval bases.[4] When it came to the question of breaking with the Taliban, the United States was keen to try and use Pakistan's links to try and negotiate first. According to Armitage: 'We said, please hold. Do not do it yet'. The United States had asked General Mahmud to go to the home of Mullah Omar and meet with him. As Armitage recalled: 'The message was that if Mullah Omar removed the Taliban from Al Qaeda, we would not attack them.' Mullah Omar said no.

For all the previous criticism of the military coup and General Musharraf's rule, when it came to a crisis like 9/11, he acted swiftly and decisively. It helped that he was in control of both the government and the army. The United States recognised this – Christina Rocca, the Assistant Secretary of State for South and Central Asian Affairs, recalled sitting at an event in Washington next to Strobe Talbott, the Deputy Secretary of State at the time. He told her that, when he saw what had happened on September 11 and realised what was going on, he thanked God that Musharraf was in charge in Pakistan.[5]

The first official meeting we had with the United States after 9/11 was a dinner with President Bush in the United States ambassador's suite in the Waldorf Astoria Towers in New York, a month after the attacks. We received a warm welcome, and President Bush assured General Musharraf that he would stand by Pakistan and not abandon it like the United States did after the Cold War.[6] It was a far cry from President Clinton's six-hour condition-laden visit.

After that, Colin Powell was the main official who usually came to Pakistan from the United States. His military background helped the four-star general forge a connection with Musharraf. Powell told me: 'Over a period of three or four years, we became extremely close. We once counted up that I had talked to him something like eighty-two times, both over the phone and during personal visits.'

The regular contact was constructive on both sides, and it helped that Powell was sensitive to the domestic challenges facing Pakistan's leadership over its closeness to America. In a memo to President Bush in November 2001, the Secretary of State wrote: 'Musharraf's decision to fully cooperate with the United States in the wake of 9/11, at considerable political risk, abruptly turned our stalled relationship around.'[7]

Powell also helped me with several economic matters. My first priority when I became finance minister was to restructure Pakistan's sovereign debt. Only with the debt spread out over many more years could it become manageable, and allow Pakistan to focus on building its economy. As Powell recalled: 'At that time we were providing military assistance, but what you really needed was economic assistance.' He jokingly added: '[Shaukat Aziz] was now finance minister, so I'm saying, OK, I know this guy. He's a banker. So of course he's going to be worried about the economy. Every time we sat down, we would talk about a few issues, and then he would say: "debt relief."'

Indeed, debt relief was at the forefront of my mind. I remember one instance during the Millennium Development Goals (MDG) summit in Monterrey, Mexico. This was a United Nations effort launched in 2000 and spearheaded by Kofi Annan and Mark Malloch Brown. I had come to lead the delegation from Pakistan, which included our permanent representative to the United Nations, Shamshad Ahmad, who was involved in organising the summit, and economic adviser Dr Ashfaque Hasan Khan. In 2015, the United Nations called the MDGs the 'most successful anti-poverty movement in history,' as the number of people living on less than $1.25 a day has been reduced from 1.9 billion in 1990 to 836 million in 2015 – a powerful example of how multilateral cooperation can tackle the most pressing issues we face.[8]

I arrived at the auditorium, where I was to chair some plenary sessions, and caught sight of President Bush sitting with Colin Powell and Condoleezza Rice. As I approached them, I saw Colin get up and start pointing vigorously at his forehead. 'I've got it, Shaukat, I've got it!' he bellowed across the room. 'It's written right here. Debt Relief!'

As the others looked on, baffled, he explained that I had been talking to him so much about debt relief that it had become ingrained. To this day, Powell likes to joke about how many times I brought it up. And it paid off – Washington cancelled $1 billion of Pakistan's debt and deferred the payment of much more, as well as encouraging crucial support in the Paris Club, World Bank and the IMF for Pakistan. Without the strong backing of the United States, we would have struggled to reduce our debt burden, which became the driving force of our economic revival.

A little-covered aspect of the War on Terror was the activity in the sphere of international finance. The United States Treasury set up the Financial Action Task Force to track illicit money transfers. The effort was spearheaded by John Taylor, the Treasury Under Secretary for International Affairs between 2001 and 2005.

In his book, *Global Financial Warriors*, Taylor recalled our work to address the issue of terrorist financing. He said: '[Aziz] knew volumes about the secretive methods of transferring funds in and out of South Asia. He suggested to me that we invite finance ministers from countries where illicit fund flows were likely to be a problem to a G7 meeting. I thought it was a great idea, and I set up such a meeting in Washington in April 2002. Aziz chaired this historical outreach meeting, and useful information about how illicit money is transferred was shared with the G7 ministers, either at that meeting or later through staff contacts set up there.'[9]

This was an excellent opportunity for Pakistan to show the financial community that we had professionals working with broad-based exposure in every aspect of banking and finance.

The aid package

Before Pakistan could get any economic assistance from the United States, the question of sanctions had to be addressed, including those imposed on Pakistan and India after their respective nuclear tests. The process to remove them had already begun before the World Trade Center attacks. On the day of 9/11, a team of state department officials were scheduled to go to Capitol Hill and begin discussions about lifting sanctions for Pakistan.[10]

Christina Rocca was involved in the process. She said: 'There was intense opposition from India, which would have preferred to have no sanctions lifted on it than to have all sanctions removed. But the decision had already been made – the administration had decided to lift sanctions as early as May 2001.' Still, it probably would have been a lengthy process, and 9/11 accelerated it. The administration was able to lift the sanctions within days of the World Trade Center attacks.

Aid began to flow. The pivotal meeting for this was on 24 June 2003, when General Musharraf paid a visit to Camp David. I was part of the delegation as finance minister. I woke early that morning in Blair House, the official guest residence of the White House. We were driven in limousines to the foot of the Washington Monument, where we boarded Marine One helicopters and flew to the presidential retreat in Frederick County, Maryland. On arrival, we were greeted by a casually-dressed President Bush and his wife Laura, Colin Powell and

Condoleezza Rice. We rode in golf carts to the meeting villa, where I chatted with Powell – no doubt about debt relief.

This came at the height of our relations with the United States and the partnership in the War on Terror. Four months earlier, the ISI had worked with the CIA to capture Khalid Sheikh Mohammed (KSM), the mastermind behind the World Trade Center attacks and Bin Laden's right hand man, in a raid in Rawalpindi. Under interrogation KSM provided valuable intelligence about Al Qaeda's operations. Around this time General Ehsan ul Haq, then head of the ISI, travelled to Washington and proposed to Vice President Dick Cheney that the two countries should formalise a new strategic relationship. Cheney was very receptive to the suggestion, although other United States officials were reluctant. The State Department pushed to hold the meetings in the White House, in what would have been a more brief and formal manner. It was only through our efforts with Cheney that the arrangements moved to the more symbolic location, Camp David.

During the meeting there, I laid out our two-pronged case for economic assistance: first, enlisting American aid would help persuade the people of Pakistan, many of whom were critical of the United States, that we were building a mutually beneficial strategic relationship. Second, improving the quality of life for the millions of people living in Pakistan was a prerequisite in the long-term fight against terrorism. Reducing poverty would be one way to undercut the recruiters. The administration recognised my arguments. Alan Larson, the Under Secretary of State for Economic Affairs, revealed a $3 billion aid package, to be given to Pakistan over five years. Half of the money would go to bolstering our defence forces; the other half was for infrastructure, education and health care projects.

The State Department and the National Security Council put together a financial assistance package for Pakistan in return for our support in the War on Terror. The plan included debt relief, direct aid and loans from the World Bank. I suggested the aid package be tied to our structural reform programme. John Taylor recalled the process: 'By linking the support to economic reforms – such as improved budgetary transparency and spending controls – that Aziz wanted to put in place, we helped him prevent others in his government from thwarting the needed reforms. To the credit of Musharraf, Aziz and the assistance package itself, economic growth in Pakistan rose dramatically in the next few years, increasing from 2% in 2001 to 8% by 2005.'[11]

The Camp David summit also included discussions about the United States resuming sales of F-16 fighter jets to Pakistan. The F-16s were a significant development for us, but their timing was a point of contention within the Bush administration. A 2006 Centre for Strategic and International Studies paper, citing an interview with a senior State Department official, said: 'The Pentagon was inclined to sell the aircraft in 2002, while the State Department argued that this would torpedo United States-India relations as Washington was trying to improve ties with New Delhi. The National Security Council decided to defer the sale.' The F-16s were high on President Musharraf's agenda in his meetings with the United States. Eventually, the reminders paid off. The announcement that America would resume the sale of the fighter planes was made in 2005.

Our respective defence departments negotiated the access to airspace and bases that were used for American troops, drones and aircraft. Pakistan gave the United States an exclusive base in Jacobabad, Sindh, as well as Shamsi base in Balochistan to use for drones and provided an air corridor from the Gulf to Afghanistan over Western Pakistan. I pushed for the Pentagon to give us reimbursement every time these were used, negotiating this during separate trips to Washington. In my meetings with Donald Rumsfeld, Paul Wolfowitz and Dov Zakheim, we drew up an agreement for payment, with usage and maintenance accounted for separately. This amounted to billions of dollars a year in so-called 'coalition support funds'. Between the 2002 and 2007 fiscal years, Washington provided Pakistan with more than $4.5 billion in assistance and over $5.6 billion in reimbursements, as well as valuable training and expertise.[12]

Camp David also helped forge a good relationship between the two leaders. President Bush, who at the time enjoyed high ratings and was at the peak of his political strength, was confident and relaxed, bonding with General Musharraf. They walked together, with Bush's dog Barney following closely. I also found President Bush very easy to get along with and skilled at putting a person at ease. When he later came to Pakistan in 2006, he embraced me warmly. The security situation had deteriorated by then, and days before his visit a bomb had killed an American diplomat in Karachi. Despite this, Bush refused to cancel his trip and insisted on staying the night. It was a welcome vote of confidence in his allies in Islamabad.

Despite Bush's notable personal chemistry, cracks soon began to appear in the relationship between the United States and Pakistan. We felt not all promises were met – including agreements to get Reconstruction Opportunity Zones (ROZs) from the United States, which never materialised. These would have provided a genuine boost to the parts of Pakistan most in need, notably the tribal areas. In addition, repeated attempts to develop trade access with the United States, which would have helped economic development, came to nothing. When we tried to negotiate a bilateral investment treaty, the conditions imposed by the United States would have affected our sovereignty, so I decided not to proceed.

As the former National Security Advisor Steve Hadley put it to me, the way Pakistan was handled meant the relationship was 'very transactional'. He said: 'It convinced the Pakistani people that the only issue we were interested in was Pakistan helping us deal with terrorists – particularly Al Qaeda terrorists, who Pakistanis did not feel were a threat to them. And so the notion was that all that matters to the United States is cooperation with Pakistan against an enemy of the United States. And we would provide our economic assistance as compensation for that. But it played into the abandonment fear which Pakistan had, based on the 1980s experience – that "when we are no longer useful to the Americans, they will abandon us once again." It suggested we didn't care about Pakistan.'

Hadley suggested separating out the fight against terrorism from the 'economic relationship that is a long-term investment by the United States in the economic reform and stability and prosperity of Pakistan. You've got to make it clear to the Pakistani people that that is not contingent, that it is not transactional – that it is a strategic commitment by the United States in the long-term to the success of Pakistan as a state. That is the right way to frame the relationship.'[13]

Sometimes this was not for a lack of effort by the Bush administration, but it came up against opposition in Congress. Rich Armitage said meaningful development initiatives were hard to win support for in Washington: 'I couldn't get any money for what would have made the real difference in Pakistan

– a big infrastructure project on energy. 9/11 didn't allow us to concentrate on Pakistan for Pakistan's sake. Pakistan got subsumed by the trauma of Afghanistan.'

The reality is that Pakistan will continue to depend on America's help, both for aid and for support in the Bretton Woods institutions. The relationship between the two countries should move towards a partnership which is strategic, not transactional – something which did not take place during my time in government. This debate goes on today.

Cracks in the War on Terror

In the first few years of the War on Terror, Pakistan dutifully fulfilled its promises to the United States and Pakistan stopped supporting the Taliban. Our American partners initially had no complaints. Rich Armitage said to me: 'I looked every single day at our intelligence about Pakistan and the Taliban and ISI, and I must say, until 2005, the only real relationship I could see was a liaison relationship. But I didn't find large amounts of weapons or money [going to the Taliban] via ISI. We couldn't find it.'

It was only later that the dynamic changed. 'In 2005, we started to see several events happen,' Armitage said. 'The Taliban dug up their weapons, because they thought maybe the Americans will get short of breath. And ISI started to involve themselves with the Taliban again – increasing not just liaison but money and some weapons. Pakistan over time went back to a more traditional policy.'

At the time, the United States was busy waging the war in Iraq and shifted its focus away from Afghanistan and South Asia. The idea of American disengagement and the possibility of a Taliban resurgence could have caused Pakistan's military and security establishment to rethink what was in the country's national interest and move back to maintaining ties with the Taliban. The argument for having a counterweight to Indian influence in Afghanistan was most likely a factor in the decision-making at the time.

There would still have been elements within Pakistan that remained sympathetic to and in touch with the Taliban. The emergence of a troop withdrawal deadline for Afghanistan and the likelihood of the Taliban returning as a political player made it more in Pakistan's interest to try and find new solutions with its neighbour. The shift had a negative effect on our relations with Washington. 'The impact was seen over here ultimately as anti-American, because Americans were dying,' said Armitage. 'But it was not done as anti-American. It was much more as "this is Pakistan's interest".'[14]

Another continuous source of tension between the United States and Pakistan has been Pakistan's occasionally ambiguous attitude towards different extremist groups. Some terrorist units which did not seem to threaten Pakistan's state maintained ties with the security services. 'I think Pakistanis were slow to recognise that there are not good terrorists and bad terrorists,' Steve Hadley told me.

Islamabad officially denied any affiliation but the fact that this perception existed at the highest levels hurt the relationship. It was something the United States struggled to understand, despite the many examples of other powers expressing support for freedom fighters, whether in Afghanistan or Syria, at different points in recent history. As Kofi Annan succinctly put it to me when we met in Geneva: 'The world we live in changes, and attitudes change. Terrorists, or "freedom fighters" that we fight against, tomorrow can become our best friends.'

Much of the criticism levelled at Pakistan in the War on Terror has been unfair, since it is not seen in the context of its growing domestic challenges. The country has been forced to grapple with the very real impact of the war in Afghanistan, with more than 5 million refugees coming across its porous borders, along with terrorists who have settled in its tribal zones.[15] The human cost to Pakistan of the two Afghan wars has been immense.

At the same time, the Bush administration began separating out its relationships with India and Pakistan and dealing with them individually, as opposed to under the umbrella of one 'India-Pakistan' policy. This had the unintended consequence of weighing on the alliance with Islamabad. The so-called 'de-hyphenation' was meant to adapt to a new world order following the end of the Cold War – India had traditionally close ties with the Soviet Union, from which it received much of its military equipment. During that time, the United States sided with Pakistan, as the regional Cold War counterweight. Over the past few years the United States has made a concerted effort to boost trade and other links with India. Notably, its arms sales to Delhi have rocketed – between 2012 and 2014 alone, India's purchase of weapons from the United States rose almost tenfold, from $139 million a year to $1,141 million, according to the Stockholm International Peace Research Institute.[16]

The policy, not always clearly communicated, has made some stakeholders in the region uneasy. Nicholas Burns, the former United States diplomat, described the process to me: 'There was a strong sense in Washington in the first term of President Bush that India was going to become one of the world's largest economic powers. That it would be more glob- ally oriented in the future, not just regionally. And frankly we wanted to make sure that the democratic countries – Japan, Australia, India, the United States – were working together as military partners in the Indian Ocean and the Pacific. So that as China rises, it would rise into a space it would have to share, not a vacuum of power.'[17]

While Pakistan is aware of the United States' desire to build relationships that may serve as a counterbalance to an increasingly powerful China, Washington's increased closeness with Pakistan's historic adversary has also made Islamabad uneasy.

As the relationship with Pakistan deteriorated, the United States increased its use of drones. These unmanned weapons, unlike traditional fighter jets, carry no risk to American servicemen and can be activated by someone sitting at a computer terminal thousands of miles away; and arguably are therefore more likely to be liberally deployed. President Bush had provided the CIA with legal authority to hunt down and kill high value targets without seeking approval outside the agency beforehand.

Drones became particularly pertinent just days before my first formal visit to the White House. On 13 January 2006, a United States Hellfire missile drone attack killed at least eighteen civilians in the village of Damadola. Although the attack purportedly targeted Ayman al-Zawahiri, there were no Al Qaeda members among the casualties. A large number of the victims were children. The incident sparked public outrage and tens of thousands of Pakistanis took to the streets in protest. There was talk that I should cancel my trip to Washington as a result of the attack. However, I felt it would be more constructive to engage and try to resolve the issue.

There was a generally accepted view in Pakistan that all these drone attacks happened with the government's connivance. While we did give them a landing strip in northern Pakistan, it is not correct to say that we were forewarned before every attack. I raised the subject of drones with President Bush as we sat in the Oval Office with Dick Cheney, Condoleezza Rice and Steve Hadley by his side. I told him that it was tragic that innocent civilians lost their lives in Pakistan because of the Damadola attacks. Bush turned to his team and said: 'I think the prime minister has a point.' The president added that there should be more real-time information sharing between the United States and Pakistan.

The number of drone strikes has risen sharply since then – there were more in the first year of Barack Obama's presidency than there were in all previous years during the War on Terror combined. Pakistan has been the target of the majority of them, with more than 300 strikes killing between 400 and 900 civilians in 2004 to 2013. A 2013 report by Amnesty International fuelled the debate, saying: 'The use of drones by the USA has fast become one of the most controversial human rights issues in the world. In no place is this more apparent than in Pakistan.' It added: 'Amnesty International is seriously concerned that these strikes have resulted in unlawful killings that may constitute extrajudicial killings or war crimes.'[18]

President Obama's administration quickly identified Pakistan as a problem area and said the main effort to combat terrorism should be shifted there, instead of focusing on Afghanistan. However, on several occasions it reverted to an adversarial approach – in its rhetoric, diplomacy and even aid programmes: the Kerry-Lugar Bill was phrased in a way that many in Pakistan saw as unfavourable. It specified that, in order for Pakistan to be eligible for a $1.2 billion aid package, the United States would regularly need to sign off on how Pakistan was contributing to the fight against terrorism and spending aid money. The Kerry-Lugar Bill tied military assistance to certification related to counter-terrorism, nuclear non-proliferation and an assurance of civilian control over the army. Certification had to confirm Pakistan's cooperation in 'closing terrorist camps in the FATA, dismantling terrorist bases in other parts of the country, including Quetta and Muridke'; that 'the security forces of Pakistan are not materially and substantially subverting the political and judicial processes of Pakistan' and that 'the government of Pakistan exercises effective civilian control of the military, including approval of military budgets, the chain of command, the process of promotion for senior military leaders.'[19] This level of demands was clearly unacceptable, and should not have been agreed to by Pakistan. The terms were eventually shot down when they reached Islamabad. The media, the political parties and the military reacted sharply. The conditions implied in the bill have only strengthened the voice of those who argue that the War on Terror is not Pakistan's fight and that Pakistan is being used as hired help by the United States, which maintains an essentially transactional relationship with the country.

The danger is that, following the withdrawal of American troops from Afghanistan, the relationship may be designated a lower priority – even though Pakistan's strategic location, nuclear capability and security challenges require continuous engagement. Both sides have to work together to reduce the trust deficit.

5
FIGHTING OUR ALLIES
IN AFGHANISTAN

Kofi Annan sat in his Geneva office, poring over the document in front of him. On the left hand side of the page was a list of about a dozen names, with different countries marked across the top. The UN Secretary-General was calling the leaders of each and running the names past them, before noting down their response with either a tick or a cross. The fate of post-war Afghanistan was being decided. Whoever wasn't vetoed would be put forward as the country's next president. 'It was an extraordinary piece of paper,' Annan's deputy, Mark Malloch Brown, recalled.[1]

The United States' invasion in 2001 had swiftly overthrown the Taliban government, but the question of finding a new leader for Afghanistan remained. Annan spearheaded the effort, while representatives from Iran, Pakistan, Russia and China regularly called him for updates.[2]

Only one person scored across the list. President Musharraf gave Annan his final tick for Commander Abdul Haq, a former prominent mujaheddin commander. However, he was captured and executed by the Taliban in 2001, before the official selection could be made.

After that, the name everybody seemed to agree on was Hamid Karzai. Until recently Karzai had kept a low profile. He had been imprisoned by the Taliban when it seized power in Kabul and escaped from jail. A former senior UN official recalled: 'UNDP got this radio message: "We found someone on the roadside, can we pick him up?" So Karzai went into exile on the back of a UNDP pickup.' The official added: 'Given the way all of this began, it is not surprising that Karzai struggled for legitimacy.'[3]

Having left Afghanistan, Karzai worked for his family's restaurant business on the east coast of America before returning after the fall of the Taliban. He was chosen by the 2002 *loya jirga* and began his role as interim president, before winning the election two years later.

For a while, the allies worked well together in Afghanistan, successfully coordinating on a multinational level. Soon, however, their attention shifted and they became primarily concerned with overthrowing Saddam Hussein's regime in Iraq. General Jones was the NATO commander in Afghanistan between 2003 and late 2006. He travelled to Afghanistan two years after the invasion and met with the United States forces there. He asked: 'What's your estimate of the number of Al Qaeda inside Afghanistan?'

'Less than 100,' they said.

Jones followed up with: 'What's the number of Taliban fighters in Afghanistan?' and was told it was no more than 3,000. He recalled ten years later when I sat down with him to discuss Afghanistan: 'The attitude was – this is done, it is a small problem, we'll focus on Iraq.'[4]

Part of the tragedy of Afghanistan's recent history is the failure of major powers to take heed of the lessons of the past. The 1979 Afghan invasion by the Soviet Union triggered the last proxy war played out between the two Cold War superpowers. The United States and its allies had a keen interest to block Soviet expansion south and prevent the spread of communism. Pakistan's strategic location bordering Afghanistan provided an easy access route and a porous border from which the mujaheddin fighters could launch attacks on the Soviets. From Pakistan's perspective, there was also the fear that, were the Soviets to win in Afghanistan, the frontline would be at Pakistan's border.

The mujaheddin fighters were recruited mostly from the Middle East – countries such as Yemen, Saudi Arabia – as well as Pakistan and the Far East. Young Muslims were funded and trained by the ISI, CIA, MI6 and Saudi intelligence in camps on the border of Pakistan, after which they were sent to fight the Soviet troops. Financial aid from the United States and Saudi Arabia to the mujaheddin was channelled through Pakistan.

The allies began a campaign to galvanise support for the mujaheddin within Pakistan. Gradually popular support was shored up for the cause and thousands of Pakistanis joined the ranks of the fighters. As millions of Afghan refugees fled into Pakistan over the course of that war, the fate of the two nations became more intertwined than ever.

The United States soon became distracted by the collapse of the Soviet Union and the events unfolding in Eastern Europe. Disappointingly, there was no clear post-conflict exit strategy and the economic side of the war effort was particularly weak. A comprehensive plan was needed to create jobs, rebuild infrastructure, and improve the quality of life of Afghans. The country needed serious money, appropriate prioritisation of projects and speedy execution to show progress. The amount assigned by the allies was not anywhere near what Afghanistan required and none of the Bretton Woods institutions came forward to plug the gap.

The West also left behind the 'freedom fighters' it had armed, with no substantial effort to reintegrate them into the societies they came from. Some countries allowed them to come back but many others said they could not return, afraid that they had been radicalised and presented a security risk. Many who had fought for eight years in the Afghan terrain went on to settle there or in Pakistan's tribal areas. The infrastructure in these parts was already underdeveloped and not enough was done, either by Pakistan or the United Nations, to establish refugee camps and schools to handle the influx of people. UNHCR helped settle the refugees in camps, but many moved to the cities including Islamabad and Peshawar. Some camps were organised, others grew into slums.

Religious seminaries, or madrassas, began to fill the gap, supported by Muslim charities worldwide. Most of the funds came from Gulf countries; some were collected by religious political parties in Pakistan.[5] Other stakeholders then used them to destabilise the area. Meanwhile, the country remained flooded with arms. While some efforts were made to recover American weapons given to the mujaheddin, for the most part these did not succeed and were soon abandoned.

Having been triumphant in defeating the Soviet aggressor, the Afghan fighters split into their original tribal factions and started wrestling for control of the country. A power vacuum left by the collapse of the government, propped up by the Soviets, made way for a vicious civil war. Eventually, many Afghans became disappointed with the mujaheddin leaders, whose infighting prevented them from getting Afghanistan back on its feet. The Qandahar and Helmand regions, which were particularly affected by the nation's economic woes, became the breeding ground for the Taliban.[6]

The opposing groups were drawn along tribal lines, each of which had allegiances to different external powers. The Northern Alliance maintained close ties with India, Pakistan's historic adversary and main security threat at the time. Cautious of India gaining influence in Afghanistan and thus being exposed on two fronts, Pakistan sided with the Taliban, which was formed predominantly from Pashtun tribes. Led by a tall, pious figure called Mullah Omar, a veteran of jihad who had lost an eye in the fight against the Soviets, the Taliban defeated the other factions and seized power in Kabul. It imposed Sharia law and its conservative approach, particularly its repressive treatment of women, was frowned upon by the international community.

Lakhdar Brahimi, the UN special envoy for Afghanistan and one of the few officials to have met with Mullah Omar, told me: 'The Taliban were demonised because of their extreme religious views, but the difference between them and others was a difference of degrees. The Taliban told Afghan people they should grow their beards, consign their women to the home. That's nothing much to ask of the Afghan. That's what he does anyway. Of course human rights activists were horrified, but not the Afghan people. Many saw them as liberators.'[7] At the time, the Taliban's focus was only on Afghanistan – even after seizing Kabul it continued to wrestle for power with the other factions.

Before the Taliban had taken control of the country, a mujaheddin fighter called Osama Bin Laden founded Al Qaeda, a terrorist group focused on waging war against the West. He came back to Afghanistan after briefly returning to Saudi Arabia, from where he had gone to join the mujaheddin in the 1980s. Al Qaeda began to carry out atrocities across the world, including bombing the American embassies in Kenya and Tanzania in August 1998.

The Taliban did nothing to expel the terrorist group from Afghanistan, despite international outcries. Brahimi recalled meeting Mullah Omar at this time and urging him to change his approach: 'I told him that I come from a similar culture. A guest is a master of your house – until he starts throwing stones in the house of your neighbour. Then you don't owe him anything. And this is what Al Qaeda is doing, they are not doing anything for you but they're acting against other people. He said: "It's not true, and they told us that they are not doing anything."'

Eventually Bin Laden developed close links with Mullah Omar and gradually gained ideological influence on the Taliban. When the Taliban refused to expel Al Qaeda even after the World Trade Center attacks, its position became untenable in the face of international condemnation.

The United States and Pakistan in Afghanistan – 'fighting each other'

'We were fighting each other in Afghanistan, and we both lost.' This is how Ryan Crocker, the former United States ambassador to Afghanistan, summed up America and Pakistan's thirteen-year war partnership to me.[8]

The United States went into Afghanistan without a clear exit strategy. The result was a protracted war, with the allied forces staying on with unclear objectives and local hostility against them mounting. President Obama's announcement of a deadline for troop withdrawal by the end of 2014 and a perceived haste to leave undid some of the progress made during the US intervention.

In any conflict, the entry strategy and the exit strategy both have to be thought through at the start. Failure to adequately do this was the error made by the allies during the first Afghan war against the Soviets – and a mistake that is being repeated today.

Once again, the economic side of the war effort was not as strong as it should have been. More could have been done to fight the drug lords growing in influence, for example. I raised this issue several times with the United States, saying drug money should not be used to promote terrorism and extremism, but felt I did not get any traction.

Those who took part in the initial reconstruction efforts in Afghanistan have been left with a lingering sense of lost opportunity. General Jones described it for me: 'The sadness is there was a regional plan that would have benefitted everybody, but it took everybody to want to work together [for it to work], and unfortunately we didn't have willing partners. Military force alone on a sizeable insurgency is generally not enough without reconstruction.'

In General Jones' view, it requires a whole combination of elements working together. He said: 'In Afghanistan, the only one that was done well was the security element, but security is not enough. There was a big drug problem in Afghanistan, the rule of law was not really taking shape and economic development was spotty at best. Now it's too late. And it's too bad.'

The world's focus has shifted to the unfolding crises in Iraq, Syria and Yemen. Afghanistan, despite going through a vulnerable transitional period, has moved down the list of priorities. Meanwhile, the problems that bred security issues and made Afghanistan a haven for terrorists in the first place remain unresolved. A power vacuum or a period of poor governance would only make matters worse, unless serious attention is paid to avoiding them.

By the 2014 presidential election, the West's relations with Hamid Karzai had completely fallen apart. Karzai was publicly criticising the United States and its allies and delayed the signing of a status of forces agreement that would safeguard an American military presence after the troop withdrawal. In part, Karzai had been trying to cement his domestic position – the United States was increasingly seen as an unwelcome presence in Afghanistan. Karzai's aggressive posture towards the United States had also been down to a mishandling of relations with the Afghan leader, as well as his concerns about his legacy.

Richard Armitage, the former United States Deputy Secretary of State, said of the Americans' dealings with Karzai: 'We were unfair to him. First of all, we were looking for a Jeffersonian democrat, when "just good enough" would have been OK.'

In 2009, leaked cables from US Ambassador Karl Eikenberry criticised Karzai, calling him an unfitting partner for the United States. The relationship was further damaged when Eikenberry was allowed to retain his position, despite the revelations.

Armitage said: 'By leaving our ambassador for [more than] another year, the message to Karzai was very bad. The United States has to think through the implications of its actions.'

Donald Rumsfeld, the former Secretary of Defense, thinks the fallout came as a result of a mishandled relations with the Afghan leader. Speaking in 2014, months before the United States withdrew its troops, Rumsfeld said: 'They treated Karzai in a very unwise, undiplomatic manner. For the United States to have a series of diplomats who criticise him publicly, push him in a corner ... in my view he really had no choice but to fight back.'[9]

Rumsfeld urged more realism in the United States handling of the issue: 'Karzai was the elected leader and his interest was in representing the people of that country. Ultimately over time there are going to be areas where our interests and their interests do not converge.'

After a thirteen-year war which caused the deaths of tens of thousands of soldiers, more than 22,000 civilian casualties[10] and cost trillions of dollars, Western troops appear to be leaving the country without an exit strategy in place. It will now fall upon Kabul's new leadership and the regional powers – namely Pakistan, Iran, China and India – to navigate through the difficult transitional period.

Afghanistan-Pakistan relations

The first trip I ever made abroad was to Afghanistan. As a student in 1967, a friend and I took a government transport service bus from Peshawar to Kabul. The fare was about $5 each and got us through the Khyber Pass. I felt excited watching the ink dry on my first ever passport stamp. We stayed in a small hotel and spent our days exploring Kabul. Movie theatres were open and music from the local radio station was broadcast in the central square. Many women wore Western clothes and the city was bustling with traders and stalls. On the way back, I boarded my first ever plane – a DC6 Ariana Afghan Airlines aircraft back to Peshawar. It was a four-engine turboprop and I remember the thrill of climbing on board.

When I returned to Kabul in 2000, the city I knew as a young man had been mutilated. Parts looked like a battle zone and I saw walls strewn with bullet holes – haunting reminders of the the war with the Soviets and Taliban rule.

As finance minister, I led Pakistan's delegation at the first Tokyo summit to discuss development funding for Afghanistan after the Bonn Conference, which set up the post-Taliban government in 2001. It was the first occasion

I met President Karzai, who at the time was strengthened by the United States' backing. Clad in a green gown and cap which helped him stand out among the guests, he gave a confident speech in the presence of several heads of state and government. In my meetings I stressed the need for a Marshall Plan-type approach to Afghanistan. While the Tokyo meeting was a welcome initiative, much of the aid was subject to many conditions and there was not enough absorptive capacity on the ground in Afghanistan at the time.

Despite our meagre resources at that point and international reluctance to commit funds, Pakistan helped Afghanistan as much as possible on the development side and initiated a programme to build roads and other infrastructure. As finance minister, I set up a joint economic commission with Hidayat Amin Arsala, my counterpart in the Afghan government at the time. He played an important role in expanding our economic relationship to speed up the development of Afghanistan. The commission was an institutional forum where we tabled all our issues and worked to increase economic cooperation on issues like trade, transit and providing technical assistance. We concluded early on that there was no point in allowing our differences to impact on the need for economic cooperation. We started running commercial flights from Islamabad to Kabul. I continued to work on the joint economic commission with Ashraf Ghani when he became finance minister. He was then my counterpart for two years and I considered him committed and passionate about making a difference and rebuilding Afghanistan.

As prime minister, I would regularly visit President Hamid Karzai, making more trips to Afghanistan than any other country. We would usually meet in the Presidential Palace in

Kabul. For security reasons, there was not much movement beyond it. The meetings were often congenial although Karzai could be unpredictable to deal with – I sometimes found him emotional and inconsistent in his reactions to various events. Understandably, he was talking to all sides in the region, staying close to Iran, Pakistan and India. Nevertheless, I believed it was necessary to keep lines of communication open and continued my frequent visits. On one occasion, Karzai took me to see King Mohammed Zahir Shah, who lived in another part of the Presidential Palace. Another time, Karzai and I were joined by the Aga Khan, who played an active role in the reconstruction of Afghanistan and regularly visited the country. He was considered a reliable interlocutor, one who was respected by all sides.

My basic premise in all these interactions was always that a strong, stable Afghanistan is the best possible outcome for Pakistan. President Karzai tried to work with us to achieve the development goals but Pakistan's dealings with Afghanistan were complex and at times fraught with challenges.

The relationship between Pakistan and Afghanistan is hampered by a trust deficit. I witnessed its scale first-hand when I addressed the joint peace *jirga* in 2007, initiated by President Bush, President Musharraf and President Karzai as an attempt to resolve existing issues. I was faced with allegations of Pakistan supporting and sponsoring elements fuelling violence in Afghanistan, and seeking so-called 'strategic depth' in Afghanistan. I asked the peace *jirga*: 'How could we escape the negative consequences of such short-sighted and disastrous policy?'[11]

In his recent trips to the United States, President Ashraf Ghani has said Afghanistan and Pakistan are once again beginning to work together. This is a positive step forward for the two countries, although there will need to be a significant effort on both sides for it to take root.

Afghanistan today

One of the most pressing challenges the Afghan government faces is how to deal with the Taliban. In 2015, it once again hit the headlines after seizing key cities in Afghanistan, including Kunduz. The consensus is now that it will need to be included in the political process. The question for Afghanistan is going to be whether the Taliban is prepared to negotiate with Kabul, and on what terms.

Some argue that the allies' failure to engage the Taliban shortly after the 2001 invasion was a missed opportunity, and one which may not arise again anytime soon – not least because its splintered nature makes negotiating hard. In hindsight, if the international community had worked with the Taliban then as it is attempting to do now, maybe relations with Afghanistan would have been different for the allies.

'After 2001, we all made lots of mistakes,' Lakhdar Brahimi told me. 'It was not possible to have the Taliban at the conference in Bonn. They would not have come, because their regime had been destroyed. But even if they had wanted to come, we couldn't have had them because of the Americans.'[12]

After the Bonn process, Brahimi said: 'We should have tried to talk to the Taliban then, in the beginning of 2002. But a lot of people were saying: "Forget about them, they are finished". This was probably the biggest mistake. If we had tried to speak to them, a lot of them could have joined the process.'

Mark Malloch Brown said of the West's approach to the Taliban: 'This American policy of co-mingling the Taliban and Al Qaeda, instead of understanding that there is a differ-

81

ence between the host and the guest – that was a real foreign policy error.'

Afghanistan consists of multiple centres of power, which will compete for influence on a national level. A fully functioning government will need to bring all of these stakeholders together. The election in 2014 ushered in a government which represented two major groups of the Afghan population – a positive step forward. So far, this National Unity Government, headed by President Ashraf Ghani, has shown promise. Abdullah Abdullah, the former foreign minister, became the chief executive of the country. It remains to be seen how it will navigate the intergovernmental relations between these two very different personalities with separate power bases.

The need for maintaining the current multi-ethnic structure of the Afghan national army is also critical to the future stability of Afghanistan and for maintaining unity between the different factions of the country. Should the coalition government break down, then one big question would be how the army would then position itself – would we see different ethnic groups within the army going their own ways and joining separate factions? Would the speed of desertions accelerate? Such an outcome would have serious ethnic implications, and Afghanistan could return to the kind of regional conflict seen in the 1980s.

The government must commit to delivering growth and curtail rising unemployment by providing jobs. It should aim to deliver higher income and better standards of living, as well as improving connectivity – only 6% of Afghans are classed as Internet users by the World Bank.[13] The government needs to be able to rise above ethnic divisions while maintaining good relations with its neighbours, reforming and opening up the economy and creating opportunity. About 36% of Afghans live below the poverty line, according to the World Bank, and the country is in need of broad-based structural reform.[14] A home-grown comprehensive economic plan is needed, as well as increased funding through active donor support, aid agencies and development institutions. Renewed attempts should be made in trying to exploit Afghanistan's mining and energy potential. The necessary budget is required to fund social programmes, improve the education system and develop infrastructure. Expanding the availability of microfinance, which allows individuals and small-scale businesses to take out loans, and incentivising small and medium-sized enterprises will provide Afghans with the tools to rebuild their lives.

Drug money continues to play a toxic role and a concerted effort is required to substitute the opium trade for other cash crops, changing the main source of rural income to agriculture and halting the spread of drug production. Alternative industry – such as Afghanistan's tradition of producing quality fruit – should be reinvigorated.

Afghanistan must build its institutions to jump the curve. It needs a strong independent central bank, development bank and commercial banks. While these exist in some form, more focus is needed to elevate them to higher standards. The government should encourage the private sector to take over as much as possible. For this to happen, it must create an enabling environment for growth with greater transparency. Informal market mechanisms such as money changers – *havala* – who are outside the net, must be brought into the system. It cannot be done by decree overnight. To give them credit, during my days as finance minister I witnessed both Arsala and Ghani try to move in that direction. With help from various institutions, they attempted to rebuild the central bank and the ministry of finance.

A tremendous amount of aid is required, and the efforts of no individual source will be sufficient. As in 2001, I still believe Afghanistan would benefit from a Marshall Plan-type approach for development, which could be funded by a group of countries including the United States, Russia, China, Japan and the EU states. While commitments after the Bonn process were made, the money either did not materialise or was not deployed in a way that made a real difference. Afghanistan should redouble its efforts to engage the necessary global development institutions; such as the World Bank, the IMF, the ADB, the AIIB, the Silk Road Fund, and the Islamic Development Bank; as well as seeking bilateral aid agencies to provide funding and expertise for development projects and help the government prioritise development.

While the situation in the tribal areas is improving, the country still risks being destabilised by ethnic and religious divides; namely between Shias and Sunnis, and ethnic divisions including the Pashtuns and the Panshiris and the Uzbeks and the Hazaras. These divisions are susceptible to exploitation by different forces who wish to test the system. The government will need to exercise decisive leadership to galvanise the different groups and strive for national unity. It will need to create the necessary space in society to allow every sectarian, ethnic and tribal group to live in peace. This is where the responsibility lies on Ashraf Ghani's shoulders to try and engage all factions and convince them of the need to build a new future for Afghanistan. President Ghani has told me of his wish to have all stakeholders come to the negotiating table, and said he was taking steps to engage with the Taliban.[15]

It will help Kabul's bargaining position if it is backed by an effective security force. It is yet to be seen whether the newly-trained soldiers in Afghanistan will be effective – particularly considering they too have their own tribal affiliations and they will return to those if the country descends into civil war.

Afghanistan and Pakistan's future relationship

Almost 1.5 million registered Afghan refugees live in camps in Pakistan located close to the border with Afghanistan – globally the largest protracted refugee population, according to the United Nations.[16] The camps have provided safe havens and hideouts for extremists and Taliban sympathisers, as well as other criminal elements. Refugee children living there receive limited madrassa education. In 2007, I used the opportunity of the joint peace *jirga* to stress the importance of relocating these refugees back to Afghanistan, although little was done as a result.

Today, the situation is even more complicated. There has been no success in stemming the flow of arms from Afghanistan into Pakistan. Moreover, certain forces have exploited the situation in Afghanistan and used it to hurt Pakistan. Kabul should foster good relations with Islamabad by not allowing extremists hostile to Pakistan and other criminal elements to use its territory as a safe haven. In 2013, the United States forces arrested the number two high commander of the Tehrik-e-Taliban Pakistan (TTP) in Afghanistan, while he was in the company of Afghan intelligence operatives.[17] The news understandably shocked Pakistanis and indicated that there are elements within Afghanistan that are working to influence the TTP. India has also been suspected of links to the TTP. Zalmay Khalilzad, the former United States envoy to Afghanistan, commented on India's support for the TTP: 'As Indian influence increases, you can see this escalating.'[18]

India has four consulates in Afghanistan, as well as its embassy in Kabul. This is similar to its representation in the UK, where the Indian population numbers more than 1.4 million people. In Afghanistan, it is estimated at about 10,000. While the Indian population in Afghanistan has faced significant adversity in recent history, which could explain the extra desire to offer it representation and protection, it is still unclear why so many consulates are needed. Pakistan has concerns that these consulates amount to listening posts and are used by agents active along the border. During one of our meetings, I asked President Karzai: 'Why are there so many Indian consulates near our border?'

I did not get a convincing response. While Pakistan should not be paranoid about Afghanistan's relations with India, all sides should make sure that Afghanistan is not used by any country for subversive activity against Pakistan.

During my time in office, our approach to Afghanistan was to consider that the countries were inextricably linked – I would regularly say they are joined at the hip. They share a common history, culture and a porous border. About 35 million Pashtuns live either side of the Durand Line[19] and Pakistan has absorbed more than 5 million Afghan refugees.[20] Afghanistan is landlocked and will always need a peaceful Pakistan to procure goods, since Karachi is its most convenient port. At the same time, Afghanistan provides a market for Pakistani products. If the countries can have a mature approach to bilateral relations, then the outcome could be a win-win for both. They must build a common infrastructure – including roads and railways – and encourage companies and banks to open branches in each other's countries. Some progress has been made but there could also be cooperation on water flows, electricity grids and trade of commodities, such as cement.

Such linkages and interdependencies will both help economic development and create a sense of trust and peace, including in the Afghanistan-Pakistan border areas.

Pakistan should play a part in helping the new government in Kabul strengthen its position by offering intelligence coordination and technical expertise. The two countries should have joint monitoring of the disputed border and security cooperation. Pakistan could help establish a dialogue with the Taliban, as it has already gradually been doing.

There needs to be a programme which includes projects where Pakistan is clearly seen to be helping, not only using leverage. This must be done in a proactive way, to show the country's goodwill towards its neighbour and its investment in Afghanistan's success. A reserve of trust must be rebuilt, on both sides. After the strain caused by the absorption of millions of refugees and the influx of terror in Afghanistan and Pakistan, both countries need to convince each other that they mean well.

I had breakfast with President Ashraf Ghani while he was on an official trip to London in December 2014 and we talked about Afghanistan's future, as well as its relationship with Pakistan. He told me he wanted to 'change the undeclared state of hostility to a peaceful one.'[21] He thought Pakistan and Afghanistan have a 'special relationship', and that the two countries needed to normalise their dealings with one another, clearly defining its parameters. The two countries should focus on developing 'mutual dependencies' to build up trust – for example, cooperation in electricity generation and linking up grids. It is important to attract investment and get the economy moving. In this, China could play an important role in investing, boosting development and promoting peace, in addition to the United States, the European Union and Islamic countries.

President Ghani shared his vision for Afghanistan with me: 'My outlook is that Afghanistan could be the Asian roundabout, a hub of connectivity for energy, logistics – and a centre for agriculture, water management and irrigation.' He said: 'We have an army of about 300,000 troops and a trained police force. There is no risk of the state collapsing and we will not allow any parallel governments to be established. The writ of the government will be maintained at all costs.'

Asked about the issue he faces with the Taliban, the Afghan leader added: 'We are trying to get a deal with the Taliban. The majority will agree this is needed but we should give them incentives to bring them into the fold. We must resolve our issues politically, not militarily, and we should have a partnership with them.'

We agreed that the joint Pakistan and Afghanistan economic commission, which was started in my time, should be reinvigorated and meet regularly in order to explore areas in which the countries can cooperate, such as linking electricity grids and building dams. The commission could also be a forum in which any issues can be settled as and when they arise.

The two countries should treat points of difference with patience. 'Every problem is not a nail to be hit when you want action,' said Ghani. 'We need to heal the wounds between the two countries.' The governments in Kabul and Islamabad need to seize the moment and work together to build a mutually beneficial relationship. This will help resolve other issues which have lingered for a while.

The United States and Afghanistan

Ashraf Ghani succeeded Karzai when the relationship with the United States was at a low point and took steps to repair

1&2 On a family holiday in Italy with my mother and my sister. It was the first and only time I boarded a plane until my student days, when I flew to Kabul, Afghanistan.

3 My father walking in Champaign Urbana at the University of Illinois, United States, where he did his masters in electrical engineering.

4 As a student at the Institute of Business Administration in Karachi. I was in charge of collecting hostel fees and the funds were used to pay for food in the cafeteria. I earned an allowance of forty rupees a month.

5 At Abbottabad public school with two prefects, Imtiaz Alam from Dacca and Razzak Bandukda from Karachi. My education was entirely in Pakistan.

6 With Rukhsana in our wedding photo. The ceremony was performed at the InterContinental Hotel Rawalpindi, by H.E. Gilani, the Iraqi ambassador to Pakistan and a religious leader. We honeymooned in the Swat Valley in Northern Pakistan.

1&2 My thirty-year career at Citibank gave me access at the highest levels around the world. I travelled with both Margaret Thatcher and George H. W. Bush while they were on speaking tours for Citibank shortly after they had each left office.

3 Prime Minister Benazir Bhutto, along with her husband Asif Ali Zardari, paid a surprise visit to my Citibank residence in Singapore.

4 With the Malaysian prime minister, Mahathir Mohamad.

With the Citibank chairman, John Reed, and his wife Cindy at their home in Boston in 2014, where John was chairman of the MIT Corporation board of trustees.

&3 Citibank executives, past and present. Sandy Weill, John Reed's co-CEO after the merger, with Joan Weill; and the current CEO Michael Corbat with Vice Chairman Alan MacDonald.

With Paul Collins, the vice chairman of Citibank and his wife Carol.

In Karachi at the Institute of Business Administration campus. With Julio de Quesda, head of Citibank; Dr Abdul Wahab, dean of the IBA; Dr Mukhtar, founder and former dean of the IBA; Dr Mateen, former dean of the IBA; Mr Inayat Din; Fazle Hasan and other faculty members.

With Richard Huber, who I worked for in several different positions at Citibank.

1 In Geneva opening an office of SAMBA, Citibank's Saudi Arabian affiliate. L-R: Hafid Alawi, Zakaria Kabba, Chairman Abdul Aziz Al Gosaibi, Dr Khalil Kordi, Dr Mulla, Sam Mikdashi, Rashid Romaizan and Tariq Tamimi.

2 Many of my fellow Citibankers went on to hold government positions. Pictured: Shuaib Ahmed, one of the people who hired me; Salim Raza, who became governor of the central bank in Pakistan; Shaukat Tarin, who became minister of finance and Zubyr Soomro, who became president of United Bank Limited.

3 In Bahrain opening Citibank's first Islamic bank, photographed with the board of directors and HRH Shaikh Khalifa bin Salman Al Khalifa, prime minister of Bahrain, and H.E. Sheikh Ebrahim K. Al Khalifa and Mohammed Al-Shroogi.

1   I had never met General Musharraf until he called me, out of the blue, and asked me to join his government and turn the economy around. Pictured at the National Command Authority meeting with General Musharraf, General Ehsan ul Haq, General Kayani, General Kidwai and others.

2   The handover ceremony of strategic missiles to the strategic forces command group at a military base.

3   Attending the annual Republic Day parade with General Ehsan ul Haq, President Musharraf, Admiral Tahir and General Ahsan Hayat. I am pointing to the airforce fly past, led by Airforce Chief Tanvir Mahmood Ahmed.

4   The opening of the defense products export exhibition in Karachi. I am being received by the chairman of joint chief staff, General Aziz, along with Governor Sindh, Dr Ishrat Ul Ibad, and Major General Ali Hamid.

Although the military takeover had been bloodless, many viewed the new government with trepidation. Months after it had taken place, the former prime minister, Nawaz Sharif, remained detained. US President Bill Clinton and King Abdullah bin Abdul Aziz Al Saud of Saudi Arabia, rallied to get Sharif released.

1   Years later with Bill Clinton, singer Bono and former Congressman Joe Scarborough at a gala in Washington.

2   Meeting King Fahd Bin Abdul Aziz of Saudi Arabia at the Royal Palace.

3   With King Abdullah bin Abdul Aziz Al Saud of Saudi Arabia.

4   With King Abdullah II Ibn Al Hussein of Jordan, the country where I spent my early banking days as head of Citibank Amman.

5   I accompanied General Musharraf when he met with Sheikh Zayed bin Sultan Al Nahyan, ruler of UAE, at his palace in Abu Dhabi. Sheikh Zayed urged General Musharraf to co-operate with the United States in our dealings with Afghanistan.

After the 9/11 attacks shocked the world, the focus shifted to Afghanistan and the hunt for Osama Bin Laden. Pakistan's strategic position made it a vital ally in the War on Terror. It gave legitimacy to the new leadership in Islamabad and the West welcomed us with open arms.

1 Taking a stroll with George W. Bush in the garden at the White House.

2 Rukhsana with Laura Bush in the White House.

3 Talks with George W. Bush at the Oval Office.

4 With Prime Minister Tony Blair outside 10 Downing Street.

5 Catching up with Vice President Dick Cheney during a visit to Washington.

President Musharraf and Prime Minister Atal Bihari Vajpayee came close to finally reaching a settlement on Kashmir, aided by American and British diplomats. However, a change of government in India stalled the process.

1   With Mr Vajpayee's successor, Prime Minister Manmohan Singh.

2   I was asked to be the minister in waiting for Prime Minister Vajpayee when he visited Pakistan for the South Asian Association for Regional Cooperation (SAARC) summit in 2002. He discussed a back channel peace process on Kashmir. Pictured, visiting him at his home in Delhi after he left office.

3   We started a bus service to Kashmir to facilitate travel across the Line of Control, as part of the back channel process. Pictured by the Line of Control.

4   Meeting with Kashmiri leaders during my visit to Delhi. L-R: Shabbir Shah, Yasin Malik, Syed Geelani, Mir Waiz Omar Farooq and Abdul Ghani Bhatt.

5   Distributing awards at the 'passing out parade' at the Pakistan Military academy in Kakul, near Abbottabad.

6   In Delhi at the Pakistan high commissioner's reception with Foreign Minister Natwar Singh, former Prime Minister Inder Gujral, LK Advani and Mr Inderjeet.

1   I had a one-on-one meeting with Muammar Gaddafi in Tripoli. Pictured with Gaddafi and President Hugo Chavez of Venezuela. At the time, Gaddafi had rekindled his relationship with the West. His dealings with the Arab world, however, remained complex.

2   Welcoming the Bangladesh prime minister, Khaleda Zia, on a visit to Pakistan.

3   At the D8 summit in Bali, Indonesia, with President Yudhoyono of Indonesia, President Obasanjo of Nigeria, Prime Minister Erdogan of Turkey, President Ahmadinejad of Iran and Prime Minister Badawi of Malaysia.

4   I was in Davos when I first met Recep Tayyip Erdogan, who was the mayor of Istanbul at the time and later went on to be prime minster then president of Turkey.

1   I made regular trips to see President Hamid Karzai, although the relationship between Afghanistan and Pakistan remained complex.

2   With the current Afghan president, Ashraf Ghani. We worked closely together when we were both finance ministers in our respective countries.

3   With Hedayat Amin Arsala, former vice president and finance minister of Afghanistan.

4   Opening a road, financed and built by Pakistan, from Torkham to Jalalabad in Afghanistan, along with President Karzai.

What was left of my armoured car following a suicide bomb attack while I was on the campaign trail.

Addressing Parliament in Islamabad after being voted in as prime minister.

Many thought I would pack up my bags and go back to New York after the attack, but it only spurred me on and reinforced my desire to serve my country.

I received many messages of support following the attack, including Rafik Hariri, the prime minister of Lebanon, who airlifted an armoured car from his own fleet. Just one year later he was assassinated when a bomb detonated in his motorcade. I am pictured with his son, the former prime minister of Lebanon, Saad Hariri.

With key members of my staff, when I was prime minister – a dedicated team.

1   With His Majesty King Bhumibol of Thailand
    at his summer palace.

2   With Lee Kuan Yew, the founder of Singapore.
    We first met while I was running Citibank's Asian
    business in Singapore.

3   With the Sultan of Brunei and the Crown Prince
    of Brunei, at the Sultan's royal palace in Bandar
    Seri Begawan.

4   With Lee Kuan Yew's son and current prime minister
    of Singapore, Lee Hsien Loong.

5   Cricket was always part of the discussion with
    the Australian prime minister, John Howard.

6   With the Korean president, Roh Moo-hyun,
    at the Blue House, Seoul.

7   In Phoenix Arizona with the Mexican president,
    Vincente Fox, fundraising for education.

8   With President Ramos of the Philippines, in Manila,
    which was my first overseas Citibank assignment.

With Chancellor Angela Merkel, while she was leader of the opposition.

With former German president, Hörst Kohler, in Berlin.

With Chancellor Gerhard Schröder after the welcoming ceremony at the Chancellery in Berlin.

With the Aga Khan, who has played a key role promoting development projects and humanitarian work in Pakistan, Afghanistan and other countries.

The official welcome by Thaksin Shinawatra, prime minister of Thailand, during my visit to Bangkok.

1 I typically briefed representatives of the press on the flights back from official trips.

2 With the Italian prime minister, Silvio Berlusconi, in Rome.

3 Addressing the Boao Forum for Asia with Bob Hawke, the former prime minister of Australia and originator of the APEC concept.

4 With Abdullah Badawi, the prime minister of Malaysia, at Putrajaya, Kuala Lumpur.

5 With the King of Bhutan at his palace, visiting as prime minister and chairman of the South Asian Association for Regional Cooperation (SAARC).

6 Addressing the NATO council in Brussels along with the NATO Secretary General.

Pakistan retained close military cooperation with the US, which provided us with vital aid and helped get the Bretton Woods institutions on board with our reform programme after 9/11

I developed a close relationship with Colin Powell, pictured here in 2015, outside his home.

The authors meeting with George W. Bush at the George Bush Presidential Library in Dallas, Texas.

Being received by US Secretary of Defense Donald Rumsfeld at the Pentagon.

While working for Citibank, I lived in Saudi Arabia and Jordan, and at one point ran the bank's Middle East business. I regularly travelled there after joining the government, building on Pakistan's close relationship with the GCC region.

1 The historic meeting between President Franklin D. Roosevelt and King Abdul Aziz, which cemented the relationship between the United States and Saudi Arabia.

2 Senator John Kerry hosted a dinner at his residence during my visit to Washington as prime minister. It was attended by all members of the Senate Foreign Relations Committee, including Chairman Richard Lugar.

3 With Sheikh Nahyan bin Mubarak Al Nahyan, United Arab Emirates, minister of culture and knowledge development.

4 With Prince Alwaleed bin Talal, a global entrepreneur.

it, promptly signing the status of forces agreement. America agreed to leave behind about 6,000 troops to help maintain order and create a smoother transition. Today, international cooperation, aid and reconstructive efforts are more vital than ever to set Afghanistan on the right track.

The United States is critical in the future of Afghanistan, through its potential to provide financial support and act as a stabilising force. In the past, the United States and the Soviet Union both built roads in Afghanistan – resuming such investment in infrastructure would be a boon for the country. While an American security presence is needed, it is important that it remains a soft one, so as to not look like an occupying force. It would be helpful for the United States to maintain some airborne capability to intervene at the request of the Afghan administration. This, along with drones and elite troops, could target pockets of trouble and help create stability in the country.

However, it is unclear whether the United States will stay invested in Afghanistan, considering its domestic mood and budgetary pressures. General Jones, who was NATO commander and was given the mission of writing the operational plan that brought NATO into Afghanistan, said: 'I see a danger of doing what we did in Vietnam When we left, about two years later Congress cut off the money to Vietnam, the north invaded the south and it collapsed. I think there is a danger history could repeat itself.'

Some have taken a more bearish view of the country's future in terms of security. The former US National Security Advisor Brent Scowcroft told me: 'I think Afghanistan is likely to be a problem for all of us for a long time. We shouldn't occupy it, we shouldn't try to steer it too hard, but it's going to be a problem for a long time, exporting trouble.' Whether this can be avoided remains to be seen, but it is clear that, for the benefit of the region's security and stability, a greater level of attention and aid should be committed to help Afghanistan get back on its feet.

I am optimistic about Afghanistan's future and believe its potential can be realised, but this requires political will, leadership and a substantial amount of external help. The sooner the international community realises this, the better for the security of the region and the wider world.

6
GADDAFI'S SURPRISE

'Come, let us go in,' Colonel Gaddafi said, putting his arm around me and leading the way into a banqueting tent on his compound. It was my first time face-to-face with the Libyan leader.

After landing at Tripoli airport for an official visit to Libya in 2006, I was greeted by Prime Minister Al Baghdadi Ali Al Mahmudi, the cabinet and a host of dignitaries, along with the guard of honour. He travelled with me to my hotel and was meant to host a dinner for me that evening.

The day took an unexpected turn when I was informed of a change of plan – Colonel Gaddafi himself would host the dinner. I received the news with a mixture of curiosity and trepidation. That evening, I was driven to Bab al-Aziziya, the presidential compound made up of a maze of houses and bedouin tents.

'Brother Leader is ready for you,' I was told as I entered a small tent next to the banquet. To my surprise he was accompanied by President Hugo Chavez of Venezuela – I was not even aware the Venezuelan president was in Tripoli.

Gaddafi's arm weighed heavily on my shoulders. I glanced to my right and saw that he had placed his other arm around Chavez. Several hundred guests stood up and greeted us as the Libyan leader made his grand entrance and we proceeded to the head table.

91

After dinner, Gaddafi pulled me aside. 'We will meet again tomorrow,' he said. We agreed to arrange a time and I rose to go back to my hotel. As he was seeing me off, Gaddafi asked: 'Have you seen the remains of the bombing?'

In 1986, his compound had been the target of an American attack, following the bombing of a Berlin nightclub in which US servicemen died and which was linked to Libya. In retaliation, the United States bombed the compound but Gaddafi survived. He then erected a monument on the site of the incident – a left-handed fist crushing an American fighter plane. He suggested I go see it, before adding: 'See how they attacked me and my family.'

As a man who had enjoyed absolute power for decades after seizing control through a military coup in 1969, Gaddafi had seen his relationship with the outside world see-saw. It became particularly adversarial due to his links with certain extremist groups. Sanctions were imposed on Libya after the terrorist attack on a Pan Am plane in 1988 shocked the world. However, observing the World Trade Center attacks and the subsequent invasions of Afghanistan and Iraq reportedly caused him to change track. He renounced Al Qaeda's actions, stopped Libya's development of weapons of mass destruction and nuclear programmes and built friendly ties with the West. In return, he began to be met warmly by European leaders and foreign companies looked to invest in Libya.

During my brief stay in Tripoli, I witnessed signs of Colonel Gaddafi's new friendship with the West. The top two floors of the Corinthia Hotel, where I was staying, were occupied by an American advance team preparing to open a US embassy in Tripoli. They shared the hotel with European tourists setting off on day trips to Leptis, the grand roman ruins outside the capital.

It therefore took me by surprise when, during my meeting with Gaddafi the next day, he turned to me and said: 'Let me tell you: do not trust the Americans.'

We were sitting in another, simpler tent. It had a small old-fashioned television and a disconnected phone on the table with the wire hanging from it.

'But, Brother Leader, my hotel is full of Americans,' I said. 'You are being so friendly with them and you are telling me not to trust them?'

'Yes,' He said. 'I do not trust them, but I have to live with them.'

As I prepared to leave, I invited Gaddafi to visit Pakistan. I was taken aback by his response. 'I will not visit Pakistan,' he said. 'I cannot forget the fact that your country killed my brother and friend Zulfikar Ali Bhutto.' The Libyan leader added: 'I can never forgive that. He was somebody I liked and respected a lot.'

I told Gaddafi it was regrettable that he would not be visiting Pakistan, and suggested he reconsider before paying my respects and leaving. Even though he did not come, Pakistan maintained close ties with Libya as we were eager to attract investment and send more Pakistani workers there.

Kofi Annan, the former UN Secretary-General, gave me his views on Gaddafi's relationship with the West: 'It is something that maybe history will judge. But he did manage to get the West around him, he did manage to convince them that he had changed his approach, and he was willing to join the international community and accept the rules.'[1]

Gaddafi's relationship with the rest of the Arab world, however, remained complex. I recall a meeting with the then-Egyptian president, Hosni Mubarak, when his country hosted the World Economic Forum in 2006, which many other heads of state and government attended. I met Mubarak on the manicured lawns of the golf course at Sharm el-Sheikh and raised the subject of Gaddafi. 'We have to live with him,' was Mubarak's unenthusiastic response.

Five years later, the world watched Colonel Gaddafi's downfall. In 2011, following a popular uprising, NATO intervened with air strikes to help rebel forces topple his government. Gaddafi ended up on the run, with a $2 million bounty on his head. Eventually he was tracked down and killed in his home town, Sirte.

Little has been revealed about the behind-the-scenes discussions which were taking place with Gaddafi before his downfall. While these included two calls made in a 'personal capacity' by Tony Blair,[2] there was also a more organised effort to liaise with Gaddafi. I met with the former French prime minister, Dominique De Villepin, who was involved in trying to negotiate with Gaddafi after the revolt, urging him to step away from power. He told me: 'I was part of the negotiation with Gaddafi's people, until the last moment. We almost reached an agreement. Qatar, France and Japan were involved, as well as the closest people to Gaddafi.'[3]

This was before the fall of Tripoli. Those negotiating with Gaddafi told him: 'You can keep some responsibility, but you must accept a united national government and step aside. We do not want to destroy what existed. You have been giving your life to create a certain order in Libya. We want to have a more stable Libya, and we want to solve the problem.' The key requirement was for Gaddafi to step down.

However, these were not direct negotiations. On Gaddafi's side, they were held through Bashir Saleh and other members of the Libyan leader's close circle. 'That was part of the problem, we could not get to him directly,' De Villepin said. He added: 'It was his lack of trust in his allies that prevented him from making a deal in the end.'

The biggest issue with the Western intervention in Libya was that it had no developed post-conflict strategy, which left the country in a weak state. Sending in NATO, an organisation built to contain communist expansion, to carry out regime change in north Africa was flawed from day one. Although it was understandable to take issue with the human rights violations carried out in Gaddafi's time, military intervention set a poor precedent in removing a head of government. The fabric of the state deteriorated with no viable alternative to take its place. Meanwhile, the problems the Libyan people faced under the old regime – poverty, lack of freedom, an environment of fear – remain.

After Gaddafi's downfall, the world made the mistake of assuming that new leaders would emerge and take part in a democratic election and that the government would gradually start functioning as normal. Instead, the authority of the state disintegrated, security deteriorated and the economy stagnated. When the writ of the government no longer functions, it creates a power vacuum and non-state actors may step in to fill the void. The lack of post-conflict strategy left the country in an unpredictable situation, with no local capability to take charge and assure a reasonable level of governance. Moreover, when the fabric of the state crumbles in a tribal society like Libya, the administrative system ceases to function effectively and people gravitate toward pre-existing tribal loyalties.

The country effectively imploded and became a safe haven for terrorists and an unreliable supplier of oil. The power vacuum and existing tribal fault lines have played into the hands of terrorist groups which have benefitted from the instability. In some parts, non-state actors took over the state's structures of raising revenue. Chaos ensued and violence escalated – in 2012, heavily armed militants attacked the American embassy compound in Benghazi. The United States ambassador, J. Christopher Stevens, was killed during the attack, along with three other Americans.

Dominique De Villepin told me: 'Gaddafi, with all his faults, was able to unite the tribes in Libya. The problem is, if you just go into these countries, you will get the same results after a couple of years of civil war. At the end of the day we are going to support the same kind of regimes.'

Any externally driven regime change involving military intervention instead of democratic process is fraught with danger. To use military power to remove a government and promote rebel forces, with no clear post-conflict strategy, is highly damaging in the long-run. It is a simplistic approach to complex problems without giving full consideration to the realities on the ground. Regime change can lead to balkanization, state collapse and the strengthening of non-state actors – scars which take a very long time to heal.

De Villepin said: 'Regime change, through the eye of the United States, UK or even France, is always meant to bring a friendly regime to the Western world. This is a big mistake. The important issue is for these regimes to be legitimate and able to do better for its people.'

For a transition to take place smoothly, a new government should ideally integrate part of the deposed one. After Colonel Gaddafi was killed, people in Libya were willing to work with those from the former regime. But the democratic countries, which had carried out the intervention, opposed this.

The press surrounding the public appearances made by British Prime Minister David Cameron and French President Nicolas Sarkozy in Libya after the invasion did not help the perception of the West in the region. Alain Minc, who was an adviser to Sarkozy at the time, later told me: 'It was a matter of internal politics. Both of them needed it for public opinion.'[4]

As the international debate rages over what could be the best approach to Syria and Bashar al-Assad's regime, we have to ask ourselves – can toppling a government ever work? And if we decide to resort to it, have we made a realistic assessment of the situation, and considered the potential fallout such a military intervention could bring?

7
THE COLD WAR ON TERROR

On 12 November 2015, Pentagon officials declared that an American drone attack in Syria had killed Jihadi John: one of the most harrowing figures of the Islamic State and the hooded star of its brutal execution videos. His death appeared to be a victory in the fight against global extremism. The euphoria did not last. Only a day later, a series of coordinated attacks terrorised Paris, killing 130 people. The president of France, Francois Hollande, declared a state of emergency.

Fourteen years had passed since the 9/11 attacks sparked the War on Terror. In that time, the enemy has morphed and adapted. We have seen the emergence of terrorist armies and, with the Islamic State, extremists seizing and running territories.

In 2014, I spoke with the former United States Secretary of Defense Donald Rumsfeld, who launched the War on Terror, spearheading the toppling of Saddam Hussein and the fight against Al Qaeda in Afghanistan. I asked him how he perceives today's threat from the spread of extremist groups and what could be done to combat them. He said:

'My instinct tells me that it is more like the Cold War. It is not a war that is going to be fought or won with bullets. It is ideological, and will take time and patience, just like the Cold War took several decades. The ideas that radical Islamists want to promote have a degree of persuasiveness in the world. They are still able to raise money, and they are still able to recruit. [While] the pressure put on them has been beneficial, the battle ultimately is going to be won not by the West against them, but more within that faith, by people who come to the conclusion that the course of radicalism is not going to be beneficial for their people, and that support will erode over a period of a decade or two.'[1]

Rumsfeld's prognosis worried me.

We must ask ourselves – what have we done wrong? What could have been handled differently?

I remember discussing the changing threats facing the world with the British prime minister, Tony Blair, at the Commonwealth summit in 2005. Following the military takeover in 1999, Pakistan had been suspended from the Commonwealth and only allowed to re-enter six years later. As prime minister, I led our delegation to the summit in Malta, which was attended by Queen Elizabeth II and Tony Blair, as well as President Thabo Mbeki of South Africa, President Olusegun Obasanjo of Nigeria and Prime Minister Abdullah Ahmad Badawi of Malaysia, as well as many other dignitaries.

During the summit I met Blair at the British high commissioner's residence in Malta. It was just months after bombs had struck the transport systems in London, in the most devastating coordinated terror attacks the UK had ever seen. Once we had finished with the pleasantries and got down to business, I turned to the subject of terrorism and said: 'Your government needs to do more to integrate Muslim communities living in the UK into British society. They should not be a marginalised community – there is no reason why they cannot be part of the mainstream. Young people have to be given opportunities in education and the job market and a chance to compete on a level playing field. Failure to do so can open up the risk of their frustration being expressed in extreme ways.'

When I met with Tony Blair again in 2014, seven years after he left office, we reflected that the threat of terrorism had only grown, morphing into a new phenomenon with the emergence of the Islamic State. He recalled our meeting in Malta, and said:

'I remember you really gave me a very concise and direct message on the threat of extremism, and the threat in Britain too. This is the first time I had this explained to me on such clear terms. It made me realise I think for the first time that we were going to be dealing with something of a fairly profound nature in our own country.'[2]

I asked him what he thought of the threat of extremism in Britain today. Blair said: 'I think it has increased I'm afraid. I think the problem is still here, and it is not diminishing.'

While some progress has been made, much more is needed to be done to integrate Muslims and make them a functional part of British society. The UK has one of the biggest global diasporas of Pakistanis, about two thirds of which are in the 'low income' earnings bracket, more than any other ethnic group.[3]

Rooting out these problems begins in the community – through creating jobs and opportunity, improving education and promoting a feeling of fairness and equity. At the same time, Muslim communities should also be aware that in a country like the UK, they need to be educated, have the relevant skills and be active and constructive members of society.

The crisis in the Levant, encouraged by internal and external stakeholders, has impact well outside its borders. The Islamic State, also known as Isis and Isil, began as one of many groups formed during a sectarian conflict in countries ravaged by civil war or which had gone through externally-driven regime change. Saddam Hussein had ruled on behalf of a Sunni minority in a predominantly Shia Iraq. The subsequent refusal of the new Shia-led government to include Sunnis in the political process led to a furious backlash, contributing to a weakening state.

Several mistakes were made in Iraq. For one, not enough economic activity was generated in the war-torn country. In any post-conflict environment, there needs to be a well thought-out economic revival plan, with support from key countries and the Bretton Woods institutions, as well as credible structural reforms. When it came to the war in Iraq, a comprehensive plan covering infrastructure development, growth and job creation was distinctly lacking.

One former senior United States official told me in 2014: 'I was there at the State Department and the United States was spending about as much on the economic development of Iraq as the cost of one day of meals and support for US troops.'[4] Economic development would have helped give assurance to various rival factions that the country was heading in a positive direction. Instead, the state of flux following the war played into the hands of groups seeking to destabilise the region.

The world needs to focus on a strategy to deal with these developments, and the sectarian, tribal, ethnic, nationalistic and religious issues they encompass. It is still not fully understood how these groups develop and gain ground. More sophisticated intelligence is needed to grasp how they are funded, how their command and control structure works, what their ultimate objectives are and how the different terrorist groups are linked.

International terrorism presents an existential threat to the state of every country it targets. In June 2014, the Islamic State hit headlines across the world when it seized Mosul, one of the largest cities in Iraq, and announced itself as a 'caliphate'. It reportedly holds an area with an estimated population of more than 6 million people, which it rules over with an iron fist, carrying out acts of terror as well as controlling resources and generating income.[5]

Migration

As the battle with the Islamic State rages on, millions of refugees have already fled the conflict zone. The majority have settled in neighbouring Jordan, many have travelled to Turkey and Europe. Each day, as many as 5,000 people reportedly attempt to cross the Aegean Sea to get to Greece.

While the humanitarian reasons for accepting the people affected by war is undeniable and this crisis requires careful handling, a failure to manage the flow of migrants could have troubling consequences for Europe.

Speaking from the experience our government had with absorbing more than 5 million refugees from Afghanistan, I believe the inability to control the movement of migrants could result in long-term problems for Europe today.[6] In Pakistan's case, refugees came as far as Karachi and set up camps, which became prone to infiltration by extremists. As in Europe today, they were not transit migrants and they stayed in Pakistan even when the situation in their home country normalised. Attempts to resettle them did not work.

As the crisis in Iraq and Syria unfolds, European policy-makers should look carefully at their approach to the migrants coming from the afflicted region and the security risks they may pose. In 2015, I met with Herman van Rompuy, the former European Council president and ex-prime minister of Belgium, and asked for his views on the issue. He said: 'The challenges for Europe are mainly economic and demographic – migration is in some ways part of the solution, but it is very difficult to sell this to the public.'[7]

He added: 'If the European population declines by 40 million by 2050 and we have migration of 55 million, based on current trends, the question is: do we have a societal base for migration, even if it is needed? It is now felt otherwise, because of slow growth and limited social security systems.'

If moderate, centrist leaders do not handle this migration crisis properly, nations could become increasingly polarised, which would play into the hands of nationalist movements and far-right parties. The world requires leaders who can bring all the various factions together and create a sense of nationalist spirit, making it harder for more hardline elements to call the shots.

What can be done?

Unlike with past, more conventional warfare, our highly connected, globalised world gives these conflicts an unprecedented reach. Technology allows them to recruit abroad and connect with other terrorist groups. They use a sophisticated Internet and social media strategy, even devising their own mobile apps. The global and cross-border scale of the problem means we cannot afford to let this play out for decades.

These problems are not isolated in the regions these groups operate in. Terrorist organisations have been able to successfully recruit foreign fighters to join their cause. Over three years, to the end of 2014, an estimated 20,000 foreigners have travelled to fight in Syria and Iraq.[8] About 4,000 of them have been from Western Europe. Of these, the largest number have come from France, followed by Britain, Germany and Belgium. We have seen young people travelling from as far as Canada and Australia to fight in the Middle East.

Terrorists spread by preying on the disillusioned. They hit hard to the very heart of our own societies, targeting the vulnerable and disaffected. Their feelings of deprivation are channelled into what has emerged as an effective message by radical elements, which fuses a reaction to modernity and globalisation with a move to preserve an anachronistic impression of the first caliphate.

We have been too focused on treating this as a security and intelligence issue, but it is much deeper than that. It concerns the disenfranchised, the neglected, who are being seduced by a powerful message that has broad appeal. Instead of a military solution, we must focus on winning hearts and minds through a more emotive approach.

General Jones said to me: 'Generally, whether it is in Vietnam or Pakistan or Afghanistan, insurrections [feature] a cause that offers a better life. If you really want to defeat terrorism, you start going and solving the root causes of people's unhappiness. Which is food, clothing, shelter – the basics.'

This requires a holistic effort, encompassing aid, technology, communication, human development, job creation and the availability of education. A key method in addressing the spread of terrorism is finding a way to give people a sense that they have a bright future and alleviating their feeling of hopelessness.

The conflicts in the Middle East today must not be viewed in isolation. In many cases, this starts at home, within our own societies. The importance of having strong family units which look after each other should not be underestimated. Sectarian, tribal, religious and ethnic issues are gradually globalising, which makes the threat of terrorism even more widespread; marginalised communities anywhere in the world can become a preying ground for extremists. This problem is only set to increase as our societies are faced with a growing problem of inequality.

As was the case in the UK in 2005 when I spoke with Tony Blair, governments and communities need to focus on encouraging inclusiveness, on making these people feel they are valued and valuable members of society. There are also many invisible fault lines which need to be discussed more and addressed. These include racial and economic prejudice, the rich poor divide and religious divides. We need to start by acknowledging these fault lines exist and gradually work to build tolerance and change the mindset which perpetuates them.

Germany is one of the countries which has seen its people join the jihadist cause, with more than 800 reportedly leaving for Syria or Iraq.[9] I asked the former German chancellor, Gerhard Schroeder, about this problem and he said: 'In the long run, the fight against terrorism can only be won if people feel there is a degree of success in their lives. The dividend of peace must not just be theoretical – it must provide a tangible reward. In order to withdraw the breeding ground for fanaticism, we must ensure political, material and cultural security around the world.'

More work is needed to prevent the radicalisation of disaffected citizens. Research has shown that most initial recruitment into terrorist groups continues to take place in person – not online – which is why we need to redouble our attempts to pre-empt this in 'vulnerable environments' such as educational institutions, prisons and local communities.[10] In the UK, Maajid Nawaz and his foundation, Quilliam, have done valuable work in spreading awareness of the realities of radicalisation and how it can be countered. More such efforts are needed.

We need to address the often-cited narrative of a 'clash of civilisations' by focussing on promoting understanding between different cultures and highlighting their commonalities. Alongside this, there should be a greater focus on 'soft power', as initially propagated by the Harvard academic Joseph Nye. This concept refers to boosting the appeal and attraction of our own society and encompasses increased spending on development and the use of a variety of mediums, from films to the Internet, to publicise our values. We are quick to criticise the horrors of the propaganda put out by the Islamic State, but have not been doing enough to promote our Enlightenment views. Instead, we need to use all means at our disposal to counter the message delivered by extremists. So far their calls to violence have resonated with tens of thousands across the world and not enough is being done to create a compelling counter-narrative.

Islam

Islam is a religion which promotes peace, tolerance and respect for other people's beliefs, security and safety. I felt my childhood illustrated this well, as I spent my days at a school run by Christian missionaries and, during the evenings, studied the Holy Qur'an at home with a tutor. However, the moderate, tolerant Islam I know is now being distorted by the narrative from extremists who have been successfully spreading their message of violence and hate.

Terrorism does not belong to any religion or moral creed. While the hardline militancy we are faced with most today stems from distortions of the faith, it has more in common with historic terrorist organisations, such as the Baader Meinhof group and the Red Brigade, than it does with the religion it claims to represent. Terrorism is an affront on humanity, packaged with effective propaganda and recruitment techniques.

The Western interventions in the Middle East had the adverse effect of fuelling their message. Existing sectarian, tribal and ethnic divides have been exploited by those who wanted to seize power in the region. Today it is important to encourage the different sects to learn to live with each other, to prevent any further escalation of violence. The challenge is to reclaim the original teachings of Islam by going back to the holy texts to counter the terrorists' distorted message.

However, governments around the world are struggling to combat its spread. We should look at the lessons from countries which have been successful in containing the growth of terrorism. One noted example is Malaysia, which has a large Muslim population but a stable security situation. Having lived there, I had the chance to observe the country's progress. I was also able to meet the former prime minister, Dr Mahathir Mohamad. As the longest-serving Malaysian prime minister, he steered the country through rapid modernisation and structural reform. Dr Mahathir showed the world that different ethnic and religious groups could live together, bringing together previously divided communities. He presided over a coalition of Malays, Chinese and Indians and gave Malaysians a sense of pride in their country, while putting it on the path to growth. He also focused on spreading the benefits of the country's increasing wealth to sectors that had previously lagged behind, such as those in rural areas.

In 2014 I met with Dr Mahathir to ask for his views on these complex issues facing the Muslim world. I spent an hour with him in his office in Putrajaya, outside Kuala Lumpur, to hear his insights. He said the involvement of Muslims in terrorist activities began with erroneous religious teachings and the misinterpretation of the Holy Qur'an.

Dr Mahathir said: 'I was recently invited to Egypt, where they asked me what Muslims are doing wrong. I told them that Muslims have no clear strategy, which means knowing what you want to do and can do. The justice systems are weak. Muslims do not read the Holy Qur'an properly. The Muslim leadership must go to the original teachings of Islam, and not people's interpretation of them for their own agenda.'[11]

Commenting on jihadist movements that have also convinced Muslims that it was acceptable to kill fellow Muslims from a different school of thought, he said: 'There is only one Islam. We give too much importance to sects. We are Muslims first and we are one, everything else comes second. Islam and Islamic cultures should strictly follow the Holy Qur'an and not get into sects.' He highlighted that divisions in Islam are hurting the *ummah*, which refers to the global community of Muslims: 'We must think of it as a common faith and bridge the differences.' We agreed that international bodies, such as the Organisation of Islamic Cooperation, had a role to play in creating unity in the Muslim world.

Dr Mahathir called for tolerance and harmony as propagated by the Prophet:

'We must learn to follow the Holy Qur'an. The glue which will drive us together is that we all share a common faith. The culture of violence is very difficult to get rid of. Violence starts with the training of children. They have to be taught the value of peace, sharing and harmony.'

International community

In the face of the spread of global terrorism, the case for international engagement is stronger than ever. Only a truly coordinated effort will allow us to face this existential threat.

It is therefore all the more crucial to have the major world powers rise above their differences and work together – this means the United States, China, Russia, European and Islamic countries.

Extremists will not be defeated by traditional means of warfare or statecraft. Kofi Annan shared valuable insights into the challenges we face when he recalled his personal interactions with the Afghan Taliban leadership with me. Annan had been one of the few to speak to the foreign minister, Wakil Ahmad Muttawakil.

He described the conversation to me: 'When I talked to him about rule of law and doing things legally, he said: "Under our system, whatever we do is legal". I told him: "You don't have many friends, if you do this, you are going to lose the few you have, and there will be sanctions." He said: "Sanctions? What sort of sanctions?" I said: "You may not be allowed to travel, you may not be allowed to transfer your money." He said: "Travel? Where do we have to go?"'[12]

Annan said: 'We sit in New York and think everybody shakes when we mention sanctions. But he did not even have a clue what sanctions were, and they do not care. They have ways of moving their money that they don't need our banks. And so we don't have a real hold on them. This is a problem we see in the world when people have different standards, different perceptions. You think what is important to you and applies in your corner of the world also applies to them. How do you make sure that the people you are dealing with at the other side of the world understand rule of law, sanctions the same way you do? Because if they don't, and they do not care,

109

all your ways and your security council resolutions are wasted on them.'[13]

Much more thought must go into developing new ways of tackling non-state actors. As Annan said, it is difficult to affect them with sanctions because they are not in the system. They have developed untraceable ways to transfer money. Traditional ways of tracking communication also do not work adequately in the face of these modern challenges; the United Nations and the world as a whole have not done enough to focus on finding solutions.

We need to encourage a proactive approach to intelligence and security. In the past we have been reactive, responding only after being stirred into action, for example after the World Trade Center attacks in 2001. Jack Straw, who served as Home and Foreign Secretary, offered me an insight into how the British approach to terrorism changed after 9/11: 'The whole focus of our intelligence agencies post 9/11 was shifted like a laser onto Al Qaeda and Islamist terrorism, in a way it wasn't before. It should have been. When I was Home Secretary and responsible for MI5 and the security service, they were looking for a role, because their counter espionage against the Russians had gone down and the Irish threat was going down. So the security services shifted to doing quite a lot of serious crime, just straight gangs in the UK. That all changed.'[14]

Return risk

The problem is not only with identifying young people who are susceptible to being recruited and preventing them from fighting in these causes. Arguably the bigger issue is what happens when they wish to return to society. We must develop a re-entry strategy for extremists who have gone abroad, which includes programmes to rehabilitate them and ensure that they are not a threat to others. The re-assimilation of these people must be looked at much more carefully.

Some have called for a statutory de-radicalisation programme for returning fighters, which would address, among other things, societal deviations and consequential psychological problems that they may suffer from. Such programmes should aim to eventually reintroduce extremists into society and provide an alternative narrative to the radical one they have been given.[15] At the same time, we need to identify and take action against those likely to convert more people to their cause.

All this is largely not a task for local police and calls for specifically trained professionals. Local police should be specially trained to combat radical elements, to identify and take action against advocates of violence. Our police forces will require funding to address this.

A global strategy is required to deal with the record numbers of fighters that have been travelling to the Middle East. Many are already coming back, which means that countries are having to deal with unprecedented numbers of returning foreign combatants and home-grown extremists. Unless there is a concerted world effort to reintegrate them, we will see history repeating itself. Not enough was done to rehabilitate the mujaheddin fighters after the Soviet Union was defeated in Afghanistan. We must try to avoid the mistakes of the past.

We can learn from the examples of countries such as Tunisia, which managed to transition to a democracy while navigating the existence of different factions in the aftermath of the 2011 revolution. The different stakeholders were brought into the process and given a sense of ownership, allowing for the transition to take place. The transition was guided by President Beji Caid Essebsi, who had the necessary clout to lead the country. While this is not a paradigm which will necessarily last forever, there are lessons other countries in the region can learn from this period in Tunisia's history.

External intervention in the region is not the answer. As one senior former US official told me, speaking of the current crisis in the Levant: 'There is nothing the Islamic State wants more than American boots on the ground – it would allow them to paint the West as the aggressor.' Instead, a coordinated and considered multilateral effort is needed. Many of the actions taken to date have been knee-jerk responses to events; the global community should develop a long-term strategy for tackling the spread of extremism.

The president of Turkey, Recep Tayyip Erdogan, has shown considerable leadership amid testing times. I first met Erdogan at the World Economic Forum in Davos in 1999 – my first as finance minister. He introduced himself as the former mayor of Istanbul saying he hoped to be the next prime minister of Turkey. We bonded over lunch, sitting with Klaus Schwab, the head of the World Economic Forum. I mentioned how Turkey had historically stood by Pakistan and the affection our people have for it. Turkey is a major country in the Muslim *ummah* and a source of strength for the Muslim world.

Since becoming prime minister in 2003, Erdogan has developed his country's economy and raised its prestige, making it a significant regional power. It has played a pivotal role in the migration crisis unfolding in Europe, as Turkey has absorbed millions of refugees fleeing the war-torn Middle East.

Together with other regional countries such as Saudi Arabia, the UAE, Egypt, Iran, Qatar and Jordan, a coordinated multinational peace effort is needed. The United States has an important role to play in bringing the different stakeholders together, with help from China, Russia and Europe.

Combating global terrorism is one of the toughest challenges the international community has ever faced. In the years since the War on Terror began, our world has only become more dangerous. Individual countries are not in the position to meet these challenges by themselves. Coordinated multilateral solutions are the sole viable response. Only by presenting a united front can we have a real chance of defeating this existential threat.

8

NUCLEAR PEACE WITH INDIA

As a young bachelor I rented a small annex of a house in the Defence Society, one of the well-to-do suburbs of Karachi. I shared it with a fellow banker, Abdul Baqui. He was from East Pakistan and had been hired by Citibank to prepare the opening of its branch in Dacca. Those were easy, carefree days. We would drive around the city in my car, a cream Volkswagen Beetle which I had bought second-hand for 10,000 rupees.

On 4 December 1971, following a lengthy covert operation to stir up rebellion and fuel the Bengali separatist movement, India moved its armed forces across the international border into East Pakistan. At the same time, the Indian Navy launched a speedy strike on the Pakistan naval base in Karachi. It was an attack on two fronts as India tried to break up its smaller neighbour. After a thirteen-day war, the Indian offensive caused Pakistan's forces to surrender and the country I knew was dismembered. East Pakistan seceded and became an independent Bangladesh. Delhi had designs on West Pakistan as well, but caved in under international pressure.

I was careful not to broach the subject with Baqui and for a while we carried on living together as usual. Yet the tension and humiliation of defeat were hard to escape. Overnight, many Bangladeshis living in Pakistan felt like aliens.

One evening, I was late coming home from work and went straight to bed. When I woke up the next day, there was no trace of Baqui in the house – he had packed his bags overnight

114

and gone home. I was upset he left but understood his reasons for doing so. The loss of my roommate paled in comparison with the strife of the millions of families that were torn apart. About 90,000 Pakistani soldiers became prisoners of war. The humiliation suffered by Pakistan continued to affect the actions of every policymaker, military officer or patriotic Pakistani for many years.

India's strike was a culmination of a decades-long effort to substantially weaken Pakistan. The far-reaching intelligence agency, RAW, was founded in 1968 with the specific aim to lay the ground for encouraging the split. Still, India's instrumental role in the breakup of East and West Pakistan had been an open secret until as recently as 2015, when Prime Minister Narendra Modi publicly confirmed it.[1]

While ostensibly India is now trying to carve a bigger role for itself in the region, the bulk of its army – eight out of thirteen corps – remains deployed against Pakistan.[2] In 2014 a senior British diplomat told me:

'India has its own agenda. All their training is based on attacks against Pakistan. The counter point of that is the military doctrine of Pakistan, where the training is all focused on India.'[3]

Today India is engaging in more dangerous means to undermine Pakistan, without resorting to open conflict, by actively supporting extreme elements within Pakistan. In May 2015, India's defence minister, Manohar Parrikar, publicly warned that Delhi is capable of actions which could try to destabilise Pakistan. Speaking at a media event in the capital, he described a tit-for-tat approach in dealing with Pakistan. He said: 'To remove a thorn, you need a thorn.'

Days later Sartaj Aziz, the foreign affairs adviser, said: 'This confirms Pakistan's apprehensions about India's involvement in terrorism in Pakistan. It must be the first time that a minister of an elected government openly advocates use of terrorism in another country on the pretext of preventing terrorism from that country or its non-state actors.'[4]

While it may be tempting to dismiss the Indian defence minister's statement as spontaneous verbosity, it does seem to confirm what has been a long term policy of aggression towards Pakistan. Government officials speaking so candidly about India's potential to destabilise and undermine its neighbour points towards a worrying new dimension to the threat it historically posed. Why would Delhi need to resort to such tactics? Primarily because it can no longer rely on its larger conventional force, as it did in 1971. This is due to the acquisition of nuclear weapons by both countries, which raised the stakes of conflict so high that traditional methods became unusable. For decades, Pakistan's strategic weapons have served as a guarantor for peace.

The Cold Start

On 18 May 1974, India carried out its first nuclear test, underground at the Pokhran test range in Rajasthan. Pakistan moved quickly to build its own nuclear programme. In 1998, both countries tested their weapons and declared their nuclear capability to the world. While Pakistan could never afford to reach conventional military parity with India, it could rival its strategic capability instead.

As Pakistan grew its nuclear arsenal, India decided to go back to focusing on conventional weapons. It developed the Cold Start military doctrine, which was announced in a speech by General V.K. Singh of the Indian army, in 2004. The motivation behind Cold Start was the desire to develop a faster mobilisation system to be able to strike Pakistan on a limited scale. These short, swift military offensives were supposed to provide India with options for conflict without escalating to nuclear war.[5] The fast mobilisation would also allow India to achieve its objectives before being affected by external pressure. As Mark Lyall Grant, national security adviser to David Cameron and previously the UK's ambassador to the UN and before that Pakistan, told me: 'The Cold Start meant they could mobilise much faster, before the international community could react.'

Colonel Ali Ahmed, a retired Indian officer who has written extensively about India's plans, quotes the doctrine, saying: 'It calls for a synergised effort by all instruments of the government to ensure that these forces are moved to their areas of operations, fully-equipped and within an acceptable time frame.'[6]

Lieutenant General Khalid Kidwai was the adviser to Pakistan's National Command Authority and pioneer director general of Pakistan's Strategic Plans Division, which he headed for nearly fifteen years. He spoke about Pakistan's nuclear capability at a conference in 2015 in Washington DC and described India's Cold Start doctrine as: 'Equal to a pre-programmed, predetermined, shooting from the hip posture, commencing at the tactical level, graduating rapidly to the operational strategic level.'

Critics say India does not have the resources to implement the Cold Start doctrine. In a leaked cable to Washington, Ambassador Tim Roemer in New Delhi wrote: 'The Indian Army's "Cold Start Doctrine" is a mixture of myth and reality. It has never been and may never be put to use on a battlefield because of substantial and serious resource constraints, but it is a developed operational attack plan announced in 2004 and intended to be taken off the shelf and implemented within a seventy-two-hour period during a crisis.'[7] Still, the doctrine is one Pakistan could not ignore.

At the same time, India has continued to build its conventional strength, becoming the biggest global arms importer in the world in 2014, according to the Stockholm International Peace Research Institute.[8] Between 2002 and 2011, Indian defence spending grew at the eighth fastest rate of all countries, behind the five UN Security Council permanent members, Japan and Saudi Arabia.[9] India has been acquiring advanced long-range and short-range aircraft, early warning systems, satellite systems and – most importantly from Pakistan's point of view – anti-ballistic missiles. Between this and the Cold Start, Pakistan cannot ignore the aggressive signals emanating from its larger neighbour.

Tactical nuclear 'weapons of peace'

Unlike India, Pakistan does not have the ability to invest in conventional weapons on such a large scale – nor does it have access to the same markets for high-tech arms. Instead, Pakistan has shifted its focus to developing tactical nuclear weapons.

When Peter Lavoy, a former United States national intelligence officer, first visited General Kidwai's office in Rawalpindi, he noticed a few photographs on the wall of some of the missiles that Pakistan had tested. On his last visit, not one but two walls were noticeably full. One photograph caught his eye, however – the Hatf IX (Nasr), a sophisticated short-range surface-to-surface missile, capable of carrying nuclear warheads.[10]

In November 2013, Pakistan officially revealed its tactical nuclear weapons capability during the army's annual exercise.

It saw the live firing of a Hatf IX (Nasr) missile, which was demonstrated in front of foreign dignitaries, including the Indian defence attaché. The nuclear-tipped Nasr would form an integral part of the nuclear doctrine of Pakistan. More recently, Pakistan tested the Shaheen-III, which is an intermediate-range ballistic missile with a much longer range than the Nasr, at about 2,750 kilometres.[11]

Now out of office, General Kidwai has shared his insights on Pakistan's development of 'full spectrum deterrence'. He said: 'Pakistan took the [Cold Start] doctrine seriously, because it had a direct bearing on our security, and to prevent destabilisation in an environment of conventional asymmetry. To deter the unfolding of operations under the doctrine, Pakistan opted to develop a variety of short-range, low-yield nuclear weapons, also dubbed tactical nuclear weapons. By introducing the variety of tactical nuclear weapons in Pakistan's inventory, and in the strategic stability debate, we have blocked the avenues for serious military operations by the other side.'

Pakistan's new generation of tactical nuclear weapons is intended to lower the threshold at which it will resort to using its nuclear weapons. The idea is to close the gap that India sought to fill using its Cold Start doctrine.

The thinking behind their development is nothing new. Tactical nuclear weapons were a large part of NATO's arsenal during the Cold War. They were based in Germany and intended to stop a core thrust to the West by the Soviet Union. Their primary role was to send a political message to the adversary, signalling resolve.

There is another potential reason for developing tactical capability. These weapons could allow Pakistan to, if faced with an attack by India, launch a short-range tactical nuclear response to Indian troops on its own soil, which Colonel Ahmed describes as the 'Sehjra option'. This would amount to defensive 'first use' of nuclear weapons within Pakistan – without risking total international retaliation.

The integration of tactical nuclear weapons is a vital component of the country's national defence strategy, extending the nuclear deterrent from full-scale wars to small-scale ones too. It will reduce the 'space' for short, swift conventional battles and virtually close the option of military aggression by the adversary.

By lowering the nuclear threshold, the risk of an escalation from small-scale use to a strategic nuclear war rises. This puts the responsibility on both sides to limit provocations that could spark even a small confrontation. That said, I believe nuclear capability has been a guarantor for peace in the region. General Kidwai even went as far as saying: 'I am fond of calling these weapons "weapons of peace", because they have deterred the urge of aggression.' He went on to say they have 'closed the door to war being used as an instrument of policy.'

However, the development of tactical capability by Pakistan makes other powers uneasy. The fear is that, in a crisis, events move quickly and can be triggered by miscalculation, accident or a breakdown of command and control. We must take extra care to prevent violence and unconventional or proxy warfare from turning into nuclear war.

This is particularly true of tactical nuclear weapons. The former United States National Security Advisor Steve Hadley told me: 'The smaller they are, the more operationally useful they are, the harder they are to control, the greater the risk that they will fall into the hands of terrorist elements.' I do not agree on the latter point. Pakistan's strategic weapons are professionally stored and carefully maintained. When asked about this, General Kidwai said of the safety of the country's nuclear weapons: 'We have invested heavily in terms of money, manpower, equipment, weapons, training, preparedness and smart site security solutions.'

When asked about Pakistan's nuclear submarine plans, General Kidwai said: 'A submarine is just a platform. There will be a time when there will be a platform as well. There will be a time when there will be a weapon. I can say with confidence that we are not too far away from it. I think this capability will come into play in the next few years.'

The general added: 'Pakistan has only met 95% of its goals. Pakistan should be looking at a second strike capability.'

While I believe a comprehensive deterrent capability has prevented confrontations from escalating, certain fault lines which could spark tension remain. This became clear months before I joined the government, in 1999, when Pakistan and India fought in the high altitude planes of Kargil. General Musharraf, then army chief, had led the operation.

As a result of Kargil, trust levels between India and Pakistan were low at the turn of the millennium. In addition, Pakistan's new closeness with the United States as part of the War on Terror became another source of tension. I met with Nicholas Burns, the former United States permanent representative to NATO, at the John F. Kennedy School of Government at Harvard University in 2014. He described the shift which accompanied the War on Terror:

'We had a closer relationship with Pakistan on Afghanistan – a strategic engagement. Pakistan was a more important country and that was not something the Indians were happy about. The Indians would say: "Why can't you work with us?"

121

We would say: "Well, Pakistan is more centrally involved, Pakistan has a border with Afghanistan."'

A 2006 study by the Centre for Strategic and International Studies said that in Autumn 2001 'Indian leaders were bitter that Pakistan had become a primary beneficiary of the Bush administration's global War on Terror.' The study quoted a senior United States official as saying that 'every meeting with Indians had one topic: Pakistan'.

These tensions can spill over into conflict if a trigger event occurs. In my time, we witnessed a troubling chain of events unravel after December 2001, when terrorists breached security in the parliament in New Delhi. They drove through Gate 12 and tried to reach Parliament House but were intercepted by the guards and blew themselves up before they got to their targets. Fourteen people were killed in the attack, including five terrorists, and India squarely blamed Pakistan.

India's BJP government felt it had to show a strong response to appease domestic opinion and put pressure on its neighbour. Within five days, India had deployed 500,000 men and three armoured divisions along the border between Pakistan and India. They stood in an aggressive formation, ready to strike. Pakistan responded by mobilising over 300,000 troops. It was referred to as the 'two million eyes' incident, as the troops stood eyeball to eyeball. Both armies remained deployed and ready to strike.

President Musharraf called an urgent meeting in the operations room of General Headquarters. He said an attack on Pakistan would bring the Indian army within mere miles from Lahore. As I was finance minister at that time, I was asked to discuss the implications of conflict on the economy, the availability of cash resources and our ability to spend where needed. I told them the state of the budget and what it gave us room to do. The generals proceeded to discuss Pakistan's options. They felt the need to grab the attention of the international community and the two or three countries that could have sway with India, particularly the United States. With the world's eyes watching its movements, India might show restraint. But the main message was clear – if provoked, Pakistan would resort to using all means to protect itself.

The mobilisation on both sides lasted through the year. On several occasions during 2002 we were apprehensive that an attack was imminent. During that time, we passed discreet messages to some friendly countries to tell India not to push Pakistan into using its strategic defence capability.

As months went by, the situation escalated until, with the stakes so high, there was no easy way out for either country. The BJP government, led by Prime Minister Atal Behari Vajpayee, risked losing face by withdrawing its troops. On 24 May, Pakistan carried out a series of missile tests, including nuclear-capable weapons.

That month, Pakistan detected that an Indian strike corps was moving along the pivotal western front of the border. India apparently believed it could take Lahore without triggering a nuclear response from Pakistan.[12] The Indian military's plans were reportedly 'so audacious they had never been war-gamed before.'[13] A terror attack which struck the family members of Indian troops stationed in Jammu heightened the tension.

Soon both sides began to drop greater hints about using nuclear weapons. Colin Powell, who was US Secretary of State at the time, recalled to me: 'They were deadly serious. The [Indians] moved up stocks, moved up headquarters, moved up ammunition. Musharraf started saying things like: "Whatever the Indians do, we have means to deal with this."' Powell added: 'It was getting out of control, because the Indians knew what he was saying, and they started to respond in the same way.'

An international effort to calm the situation followed. The UK, the United States and Japan became involved, with cooperation from China and Russia. The countries sent officials to speak with their Indian and Pakistani counterparts.

Christina Rocca, the Assistant Secretary of State for South Asian Affairs, travelled to the region almost once a month throughout the crisis. She recalled: 'Planes with foreign delegates were waiting in holding patterns above the capital. It was an all-out world effort. We were planning for nuclear war. I sat through so many meetings where we were talking about evacuations of American citizens, how many casualties there would be, where would the follow up go, and what were the weather conditions.'

The Americans published a Defense Intelligence Report that claimed the worst case scenario would see between 9 and 12 million people lose their lives with millions more later dying from radiation.[14] Still, neither power would back down.

Colin Powell was in Paris at the time, accompanying President Bush on a tour of Europe. He sensed the magnitude of the situation: 'We were nervous – and we should have been nervous. If there had been one more incident like the one that caused this to get started, there would have been a war.'

Powell went to the United States ambassador's office in Paris and called President Musharraf directly. He told him: 'Let's speak general and general today, not president and secretary.'

When President Musharraf agreed, General Powell said: 'General, you're scaring us. You and I both know that nuclear weapons cannot be used. Neither you nor the Indians will be the first ones to use a nuclear weapon in an ultra-existential way, after the Japanese were bombed in 1945. You've got to help us calm down the situation.'

Many stakeholders made efforts to try and diffuse the tension. On the Pakistan side, the suggestion that it would not be afraid to resort to using nuclear weapons counted. The army had published the Kidwai doctrine, which said nuclear weapons would be used in three circumstances: if Pakistan is attacked and is facing imminent defeat, if its nuclear weapons or nuclear installations are attacked, or if Pakistan is blockaded.

On 25 June, Munir Akram had just taken his post in New York as Pakistan's permanent representative in the United Nations. He was asked to hold a press conference about the crisis, during which an Indian correspondent asked whether Pakistan would use its nuclear weapons.

Akram recalled his reply: 'I said: "We have developed them and deployed them, they are not a game. Our doctrine has very clearly outlined under what circumstances we will use them. This should not be taken as academic."'

After the press conference, President Musharraf called Akram. 'How could you say that?'

The ambassador replied: 'I did say it, you can deny it and say he's talking out of turn, but the fact is we have put the doctrine on the table.'

Newspapers around the world ran headlines on Akram's comments. The Bombay Stock Exchange fell, expatriate embassies started evacuating their staff's families and the Indian business community voiced its concerns. After all this, Akram said: 'India stepped back and agreed to disengage.'

Eventually, Delhi withdrew its troops and the ten-month-long tension finally wound down.

Even though many of the people involved played a part in diffusing the tension, in the end it was the existence of a nuclear deterrent which pulled both countries back from the brink of war. While the threat of either side using its nuclear weapons undoubtedly heightened the tension throughout the crisis, it also paved the way for eventual de-escalation.

Pakistan, India and nuclear capability

Nearly a year after the mobilisation began, we could finally breathe easily once more. However, Pakistan's acquisition of nuclear capability continued to be a source of anxiety for the Western world.

In 2005, the United States signed a Civil Nuclear Agreement with India, legitimising the latter's nuclear status. Pakistan was left out, which, in my view, was a missed opportunity. Officially, this happened for many reasons – Pakistan's history of proliferating nuclear technology being the main one. In addition, Indian lobbying in Washington meant that any attempt to bring Pakistan into the agreement in some capacity would have struggled to make it past Congress, according to a State Department official from that time.[15]

Since the 1990s, the United States had been taking steps to change its foreign policy approach in South Asia. There was a trend towards 'de-hyphenation', which moved away from approaching the region under the banner of 'India-Pakistan' and tried to develop individual policies toward each state. The Civil Nuclear Agreement was part of the Bush administration's effort to develop its relationship with India as its own entity. In doing so, it only pushed Pakistan away.

Instead, similar treaties should have been signed with both countries. This could have given them the opportunity of being accepted into the nuclear club and shouldering the responsibilities which come with it. The agreement with India dealt a significant blow to Pakistan's confidence in the United States. The one-sided treaty did nothing to temper the nuclear race in South Asia.

I mentioned that Pakistan should have been included to President Bush during my official visit to the White House in January 2006. To my surprise, he agreed. Several years later, I raised the matter with Steve Hadley, Bush's national security advisor. He said: 'I think it is worth doing now. We couldn't do it at the time, because of A. Q. Khan. For all you say about India, they were not a nuclear proliferator. We had trouble getting India through the treaty – if we had tried to do it for Pakistan, they would have laughed us out. But now, I think you might be able to do that.'[16]

In 2015, the Obama administration reportedly started exploring the possibility of a similar deal with Pakistan.[17] It remains to be seen if this can progress.

Kashmir - the back channel

There were tensions over Partition from the start. Many people thought India should have remained as one country and never agreed to the creation of Pakistan. South Asia was made up of hundreds of princely and autonomous states, bound to Delhi by treaty and inferior military capabilities. In some cases, Muslim princes ruled over Hindu majority populations and, in others, Indian princes ruled over Muslim majorities. When the country was divided, the princes that ruled these states were told to choose to be part of either India or Pakistan. However, India quickly used force to incorporate Hyderabad and Junagadh – both Hindu majority states with Muslim rulers – which bred anger about Indian aggression.[18]

Even though Kashmir was a Muslim majority state adjacent to Pakistan and governed by a Hindu ruler, different standards were applied. This was a significant flaw in the process and the question of Kashmir – and other former princely states – was left unresolved. After the first conflict over the disputed territory, the UN drew the Line of Control, splitting Kashmir in 1949. The most politically sensitive part – the Valley of Kashmir – has a Muslim majority population and is under Indian administration, along with Hindu-dominated Jammu, which is also occupied by Indian troops. The remaining parts are administered by Pakistan and constitute Azad Kashmir.

Neither country accepts the validity of the Line of Control. India lays claim to all of Kashmir, because the maharajah of Kashmir acceded to Delhi during Partition. Pakistan supports the UN resolutions, in place since the first India-Pakistan war over Kashmir in 1947, which say the fate of the Kashmiris should be decided by them through a plebiscite. Both countries say control over Kashmir is necessary to the fulfilment of their national identities. As a result, the territorial issue of Kashmir has languished for decades with no resolution in sight.

During my meetings with Kashmiri leaders from both sides of the Line of Control, I reinforced Pakistan's unwavering support to their legitimate struggle for a plebiscite in line with UN resolutions. The Kashmiris have fought with courage and determination in the face of adversity and repression for decades. Generations of Kashmiris have grown up under the shadow of a gun, lost their homes, family members and friends to the seven-decade-long struggle. Kashmir remains vital to both countries strategically and for water – many key South Asian rivers have their source there. For both sides, Kashmir has become an emotional as well as a strategic issue.

An early attempt between President Musharraf and Prime Minister Vajpayee to begin talks about Kashmir had not succeeded. In July 2001 the two leaders met in Agra and attempted to draft a joint statement on terrorism and Kashmir, although India pulled out at the last moment. Prime Minister Vajpayee's party, the BJP, was traditionally unsympathetic to Pakistan, and the effort was stalled at his end. It was the close nuclear call of the 'two million eyes' incident of 2002 which prompted Vajpayee to change track.

In April 2003, Vajpayee offered fresh talks with Pakistan by opening up the option for a 'composite dialogue' on a range of issues, including water, trade and Kashmir. There was an effort to normalise relations. Crucially, a discreet back channel process began.

On the Pakistan side it was spearheaded by Tariq Aziz, a senior civil servant who was close to President Musharraf. India was represented by Brajesh Mishra, the national security adviser. Pakistan had given a clear understanding to India that it would seriously address Indian concerns on the issue of terrorism. Tariq and Brajesh had the blessings of their respective principals and agreed to explore 'out of the box' solutions to the problems between the two countries, especially the dispute over Jammu and Kashmir.

The British were brought in to get the back channel moving. Mark Lyall Grant, at the time Britain's envoy in Pakistan, revealed to me: 'Tariq Aziz had asked me to do the logistics for the very first meeting, which was very sensitive.'

This initial encounter took place in Bangkok, Thailand – chosen because it was well connected enough to all parts of the world, but not somewhere that might raise suspicion. London would have been too visible. Lyall Grant recalled: 'They didn't want to let the Pakistani embassy of Bangkok know, so the

British embassy of Bangkok organised the logistics. That was the first meeting, and ever since then I was a little bit involved. They established these back channels, which progressively became serious in terms of working out documents. General Kayani was involved in some of the later meetings.'

These diplomatic efforts set the stage for a notable meeting between President Musharraf and Prime Minister Atal Behari Vajpayee in January 2004. Vajpayee was in Islamabad for the South Asian Association for Regional Cooperation (SAARC) summit. Pakistan had previously been scheduled to host the summit in 1999, but this was delayed as a result of the coup and the Kargil episode.

At SAARC summits, it is customary for visiting heads of state to pay courtesy calls on host leaders. After some subtle diplomatic consultations, Prime Minister Vajpayee called on President Musharraf on 5 January. It was a delegation-level meeting and covered the prospect of normalising relations between the two countries. Here, the ongoing Kashmir negotiations were discussed in an official setting for the first time, in the presence of our foreign minister, Khurshid Kasuri, India's foreign minister, Yashwant Sinha, Tariq Aziz, Brajesh Mishra and others.

The talks also revolved around the finalisation of the draft joint statement. President Musharraf indicated he was happy with the text prepared by Tariq and Brajesh. Significantly, Pakistan made a concession on the issue of terrorism, and, in exchange, India agreed to resume the composite dialogue process, which had been suspended since the Kargil incident in 1999.

I was assigned as Vajpayee's minister in waiting, accompanying him during his stay and at all his meetings – this was an unusual task for a finance minister but it gave me an opportunity to see the two leaders in action. It was an interesting experience to get to know Prime Minister Vajpayee during that trip – I had two days of personal time with him, as well as observing him in the official meetings. We talked at length about the state of the world and where it was going and I found him to be a man of tremendous wisdom. He had a great way with words and a keen sense of humour, although Western leaders would often find it a challenge to talk to him due to his quiet manner. My impression over those days was that both Musharraf and Vajpayee wanted peace between India and Pakistan.

We also bonded over our love of music and cricket. At one point, he was sitting in his suite, watching a cricket match during some downtime, and I got up to walk out and leave him to relax. I told him I had to go because I had a lot of files to go through, but he urged me to stay, joking: 'You finance ministers, you are always working.' We sat for hours watching the India vs. Australia cricket match in his suite at the Serena Hotel in Islamabad, built by the Aga Khan's company. Prime Minister Vajpayee was very warm and personable, even praising the *sherwani* I was wearing. After the summit, I commissioned Amir Adnan, the well-known Pakistani designer, to make a *sherwani*, a short coat and other items for Vajpayee. We flew Adnan to Islamabad to take the prime minister's measurements and make the clothes. These were then delivered to him in New Delhi personally by Amir Adnan, on my behalf.

Meanwhile, the back channel continued to gain momentum. The British used their experience of the Northern Ireland peace process to advise us. Mark Lyall Grant told me: 'We took some of the Pakistani people involved to Northern Ireland, because it was very clear that what was emerging was very close to the

131

Good Friday agreement. When the deal was basically done, it was the Good Friday agreement – soft borders, cross border institutions, free movement. I don't think they intentionally used it as a model, but it was similar. It worked in Northern Ireland, because there the Irish constitution has a constitutional claim to the whole of Ireland. They weren't prepared to repeal that for obvious reasons, in the way that India and Pakistan both have claims.'

Eventually, Musharraf and Vajpayee came close to agreeing a four-step approach that included the identification of regions, demilitarisation, self-governance and joint management in Kashmir.[19] There were to be open borders and open trade between the Indian-occupied Kashmir and Azad Kashmir. It was a highly forward-looking arrangement.

We had been consulting with Kashmiri leaders – whose involvement in any settlement is crucial – and had already begun some initiatives, such as a bus service between the two parts of Kashmir. I took several cabinet ministers along with me when I travelled on the bus to the Line of Control. I felt that progress was within reach and the whole process was moving very fast. There was a real sense of opportunity in the air and a willingness on both sides to move forward.

The main reason this was possible was because the leaders on both sides were in strong domestic positions. Musharraf and Vajpayee also recognised that a settlement over Kashmir could bring long-term sustainable peace.

Kofi Annan later described a conversation he had with the Indian leader. He told me: 'I recall talking to Vajpayee, who said: "Secretary-General, I'm a bit encouraged now, I think we may be able to do something with Musharraf. The problem we've had with Pakistan is we deal with political leaders who often have no control of the army, and when we appear to be making progress, the army seems to step in and pull it in a different direction. For once, I have a man in front of me who has both military and political influence. And so with a bit of goodwill, we should be able to make progress".' Annan added: 'I was very touched when he said he can do something with Musharraf.'

Just when, as Lyall Grant said, it was 'all done', fate intervened and the BJP lost the election in 2004. The Congress party, with Manmohan Singh as prime minister, assumed office and, soon enough, the process stalled. Lyall Grant expressed his disappointment with the way events eventually unfolded. He said: 'I think India made a fundamental strategic error in not going with that deal.' Around this time I had become prime minister and saw first hand that the Indian establishment was in favour of cooling off relations and not signing an agreement.

In 2007, President Musharraf's domestic position had weakened as he faced the lawyers' movement, a mass protest triggered by the suspension of the chief justice, and several other challenges. This only caused the Indians to stall more. Lyall Grant said: 'India made the classic mistake of saying: "I think we'd better wait for the transition and having a demo-cratic [government]".' But, once a civilian government came into power in Pakistan, it was too late to restart negotiations – the buy-in was no longer there from all the centres of power in Islamabad.

Generally, I found a distinct unwillingness to act by the Congress government on a range of matters that was separate from Kashmir and other sources of tension. My focus was on economic diplomacy between India and Pakistan, which I was keen to get off the ground. Increasing trade and building linkages and interdependencies is an important step forward between the two countries. I tried to push this idea whenever I went to

133

India. However, it usually seemed that the Indian bureaucracy was so powerful that it did not let initiatives progress.

In 2004, I travelled to Delhi, where I attended a bilateral meeting with Manmohan Singh in his office. I suggested an initiative whereby an Indian bank and a Pakistani bank would each open a branch in the other's country. It would have been a big step forward in encouraging trade by creating the financial infrastructure which could facilitate it. I suggested we start with a symbolic gesture of two Indian banks opening branches – one in Karachi and the other in Lahore – and Pakistani banks would then open branches in Bombay and Delhi. I was keen to announce the measure that day, to send a signal that we wanted to start trade.

Singh praised the idea initially but, after consulting his colleagues, hesitated on the proposal on the grounds that India's central bank is independent, therefore he could not announce that on its behalf. I then proposed that we declare a broad policy measure to allow the banks to open the branches, subject to approval by the respective central banks. However, nothing materialised.

Some of my suggestions and calls to build greater linkages and interdependencies between the two countries found a positive reception in the Indian media. Disappointingly, I did not have the same success with the establishment. Another measure I pushed for was cooperation over the trade of cement between India and Pakistan.

'I understand you have a cement shortage,' I told Prime Minister Singh. 'We have a surplus and we can send trains full of it here.' He responded positively and said our offices will work out the details. We were later told that an Indian official delegation would need to come and visit the factories producing cement in Pakistan – ostensibly to approve the product quality and manufacturing standards before it could be exported to India. This was a highly unusual demand for a straightforward export transaction but I authorised it to get the process moving. Even though we allowed this to happen, and the Indian delegation did come and inspect the factories, it was an indication of how far from normalised the relationship between the two countries was. Regardless of this, Pakistan eventually started exporting cement to India. Many more such measures are needed to improve the relationship between the two nations.

There is a history of anti-Muslim sentiment associated with Narendra Modi's government, which in part stems from the 2002 anti-Muslim riots in Gujarat, where he was chief minister. More than 1,000 people were killed in the resulting violence. Recent attacks by Shiv Sena, the Indian far-right group, on Pakistani artists performing in India and the ransacking of the Pakistan Airlines office do not help the situation. However, Modi's 2015 visit to Lahore to meet with Nawaz Sharif has been a positive step forward in India-Pakistan relations. Indications that global powers want the two countries to move towards a more peaceful coexistence was also demonstrated when the Obama administration reacted favourably to their efforts, which should help ease tension.

Other fault lines

Population growth, expanding cities and climate change all put pressure on future water supply issues, which are an acute problem in South Asia. As Ismail Serageldin, who served as vice president at the World Bank from 1992 to 2000, said: 'If the wars of this century were fought over oil, the wars of the next century will be fought over water.'

At the point of Partition, Pakistan and India could not agree on the division of the six main rivers of the Indus Basin – the Indus, Ravi, Sutlej, Chenab, Jhelum and Beas. The 1960 Indus Water Treaty divided the supply through a series of dams and canals. Although the treaty has been a model of successful cooperation for decades, it is in need of updating.

Furthermore, Pakistan believes several dams built by India violate the treaty's terms. These dams take away from Pakistan's water supply, and are a social and security threat.

During my time as prime minister, Pakistan invoked arbitration provisions of the Indus Water Treaty for the first time in 2005. It went before a World Bank-appointed expert after India built Baglihar Dam on the Chenab River. The verdict, announced in 2011, was unfavourable to Pakistan. However, another plea in the International Court of Arbitration in 2011 ruled in Pakistan's favour and ordered India to temporarily stop construction on the Kishanganga Dam in Jammu and Kashmir.

The huge increase in demand since 1960 and the absence of further substantial agreements mean this issue requires urgent attention. While the Indus Water Treaty laid the ground rules, Islamabad needs to be vigilant in protecting the flow of water into Pakistan. It is set to hold more sway in future – according to Robert Wirsing of Georgetown University, India is considering building thirty-three dams on parts of the Indus and its tributaries.

During my time in office, we started the preliminary work for the Diamer-Bhasha dam in Gilgit-Baltistan. Other proposed dams, like the Kalabagh dam in Punjab and the Munda dam on the Swat River, should be considered to improve water storage and irrigation. The reality is that Pakistan remains short on water, which is exacerbated by its rapidly growing population, a need for development in the agricultural sector and problems with water distribution within the country. Its agriculture depends on water coming onto its plains at critical periods during the year – a reduced amount flowing in could have a devastating impact on production and the livelihood of millions who depend on agriculture for income.

How to take care of the trust deficit

There continues to be a high degree of hostility, unease and mistrust between India and Pakistan. Both sides suspect the other of attempting to destabilise its internal affairs, and both perceive a security threat. How can this situation be resolved peacefully?

Pakistan has on numerous occasions proposed a strategic restraint regime to India, including in 1998, a few months after the nuclear tests by both countries. The suggestions received no response from the Indian side. Many other efforts to bring the countries closer together so far have not been substantial. India practices trinket diplomacy with Pakistan, essentially maintaining the status quo. Keeping the door open for dialogue, India is perceived as simultaneously interfering in Pakistan's internal affairs, supporting extremist elements. While these tactics may bring temporary gains, in the long run they only further increase the trust deficit. I believe that, as the larger, more powerful country, India should be more forthcoming and reduce the trust deficit. It should show understanding and reach out to Pakistan.

There is no reason why the two countries cannot live peacefully side-by-side. The peace dividend would be substantial, creating an enabling environment for growth and improvements in the quality of life in both countries.

Being able to normalise relations between Pakistan and India, without either side compromising core principles, would be a leap forward in building a thriving South Asia. Pakistan and India share waters, have a common border, an intertwined culture and history. These connections should be built on and expanded, while respecting each other's sovereignty and territorial integrity.

Some positive steps have been made in recent years, but more needs to happen. The temperature can be lowered on both sides through confidence-building measures, such as cooperation over trade and travel. The visa rules should be further relaxed for both countries and there should be no limits on trade. Travel and investment should be encouraged and banks should open in each other's countries – this kind of people-to-people contact will help strengthen the relationship between the two nations.

As well as building links between India and Pakistan, there needs to be a greater focus on promoting wider regional cooperation. South Asia is one of the least economically integrated areas of the world, according to the World Bank, which measures intraregional trade in goods, capital and ideas. In 2015, intraregional trade in South Asia accounted for only 5% of its total trade.[20]

Part of the problem is that SAARC, the South Asian Association for Regional Cooperation, is under-represented and poorly led. Its members send mid-level officials to represent them. When in office, I suggested that the next time we appointed a Secretary-General of SAARC, it should be a foreign minister or a Foreign Secretary-level official, but this never materialised. In its present form SAARC has not shown real leadership – instead it follows instruction from other countries. The organisation needs to reinvent itself as a catalyst for cooperation and increasing linkages and connectivity in the region. Establishing a credible South Asia economic bloc – bringing together India, Pakistan, Bangladesh, Sri Lanka, Nepal, Afghanistan, Bhutan and the Maldives – could open a lot of opportunities. For example, South Asia is short of energy, and the Gulf Cooperation Council countries and Iran could be brought in as suppliers by offering tariff concessions, providing a boost for trade and investment.

Kashmir is a core fault line to be addressed and its solution is critical to creating a sustainable peace in South Asia. Years later, I wanted to look into the lessons which could be learned from the Northern Ireland agreement in this respect, following Mark Lyall Grant's revelations.

I asked Tony Blair, who steered the historic agreement, for his thoughts. He said: 'You need the two big powers to get into a different relationship with each other, where they perceive a shared future. We would never have got the Northern Ireland agreement if the British and Irish had not resolved their own psychology with each other.

'My generation was a different type of Brit, and Bertie Ahern's generation was a different type of Irishman. And the result was that, whereas the Irish and British had hated each other for a long period of time, we were able to say: "In the world that's developing, we're both in Europe, we've got things we can do together, we might as well put the past to one side." So I think that it's almost an emotional and psychological as well as political rapprochement.'[21]

Blair added: 'We had a whole series of things we decided we were going to do together in terms of trade, business across the frontier, and cross-cultural [initiatives]. Secondly – and this is more difficult – to create a political process with a chance of success, the security situation has to come under control.'

139

Jack Straw, who as Britain's Home Secretary at the time was involved in the process, said of Northern Ireland: 'You've got to begin with rather prosaic issues, like bus journeys, building up people's confidence across the border, family reunions. Then people start to have a stake in the border being peaceful.'[22]

India must be convinced that peace with Pakistan is beneficial for both sides, and in its vital interests. It is clear India considers itself a rival to China more than to Pakistan and has been keen to position itself accordingly. This would be a mistake if it means leaving issues with Pakistan unresolved, and could leave both countries open to another crisis.

Straw added: 'Pakistan is not going to give up its aspiration for Kashmir for some time, any more than Sinn Fein and the Provisional IRA gave up their aspirations. But what they did do was to drop that down the list of priorities. That is of fundamental importance.'

The issue of Kashmir has been languishing for decades and India and Pakistan must get the peace process moving again. This has the highest chance of success when their respective leaders are in strong domestic positions. At the time of writing, both Nawaz Sharif and Narendra Modi have enough of a majority in Parliament to push an initiative through.

All stakeholders have to buy into any viable peace process. In Pakistan, the military, political and diplomatic establishments have to feel comfortable with any agreement for it to have credibility and lasting effect. Importantly, no peace settlement mentioning Kashmir would be acceptable to Pakistan unless it was in line with the aspirations and wishes of the Kashmiri people.

The relationship between India and Pakistan cannot be viewed in isolation and the international community will always have a role in helping resolve the tensions in South

Asia. Similarly, the relationships both countries have with outside powers can result in increasing tension. Just as India was uneasy about Pakistan's closeness with the United States over the War on Terror, so Pakistan has been watching carefully as Delhi expands its relationship with Washington.

While negotiations involving a lasting peace are something that Pakistan and India will need to resolve together, some countries could play a mediating role in certain bilateral issues. For example, Britain's historical ties to the region provide it with a certain insight; it also has many of the Pakistani-Indian and Kashmiri diasporas present in the UK, which gives Britain a key interest in staying involved. Clare Short, the former British Secretary of State for International Development, told me in 2015: 'I think there's been a real neglect. Obviously the two countries have the primary responsibility but there hasn't been much international effort to help, in the sense of looking for ways to peacefully resolve the problems.'[23]

Ultimately, a peace agreement between the two nations will only have legitimacy if it is entirely home-grown and supported by all stakeholders. India and Pakistan need to decide: do they want long-lasting peace or not? If it means making some compromises, the two countries should be prepared to do that. There are bound to be groups within both that will be opposed to the policy of peace and any initiative will require vision, leadership and an ability to get sufficient buy-in from all the relevant stakeholders. But it is undeniable that the two countries must learn to live with each other for South Asia to reach its full potential.

9
A BARBECUE WITH PUTIN

Emomali Rakhmon, the president of Tajikistan, tapped me on the shoulder.

'Come, you're one of us,' he said.

We were at a working lunch in Astana, Kazakhstan, during a summit of the Shanghai Cooperation Organisation in 2005, along with several other heads of government. I had come to discuss our economic and political agenda and Pakistan's role within the SCO – in other words, it was business as usual. Then my trip took an unexpected turn.

Taking me aside, Rakhmon said: 'This evening we are having a private dinner'. He told me it was to be held at Kazakhstan's President Nursultan Nazarbaev's dacha outside Astana. It was an intimate gathering with Vladimir Putin, Islam Karimov, the president of Uzbekistan and Rakhmon. To my surprise, they invited me to join them. Later during that warm summer day, I made my journey to the dacha.

The sun was still out while we had the barbecue, sitting in the gazebo in the garden. Putin seemed in good spirits throughout. He had a quiet, but substantive, presence.

Nazarbaev then took us to his stud farm on the grounds of the dacha and showed us his collection of thoroughbreds, gathered from around the world. Like many Kazakhs, Nazarbaev has a great affinity for horses. The farm had indoor and outdoor riding arenas, as well as giant temperature-controlled stables. We watched in awe as a blonde female trainer demonstrated the power and speed of the magnificent horses and described their provenance.

We went back to the house, where dinner was served in an intimate five-person booth. It was an abundance of rustic *shashlik* – barbecued meats including beef, lamb, horse – and drinks and delicacies. The celebrations continued late into the night. Nazarbaev had arranged a rich entertainment programme, with leading artists from Russia and Central Asia performing for us, along with traditional musicians and dancers.

I was the only one who did not speak Russian, so I had an interpreter standing behind me throughout. Amid the merriment, I stuck to my sparkling water and observed the dynamic between these four leaders at close range. There was a visible sense of seniority in the group. Putin's powerful personality was evident as he notably drove the conversation that evening, commanding the full attention of the table when he spoke. The other three leaders were particularly respectful around Putin, even appearing in awe of him at times.

Between them, they had been in power in their respective countries for decades. Nazarbaev has been president since 1991, Rakhmon since 1992, Putin since 2000 and Karimov since 1990. They had steered their respective countries following the breakup of the Soviet Union, with Putin and Nazarbaev benefiting from a natural resources-driven boom. It is remarkable to think all four leaders at that table in 2005 are still in power at the time of writing, eleven years later.

Nazarbaev wanted everyone to stay another evening, to celebrate his sixty-fifth birthday the following day. However, our schedules did not allow a night's delay in Astana. Instead, a formal birthday breakfast was held in the grand ballroom of a palace built for state events, to which all the country leaders were invited. We were treated to smoked salmon, caviar and other delicacies and before catching our respective flights.

About a year later, I was due to meet the same group at the SCO summit in Moscow. Here, in a much more formal setting, I again observed how Putin handled his Central Asian neighbours. It was a gathering of about fifteen heads of state and government. Only the Chinese were granted an individual meeting – Premier Wen Jiabao met with Putin over breakfast.

Meanwhile, all the other delegation heads were to gather in the Kremlin, in Putin's office. The Russian president sat at the head of a U-shaped table with the fourteen leaders assembled on either side. We were each told we had three minutes to make our remarks.

When my turn came, I said: 'While it is good to be here, we regularly attend SCO conferences and rarely leave with any tangible points of action. For the SCO to be effective, we should agree on implementing certain specific initiatives.' The other delegates looked at me, probably wondering whether I had spoken out of turn. When all the participants had given their comments, Putin did a roundup of the discussion. To my surprise, he agreed with my statement and said the SCO should be more action-oriented. Encouraged by his reaction, I asked our ambassador to try and arrange a meeting for me with President Putin. That evening, the Kremlin called to confirm I was to have half an hour with Putin the following morning.

I was keen to spread the word of Pakistan's reform efforts at the highest level. During my ensuing discussion with Putin at his office in the Kremlin, attended by Ambassador Kazi, I said: 'Mr President, there are two symbols of Russian engagement in Pakistan, dating back to the Soviet era.'

I then recalled how, as a young student in Pakistan, I would hear people talking about the steel mill and the Oil and Gas Development Corporation – projects which were set up and part-funded by the Soviet Union in Pakistan. Both used technology, infrastructure and advisers from the Soviet Union. Both now needed modernising and restructuring.

I told Putin that we were planning to privatise the steel mill and that the Oil and Gas Development Corporation needed revamping. I suggested that if Russian companies were to engage again on these two matters it would be a good symbol of Russo-Pakistani friendship. I promised him transparency and a level playing field.

Putin looked at me and said: 'Prime minister, within thirty days you will hear from us.'

A month had not passed before both delegations were in Pakistan. When the head of Gazprom, Alexey Miller, arrived in my office in Islamabad, I instantly noticed that he did not look well. After exchanging greetings, Miller sat down and said: 'By the way, what did you say to our president?' It turned out Miller had just been recovering from an operation and tried to delay the trip, but was told the thirty-day deadline had to be met. Overall, we had a productive discussion about how Gazprom could cooperate with our government and the Oil and Gas Development Corporation.

A Russian company soon launched a joint bid with a Saudi entrepreneur for the steel mill privatisation and started looking at exploration licenses for energy too. This was one of the most impressive follow-ups I saw during my time in office. It showed the extent to which Putin was in control – a serious, business-like leader who exuded command and a bias for action.

Unfortunately, the privatisation did not materialise because of legal action taken by the employees of the steel mill. A Supreme

Court judgement ruled the sale should not be allowed. The federal government immediately filed a review petition, which is still pending a hearing in the Supreme Court in Pakistan at the time of writing. I believe this is an effort worth revisiting.

In the intervening period, billions of rupees of losses have been incurred. The steel mill needs to be restructured, modernised and run by professional management. If the review petition can be heard, there is a reasonable chance the project can again move towards privatisation.

Russia expands its role

Over the ten years since that memorable barbecue in Astana, Russia has looked more towards its Central Asian neighbours as its relationships with the United States and Europe have become increasingly complex, even adversarial at times. The SCO, which is anchored by Russia and China, has been seen as a counterweight to NATO and other multilateral groups. The SCO's reach has been expanding – Pakistan and India were granted full member status in 2015, having previously been observers in the group. The gas pipeline deal in 2014 between Russia and China was another indicator of closer ties between the two big powers.

If Russia is increasingly turning towards the East, what does this mean for Europe and the West? Tension has run high with Moscow over the crisis in the Ukraine, leading to heavy sanctions on the Kremlin. I met with former German Chancellor Gerhard Schroeder shortly after Moscow shocked the world with its annexation of Crimea. Along with the collapse in oil prices, sanctions plunged Russia into recession. Double-digit inflation has eroded real wages and incomes and consumer demand has dropped.

I asked Schroeder, who had been close to Russia, for his views on the unfolding relationships. He said: 'The question is which way is Russia drifting, toward Europe or Asia? We can already see the first structures for political, economic and military cooperation in the Eurasian region. It is not in Europe's interest that Moscow is orienting itself toward Asia so strongly. Rather, it is in our interest to bind Russia as closely as possible to European structures.'

Russia has increasingly focused on broadening its role on the world stage. In autumn 2015 it began military action in Syria to support Bashar al-Assad. This was Moscow's first offensive beyond its borders since the end of the Cold War and its first military intervention in the Middle East for decades. As Russian fighter jets tore through Syria's airspace, Moscow's role in the region significantly increased. It brought into focus an ongoing geopolitical realignment that is bound to shape policy in Asia, the Middle East and the rest of the world for years to come.

10
TURNING THE ECONOMY AROUND

When I started as finance minister in 1999, Pakistan's economy was in dire straits. The country was living hand to mouth, moving from one IMF programme to another. It was hampered by low growth, precarious levels of reserves, a swelling deficit and a mountain of debt. The spectre of default was haunting us.

Pakistan had about $400 million in available reserves, its credibility with lenders was marred and it was borrowing money at high rates just to pay the bills. This meant we were struggling with illiquidity which, in a worst-case scenario, would impact on our ability to import oil, food and other essentials. Such a crisis could lead to civil strife, domestic unrest and impact the security of the country and the region as a whole.

The fact that Pakistan was on the brink of a foreign exchange crisis had other serious implications, potentially giving other countries leverage over us as we increasingly became dependent on their help. This arguably impaired Pakistan's sovereignty.

On the first day I walked into the ministry of finance office in Islamabad and ran through the numbers, I instantly knew that doing business as usual would not work. A credible reform agenda was needed. Previous governments had been stuck firefighting, trying to keep Pakistan afloat through incrementalist measures as its situation became more and more precarious. A sense of economic crisis hung permanently in the air.

The country had a huge foreign debt burden and there was no realistic way to repay it unless we pushed this mountain of debt away. Two-thirds of Pakistan's revenues were being used to service its debt. Meanwhile, the external debt burden only kept growing – from $20 billion in 1988 to $39 billion in 1999. It was an unsustainable situation. After detailed consultation with my team, it became clear that we were at a crossroads. Either we needed to reform and radically change Pakistan's approach to managing its economy, or we would carry on living from crisis to crisis. It was time to think out of the box.

The challenge was to first stabilise Pakistan's economy and stop the haemorrhaging of foreign currency reserves that was severely depleting our economic strength and credibility, focusing instead on building foreign exchange reserves. The second was to position the nation for growth and unleash its full potential. Moreover, we had to convince the country and the outside world that we were pursuing a credible and effective reform agenda. The new government had just taken power and we needed to demonstrate we could manage the economy responsibly and offer our citizens a better future. One immediate silver lining was that I had a competent finance team. They were talented, committed, hardworking and looking for leadership and direction.

Over the next few years, we managed to take Pakistan from quasi-bankruptcy to being free from the IMF and successfully raise money through international capital markets. GDP growth rocketed to as high as 7.7% in 2005 and 4.9% on average between 1999 and 2007.[1] Poverty levels declined from 32.1% in 1999 to 17% in 2007. Foreign exchange reserves grew from $991 million in 1999-2000 to $16.5 billion in 2007.[2] The lessons from Pakistan's experience can be applied to many developing and debt-ridden countries today.

Straitjacketed by the IMF

I remember going home after my first day in government and worrying about the scale of the challenges we faced. The task seemed infinitely more daunting than I had anticipated. At the same time it was a great opportunity – I felt fate had brought me into this situation and presented me with a chance for me to do something meaningful for my country. It was a way to give back to my motherland. I wanted the people of Pakistan, who were diligent and full of potential, to get the bright future they deserved. The big question was – how were we going to deliver results, and fast? I lay staring at the ceiling for quite a while that night.

The main issues to focus on from the outset were Pakistan's level of reserves and foreign exchange cash flow problems, its overall debt situation and limited resources. The only way to lift the economy out of this quagmire was through a strong period of growth, made possible by a serious reform agenda. In developing countries such as Pakistan, where an expanding population's needs are constantly increasing, equitable growth is the only true driver of success.

This was easier said than done. I soon learned there was no room for any major changes because we were living under the invisible hand of the IMF. When I had my first review with the IMF team as finance minister in 2000, I came ready with suggestions about how we could improve Pakistan's situation. However, it became clear there was no room for input or discussion. The representatives from Washington had a narrow mandate, with little autonomy to alter the programme's terms. They said: 'These are our instructions, this is what management wants – there is nothing we can do to change it.'

This became a recurring problem and I did not find the fund's quarterly reviews encouraging or constructive.

150

Whenever we made attempts to suggest changes to the programme, the IMF representatives said they had to check with management, and then the matter would usually go nowhere. Despite our best intentions, we found ourselves straitjacketed by the fund.

In some ways, the IMF's position was understandable. Pakistan's credibility with the institution was poor, after it had failed to completely follow several previous programmes. Soon after starting as finance minister, I also discovered we had a problem with fudging our figures when reporting to the fund. It was clear that we needed to rapidly rebuild our credibility.

That said, the IMF staff's approach was excessively rigid. There was too much focus on fiscal consolidation, debt management and meeting various indicators, and not enough emphasis on growth and reform. While the programme involved us taking difficult but correct and overdue measures, they were constraining and meant the fund was micromanaging the country's economy. Every quarter we had targets for tax collection, inflation, deficits, exchange rates and reserves. The fund had little interest when it came to structural reforms and encouraging growth. I also felt the IMF was not as sensitised to the impact on job creation and poverty as it should have been. This was despite the programme being called the Poverty Reduction and Growth Facility. Managing an economy involves dealing with the intricate mechanism of many moving and interconnected parts. If certain indicators are followed, it cannot be assumed that the other factors will simply fall into place. A holistic approach is needed.

The net effect of the IMF's handling of Pakistan made it hard for the country to turn its situation around and return to a healthy economy. The fundamental issues that caused the crisis remained.

The IMF is a complex organisation staffed with many competent people but they are not free from the strong guidance, and sometimes interference, of its major shareholders. The United States in particular plays a significant role – it has 17% of the vote and the power to block any big initiative. In contrast, China's share is 6%. In addition, the head of the IMF has historically been European. Its twenty-four-member board has nine European executive directors, and calls to increase representation from emerging markets have been met with resistance. Other senior roles are also taken up by a small group of stakeholders – for example, the first deputy managing director has always been from the United States.

While it is understandable that major world powers have a significant role in the Bretton Woods institutions, it can also cause their decisions to become politicised. The time has come to make the IMF truly global and its leadership selection driven by merit, not passports. It should focus on taking on the best possible talent, as many in the corporate world have been doing. When these institutions become more meritocratic, their impact across the world will also increase. Similarly, the head of the World Bank is always an American, their appointment announced by the United States before they are elected by the board. These are meant to be global institutions – merit should be the only deciding factor for such appointments.

The IMF structure was designed in 1944 and has largely remained the same since, even though our world has changed substantially. In my experience of dealing with the fund, I found its system of having a permanent executive board of directors particularly counter-productive. The IMF has talented people at its helm, but they are constrained by the resident board, which reduces management space and flexibility. Although the fund's board is necessary for oversight, the fact that it sits full-time in the IMF premises in Washington impairs the management's ability to act. In today's interconnected world, there is no need for the board to meet so regularly. Instead, it could meet quarterly, provide clear direction on policy and give the officials who run the fund much-needed flexibility. If there is a sudden need to consult the shareholders, they could be connected by video conferencing. This would lower running costs and improve effectiveness, without reducing the roles of the shareholders. As one former European member told me: 'The IMF needs to create a role of a president or chief executive who would have the necessary authority.'[3]

These issues could have been foreseen. At the time of its creation, the renowned economist John Maynard Keynes was critical of how the fund was being structured. The historian Robert Skidelsky described the creation of the IMF and World Bank in his biography of Keynes: 'Two main issues divided the British and Americans: the location of the Fund and Bank and the Fund's modus operandi. The British wanted the two institutions to be apolitical, deciding matters on technical criteria. To this end they wanted them located outside Washington and wanted the Fund, in particular, to be under the unencumbered control of the managing director and his staff, with the twelve executive directors and their alternates representing their countries or regions on a part-time basis, and [on] part-time salaries. The Americans wanted the Fund and Bank to be located in Washington, they wanted the executive directors to be full-time, and lavishly reimbursed. They also envisaged a staff of 300 technicians, whereas Keynes thought thirty would be "more than adequate to handle the business of the Fund".'

The matter was decided in favour of the Americans and Keynes 'felt a grave mistake was being made'. His concerns were prophetic, as permanent resident boards have impeded the effectiveness of the fund.

These management issues are not exclusive to the IMF. The World Bank and the Asian Development Bank also have resident executive boards. The Islamic Development Bank is almost unique in not following this model. Encouragingly, the newly-formed Asian Infrastructure and Investment Bank will also have no resident board.

As with other global organisations, there is a tendency for people in these institutions to remain there for many years. The focus must be on maintaining a high level of performance and hiring the very best for the job – this is how to ensure the human capital in these organisations is world-class. Today the role of these institutions is arguably more crucial than ever, as many countries face an uncertain economic outlook. A review of the world's financial architecture is long overdue. In order for their programmes to have a real effect, the time has come to fully reform these multilateral bodies and bring them in line with modern governance standards.

Many presidents and managing directors have taken steps to improve governance. James Wolfensohn, to his credit, carried out wide-ranging reforms while he was head of the World Bank. He restructured the institution and upgraded its staff where needed. However, reform must be a continuous process and much more needs to be done.

I met with Wolfensohn in 2015 to discuss the issues facing our global financial institutions. He agreed about the need to encourage meritocracy and stop having resident boards, and added that we need to focus on project management, fighting corruption and empowering the CEO. 'Shareholders should function as shareholders,' he told me.[4]

He agreed that countries' shareholdings should be in line with their GDP. There is a need for a reset, as the OECD countries' proportion of world GDP continues to decline and their populations shrink. Major powers should realise structural reform is needed and that some countries' roles need to be rationalised – perhaps by abolishing the power to veto by any members.

Initial progress

After that first review with the IMF I felt humbled and humiliated. I said to myself, this is no way for a sovereign country to live, and I made it my priority to devise a credible strategy to turn Pakistan around and exit the IMF programme. I knew we could not blame the fund for our problems. It was Pakistan's own fault for not managing the economy right in the first place, otherwise we would not have needed its help. Having said that, once countries like Pakistan take the IMF's medicine, it is very bitter. Breakout from traditional methods is difficult to achieve. We felt the IMF needed to work more with the host government to devise tailor-made solutions, instead of sticking to a straitjacketing approach.

Pakistan required people to think outside the box. Until then, structural reform plans initiated by the government had been driven by the objective to qualify for more IMF money, not by what was realistic and helpful to the country.

I talked to my team and convinced it of the need to break from this pattern. Rather than go for another programme, I developed a two-pronged strategy to attain economic sovereignty and ensure macro-economic stability. We had been incrementalist, and the IMF had been calling the shots. My aim was to accelerate growth and free Pakistan from the fund's constraints. To do this, we needed to make some serious changes.

We were treading on thin ice – reforms require resources, and we desperately needed both. Debt servicing consumed 66% of the budget and this had to be reduced before we could make any further changes.

We looked at various scenarios and came up with a new agenda, which required rescheduling our debts and improving our income stream by raising revenues and investment flows. We would need to commit to managing the economy better and promoting private sector growth and investment, which would eventually create jobs and boost income. Restoring GDP growth and promoting macroeconomic stability was a priority. We had to rebuild credibility in order to raise funds from the capital markets for growth and development and to encourage foreign and local investment.

Our plan was driven by a philosophy of deregulation, liberalisation and privatisation. We began by selectively bringing in people from the private sector to run public sector entities, which helped increase their effectiveness. Boards of directors were filled with professionals and subject experts. We then developed a comprehensive structural reform agenda, which touched on every aspect of the economy, including banking, energy and the social sector. There were many critics of our strategy – both domestic and international – and those with a vested interest in maintaining the status quo hit back hard. However, once we had started, we knew we had to stay on track and wait for results. Over the course of the first twelve months, we established credibility with bankers, creditors and the Bretton Woods institutions. For the first time in many years, Pakistan successfully completed its IMF reviews, tranches were released on time and momentum was re-established.[5]

Then came the medium-term problem of how we could tackle our incoming avalanche of debt. As soon as I assumed office, I started talking to countries who had been Pakistan's main donors – principally, the United States, Japan, the UK and other lenders in the Paris Club, a consortium which includes all major creditors and provides debt relief and debt management to countries under a collective arrangement. The objective was to convince them that we were serious and committed about fixing Pakistan's problems and to come up with an innovative solution.

First, we needed to build a team from within. Moeen Afzal, the Secretary General for Finance, was a capable and experienced officer who played a key role in implementing the reform agenda. We deployed our best available federal secretaries – Younis Khan, Naveed Ahsan, Tanwir Ali Agha, Dr Waqar Masood, Javed Sadiq Malik, Khalid Saeed – and other senior officials like Dr Salman Shah, Dr Hafeez Shaikh, Dr Ashfaque Hasan Khan and many others. When I became prime minister, I held on to the finance responsibilities and brought two junior ministers of state – Omar Ayub Khan and Hina Khar – into the finance ministry.

We hired a new governor of the Central Bank, Dr Ishrat Husain, a respected former World Bank official who added credibility to the team and our reform process. Interest rates were brought down to an average of under 5%, from highs of 20% in the 1990s. In the revenue division, we placed officers like Abdullah Yusuf who helped bring about considerable reform in the tax revenue collection sphere. With the assistance of donors, we funded tax reforms and reinvested in training to upgrade the expertise in the Central Board of Revenue, including hiring private sector talent.

Pakistan had already been dealing with the Paris Club regarding how to manage its debt situation, but it was always stuck firefighting, instead of finding lasting solutions. On 30 January 1999, $3.3 billion of Pakistan's debt was rescheduled on so-called Houston terms – and again on 23 January 2001, for the value of $1.8 billion.[6] This was nothing new. There are two types of rescheduling – 'flow' and 'stock'. Houston terms use 'flow rescheduling'. Their only concern is debt that is maturing in the near future. If a country is in crisis and unable to make the upcoming repayments, then the creditors can take the debt that is due and reschedule it for payment at a later time. They can package up maturing chunks of debt and push them out by a number of years – but they are only taking what is due in that consolidation period and not the entire stock of debt.

By contrast, 'stock of debt rescheduling' concerns the entire amount owed. This stretches the debt out for an agreed period and provides an opportunity to renegotiate and reduce interest rates. For example, if the interest rate was 2% then it can be reduced to 0.5% when the debt is spread out over a longer period. I wanted to build enough credibility to be able to take the whole stock of Pakistan's debt, stretch it out by many years and reduce the interest rate. The aim was two-fold – the country would get a reduction in current debt payments and, if the interest rates were reduced, the servicing costs would also fall substantially. The total payout would reduce and the debt would get a substantial haircut in present value terms, thus creating fiscal space for other needs.

This was previously unheard of for a country like Pakistan. The way the Paris Club works, certain countries are eligible for certain types of relief. Only 'highly indebted poor countries', such as Uganda, Mali and Nicaragua, are allowed blanket stock write-offs.[7] Pakistan is considered a middle-income nation – we were in the 'mismanaged' category. What I wanted was for the Paris Club to make an exception by seeing how a 'stock of debt' rescheduling would help Pakistan get back on its own feet. It was a tall order.

Our early efforts within Pakistan had demonstrated we were serious about reform. The two initial reschedulings allowed us to build credibility with our creditors. Getting the treatment we wanted, however, required a comprehensive lobbying effort and a lot of preparation to lay the groundwork for requesting a major restructuring.

I thought the matter was so critical that I should personally deliver the message to our creditor countries, in order to make the case at the highest possible level. My background working in a global bank for thirty years helped. I flew to Paris, Bonn, London, Rome, Washington and Tokyo, meeting finance ministers and senior officials. I told them Pakistan would accompany debt rescheduling with serious reform, which would then give us the capacity to issue bonds and raise money through capital markets, instead of relying on hand-outs. This would improve living standards in the country and encourage growth and investment. I was running on a mix of excitement and adrenalin throughout – I strongly believed this process, if it worked, could be a game-changer for Pakistan.

My most significant meeting in laying the groundwork for the Paris Club was with Laurent Fabius, then the French finance minister, former prime minister and later foreign minister. France has administrative control of the Paris Club, and we needed its support in order to carry this initiative through. I went to see him with our ambassador, and Fabius brought the chairman of the Paris Club to the meeting.

159

I explained to him our philosophy on rescheduling and how we needed to manage our debt burden, which should be pushed out so we can have fiscal space to conduct reforms and accelerate growth. I told him I planned to privatise assets, bring back growth, create jobs and open the country for investment.

It helped working with a seasoned politician like Fabius. He agreed that Pakistan had a credible strategy and said France would support our efforts. This was instrumental in helping us negotiate the terms of the debt reprofiling. The United States also played a major role in helping us achieve our debt rescheduling objectives. Alan Larson, the Under Secretary for Economic Affairs at the state department, led the effort. He contacted the necessary countries and lobbied them to support our debt reform programme.

As well as visiting the finance ministers of individual creditors, I met with the IMF, which has to give its blessing before a country's debt rescheduling can take place.

I had an interesting meeting with Horst Köhler, who was the managing director of the IMF – and later became president of Germany. I told him our goal was to get out of the fund's programme, to regain Pakistan's economic sovereignty and to go to the markets to raise money, rather than always look to the IMF for help. I said: 'While IMF programmes have been extremely helpful to Pakistan, we will never grow out of this debt trap until we achieve economic sovereignty. We have already completed the first phase of our reform agenda, so we are no longer effectively on life support. We intend to carry on in this way.'

While some of Köhler's colleagues looked uneasy with my statement, he emphatically said: 'I agree with your approach. Successfully raising money through capital markets would be a vote of confidence for Pakistan.' He added: 'Overall this was exactly what I want other countries to do, instead of relying on the IMF for life.'

The 9/11 terrorist attacks gave these efforts a significant tailwind. The Paris Club countries already looked at us more favourably after we showed them, in the first two or three years of our management, that we were a transparent, reform-oriented government; but 9/11 certainly helped us, once those countries recognised how crucial Pakistan would be in the War on Terror.

The Paris Club met to discuss Pakistan's proposal on 13 December 2001 in the French capital. We were there with the representatives of all the consortium's countries and the sessions went on for several days. I presented Pakistan's case and argued why we should be granted an unprecedented 'stock of debt' rescheduling. The meeting was a resounding success in achieving our objectives: we negotiated a new repayment period of thirty-eight years for $12.5 billion, of which there was a fifteen-year grace period. It concerned the total stock of bilateral debt – World Bank and IMF debt is never rescheduled – amounting to about 90% of Pakistan's total debt. This effectively reduced the amount we owed in present value terms by a third, providing us with much-needed breathing room and space for growth.[8] It was a major milestone in Pakistan's financial history and reflected the donors' confidence in our reform agenda.

The agreement came to be referred to as Pakistan Terms. It became an industry standard and set a historic precedent for middle-income countries wishing to reschedule their debt. This unique arrangement has been recognised in academic works, including the economist Nouriel Roubini's writing. When asked to comment on the changes, Roubini said: 'Pakistan's debt restructuring under Shaukat Aziz was a turning point in unleashing the true strength of the economy and increasing growth and prosperity.'

Jill Dauchy, who was part of the team from UBS advising us on the rescheduling, later told me: 'Pakistan pushed the boundaries in 2001 and paved the way for other countries to come and push the boundaries as well. This was an extraordinary achievement. It was much farther than these countries would ever have gone. What has happened in subsequent years is that the Paris Club has started to look at countries that are in that kind of situation, often when they have a political element around them, such as the former Yugoslavia and Iraq.'[9]

The Paris Club initially passed the so-called Agreed Minute, a multilateral agreement to the general rescheduling. Then, in order to make it binding, Pakistan negotiated bilateral agreements with individual countries in the consortium. Several countries, such as the United States and the UK, went even further than the terms suggested by the global agreement. Canada, Germany and the Netherlands also agreed to debt swaps, which at the time were unusual.

Others creditors were more reluctant. The Japanese resisted rescheduling the stock of debt, and the United States played a central role in convincing them to agree. Japan was Pakistan's biggest creditor. When it came to anything precedent-setting, or which implied debt relief, the Japanese were usually the most conservative. Alan Larson spearheaded the US effort to reach out to the Japanese and other creditors and helped convince them our programme was credible. In the end, Japan agreed to reduce our interest rates and extend the payment terms.

The Asian Development Bank provided extensive support for our efforts. Based in Manila, the bank was set up to focus on Asia, with the support of several countries including the

United States, Japan and others. The ADB was supportive and responsive to Pakistan's development needs. ADB Presidents Tadao Chino and Haruhiko Kuroda were helpful, as was Jin Liqun, who was vice president at the time and went on to set up the Asian Infrastructure Investment Bank, a multilateral institution aiming to finance infrastructure projects in the Asia-Pacific region. Another regional institution that supported us was the Islamic Development Bank. Based in Jeddah, Saudi Arabia, the IDB provided valuable assistance under its president, Dr Ahmad Mohamed Ali, a seasoned development banker.

Overall, the success of the Paris Club negotiations gave us the fiscal space to put our money into development projects instead of debt servicing, which fell from two-thirds of the budget to one-third. The spending was redirected to the social sector, in particular education, and the debt restructuring unleashed forces of reform and investment. Revenues went up and a period of high growth began. Foreign direct investment started flowing in and grew to $5.1 billion in 2007.[10]

One of my proudest days as prime minister was when I announced in Parliament: 'Today, Pakistan has regained economic sovereignty.'

Before coming to the session, I had instructed the ministry of finance to repay the entire balance of the IMF loans ahead of schedule. Standing in front of our assembled MPs, I said: 'Ladies and Gentlemen, I have an important announcement to make today'. I paused for breath then informed the house: 'We have repaid all our outstanding loans to the IMF.' The Treasury benches and even some of the opposition applauded.

This was an entirely home-grown plan. While we would not have been able to proceed with our efforts without the blessing and support of the IMF and the World Bank, they were not the catalysts for this initiative. The reality is that any state that wishes to achieve a similar turnaround must provide the driving force itself. This will give it a necessary sense of ownership over the process. As Dauchy put it: 'Exceptional terms and exceptional success have to be led by the country itself. No country is going to get out of their difficulty otherwise – even if it has the most talented staff member from the IMF come over and write the most brilliant paper about how to save the economy, it is not going to work. Even if all the countries write off all the debt, it is [still] not going to work unless you have technically [qualified] people within the country, empowered to create their programme and implement it.'[11]

In the end we followed our own recipe with conviction and achieved results.

It was an advantage that I had carte blanche from President Musharraf. I told him early on: 'Some of the reforms will hurt existing investors or companies who were benefitting from a less competitive industry.' He understood completely and gave us his full support.

The next step was to go to the international capital markets to raise money. For this to succeed, we had to re-establish Pakistan's brand with major investors around the world. I embarked on a series of global roadshows in Asia, Europe and North America, presenting our strategy for future growth and the case for investing in Pakistan. As with the debt restructuring, I felt it was imperative to lead from the front and use my experience of global banking to rally the international community behind Pakistan.

Raising money through international capital markets was a high-risk strategy compared to Pakistan's usual solution of approaching the Bretton Woods institutions. However, my experience and understanding of markets gained at Citibank made me confident this was the right approach. We also established a debt management office, headed by Dr Ashfaque I Iasan Khan; he conducted roadshows and dealt with investor relations, which was increasingly necessary as the number of bondholders grew.

On 12 February 2004, we issued our five-year $500 million Eurobonds and received a rave reception.[12] The issue was oversubscribed four times. It was a significant step forward in attracting a global investor base that had not previously looked at Pakistan.

The closing and pricing of the Eurobond issue took place in London. Afterwards, I went to meet Chancellor Gordon Brown at the Treasury. I was accompanied by our high commissioner, Maliha Lodhi. I updated Brown on Pakistan's reform agenda and described the success of the Eurobond issue, which would help us continue our development programme without relying on the IMF. The chancellor congratulated us on a successful bond issue and overall reform agenda.

Structural reforms

Pakistan historically revolved around IMF programmes, living from tranche to tranche. Our time was spent firefighting instead of unleashing the forces to create growth. Thankfully, the stock of debt rescheduling freed up the means to carry out the next stage of reforms.

Our structural reforms were aimed at creating jobs and growth, reprofiling our debt, promoting investment, making the economy more competitive, improving living standards and reducing poverty.

The objective was to create an enabling environment for growth, coupled with strong regulatory oversight. It was important for us to encourage transparency and create a level playing field for potential investors, while maintaining clarity, consistency and continuity of policies. This sent the signal that Pakistan was open for business.

I wanted to take the state away from factors of production and establish a more market-driven economy. It was necessary to improve our provision of services – we successfully upgraded our industry by opening up all sectors of the economy for local and foreign investment, embracing technological developments, seeking international economic cooperation and bringing in top-class managerial practices and technology. This improved our overall competitiveness, which should serve as a continuous goal for any economy.

Privatisation, deregulation, liberalisation

It is not the business of government to be in business. From the outset, I wanted to encourage the private sector to play a lead role in Pakistan's economic development. Most of its industry had been nationalised by previous governments and I believed this was holding the country back.

I had spent my life in the private sector. Citibank placed a particular emphasis on meritocracy, instead of focusing on nationality or background. I was inspired by the leaders who had believed in the free market economy: notably the Malaysian Prime Minister Dr Mahathir Mohamad, a renowned reformer; Lee Kuan Yew, the first prime minister of Singapore; and the British Prime Minister Margaret Thatcher, with whom I had spent a significant amount of time while she was on a speaking tour for Citibank. I had also closely observed Chancellor Gerhard Schroeder's record in Germany. He showed courage and far-sighted leadership when he reformed Germany's economy, setting it on track for sustained growth.

First we privatised Habib Bank, one of the state-owned institutions. We had developed a legal framework for privatisation and devised the process. All bidders had to pre-qualify by showing financial strength, credibility and managerial ability. Once investors passed the vetting process, we ensured open bidding and a level playing field.

Every industry required its own approach in privatisation. For the telephone network privatisations we brought in consultants from Canada with the help of the World Bank. They devised additional qualification criteria, because these were such vital public utilities. Often, when we privatised an asset, we kept a 30% share for the state, which could then be gradually sold. This meant that, in cases where the companies did well after privatisation, the state had the option to sell and profit from the growth. It also allowed us a means to maintain a say in the boardroom and helped create a smoother transition from the public to the private sector.

With state-owned structures, we tried to employ people with private sector experience, introducing a special pay package for those who made the move. The idea was to generate a healthy blend of private and public sector talent. We incentivised people from the private sector to run banks this way, changing the boards of directors to represent a wider range of skills. This made the atmosphere professional, streamlining the organisations and changing their mindset to being more akin to world-class corporate institutions.

The idea behind reform is to look at an issue holistically and try to improve and impact the entire chain. As an example, our structural reform of the telecoms industry illustrated the impact a reform programme can have across a wide range of areas.

We decided to privatise the telecommunications sector, which was largely a state-run monopoly with a huge landline network. At the time, there were a few small private companies offering cellular services, and overall the system was riddled with inefficiency. Service and maintenance quality had gradually deteriorated and obtaining a landline connection required a lot of influence.

We decided to auction new telecoms licences and rented the ballroom of the Marriott Hotel in Islamabad, broadcasting the event live on television to emphasise our commitment to transparency. We requested a cheque of $10 million in advance from each potential bidder to pre-qualify and demonstrate they had adequate funds.

Companies bid for PTCL, the landline state telecoms service, and the highest bidder was UAE-based Etisalat. We also auctioned three cellular phone licences. Previously, new licences were typically sold for nominal fees. In total the auction raised the government $291 million – a far cry from the previous amounts.

Overall, these changes introduced competition to the sector, which was additionally encouraged by the Pakistan Telecom Authority, newly-created to regulate the industry.

Teledensity dramatically increased, rising from 3.66% in 2001-2002 to 58.8% in 2007-2008.[13] Millions now had mobile phones and over a million direct and indirect jobs were created. As a result the service improved, coverage increased, tariffs fell and connectivity increased substantially. As the networks expanded, new cell sites were needed every few miles and fibre-optic cables had to be laid, which boosted construction and development. Shops started widely selling phone SIM cards, which had a positive effect on commerce. There were more adverts on TV promoting the new services.

All this created jobs. In this way one policy measure made economic activity more efficient, made lives easier and gave a huge proportion of the population access to communication and information for the first time. Tax receipts went up as every call made on the mobile phones was marginally taxed.

In telecoms, the profit margins of these businesses increased by 15-20%, as a result of higher connectivity. In 2005-2006, teledensity was just 26%; in 2007-2008 it had risen to 58.8% and in 2011-2012 it was 72%. At one point a million new phones a month were being issued. Broadband subscriber penetration rose as well. All this has had an even greater effect on people's lives following the introduction of mobile banking, which gave them the necessary tools of communication and finance. People who did not have a bank account or a branch near them could now transfer money through their phone. It empowered people by providing them with access to information and technology and allowed Pakistan to enter the digital age with improved connectivity.

Meanwhile, the new growth in the industry attracted investment, both domestic and foreign, in the telecoms companies. Companies such as Zong from China, Mobilink from Egypt, Telenor from Norway, Warid from the UAE and Singapore Telecom invested in the telecoms sector. The end result demonstrated how reform could have a broad and substantial impact when carried out properly.

Despite this, many stakeholders were against our privatisation programme, saying we were selling the assets of the country to local and foreign entrepreneurs, and that this would impact on Pakistan's sovereignty. This was misguided. A nation's sovereignty is a robust concept. Nobody can put a factory into a briefcase and take it away – it remains a national asset irrespective of ownership. Moreover, bringing in qualified management with the latest technology and letting industries compete in the free market encourages productivity, effectiveness and competitiveness. Constant innovation is a key to success and privatisation opens these industries up to the latest research, world-class standards and development. Not all the changes were immediately successful – for example, we encouraged the private sector to develop electricity and this happened more slowly than we expected. Nevertheless, the privatisation programme ultimately created new jobs, boosted profits and prosperity, reduced corruption and became a cornerstone of Pakistan's development in those years.

Role of the regulators

All our changes were coupled with a process of deregulation – stripping away unnecessary red tape. Bureaucratic procedures, corruption, excessive requirements for government approval and ambiguity of various rules all stifled investment in Pakistan. It is important to note that deregulation does not mean abdication by the state. We focused on setting up a strong independent regulatory system, which provided an essential check and balance. Some examples included regulatory bodies for electricity (the National Electric Power Regulatory Authority), telephones (the Pakistan Telecommunication Authority) and the energy sector (the Oil and Gas Regulatory Authority).

The latest global financial shock has only emphasised the need for regulators and financial institutions to work closely. The regulator has a clear role in ensuring banks and other sectors follow the necessary rules and adhere to disclosure and compliance requirements. At the same time, the regulator can be a catalyst for change and innovation. Financial watchdogs should encourage banks to review their processes and procedures and look to see how they can invent new ways to be in line with modern customer needs. Dialogue and collaboration between the regulator and those under its remit are crucial – there is a need for constant exchange of ideas, if we want to have a healthier financial system. The focus should be on reform, change and improvement, boosting the power of the boardroom and making the industry stronger. Rules must be clear and simple. Ultimately the regulator must be seen as having the industry's growth and long-term viability as a priority. It is not the job of a regulator to act as an adversary – they are overseers. We still have some way to progress in this respect.

Tackling poverty

One of the major challenges I saw in Pakistan was the level of poverty and finding a credible way of reducing it. Clearly, where there is absolute poverty – such as in cases of handicap, old age or illness – cash interventions are needed. During our time, we used the Zakat Programme and Bait-ul-Mal to give financial aid. The National Rural Support Programme, the Orangi Pilot Project, the Aga Khan Development Network and several other NGOs all did commendable work. I personally inaugurated several of their projects across the country. Subsequent governments have introduced the Benazir Income Support Programme, which has delivered visible results and ought to be encouraged.

We aimed to stimulate agriculture, Pakistan's biggest sector, through cheaper fertiliser, pesticides, quality seeds, water availability and introducing subsidies and incentives. We provided low cost funding through the Agricultural Development Bank of Pakistan and assistance to buy tractors and machinery. It also gave funding for research to develop high-yielding seeds. USAID and DFID dispensed much-needed technical support and funding. We also relied on the rural support programme, which carried out community projects such as building streets and developing Pakistan's water supply.

Above all, we wanted to create an environment where people had the means and opportunity to start an enterprise and generate income. We decided to comprehensively roll out microfinance – or small-scale loans – across the country for the first time in Pakistan's history. Previously, there were very few means of borrowing, except perhaps through local, unregulated lenders. We built a regulatory framework to oversee microfinance and introduced access to it on all levels – local, provincial and federal. People could get funding for new ventures or take out a small loan, be it to open a shop, produce handicrafts or to raise poultry. Unsecured loans of as little as $50 became available for the first time. The Asian Development Bank, with the support of President Tadao Chino and his staff, provided technical expertise and training; it helped establish the Khushhali Bank, the first microfinance institution in Pakistan, which was ably led by Ghalib Nishtar. Some banks catered specially for women and as a result a large proportion of loans were taken out by female borrowers. Several other banks opened in rural and urban areas. All this allowed millions of people access to credit for the first time.

I was inspired by Dr Muhammad Yunus, the Nobel Peace Prize winner and founder of microcredit, who I had met over the years at various conferences. I recall a proud moment at the microfinance summit in Halifax, Canada, in 2006, which I attended as prime minister alongside Dr Yunus. We spoke in the presence of Queen Sofia of Spain and Peter MacKay, the foreign minister of Canada. It was heartwarming to hear Dr Yunus mention Pakistan's efforts in his speech, acknowledging that it was one of the first countries in the world to introduce a regulatory framework for microfinance.

Attracting investment

A developing country like Pakistan always needs to generate investment to meet its needs. It requires more than domestic savings to create accelerated economic growth – hence the need for foreign debt and local and foreign investment. If used correctly, it can be a crucial driver of growth.

By 1999, foreign direct investment (FDI) in Pakistan had dried up to a pitiable $300 million. This was mostly in pharmaceuticals, where foreign companies were involved; overall it was a limited amount for a country with such a large and rapidly growing population.

The challenge was to generate opportunity, promote transparency and create a level playing field for potential investors. We needed to increase investor confidence, which meant building the government's credibility through transparency, consistency and continuity of policy.

Company registration time was reduced to days, rather than months. We also encouraged companies to publicly list on the stock exchange, sometimes granting them lower tax rates as an incentive. This provided an additional check and balance – between the stock exchange, their shareholders and the Securities and Exchange Commission, companies had all the more reason to perform well. The commission also oversaw considerable reform of the stock market, which allowed the market to increase its liquidity and attract local and foreign investment. It became another avenue for companies to be active in Pakistan.

Modernising the infrastructure was another valuable part of the structural reforms – improving ports, airports, hotels and travel within the country. All this helped bring money in and encourage development.

The efforts paid off – investors began talking about Pakistan as a place of possibility and opportunity. As its credit rating was upgraded, the availability of credit increased substantially. Pakistan's risk level was deemed acceptable, allowing further capital expansion in the industrial sector. Eventually the funds began to flow in, accelerating the speed of development and boosting growth rates.

Corruption

Corruption in Pakistan remains a problem, as in other parts of the developing world. According to Transparency International's corruption rating, it is listed as the 126th most corrupt country out of 175 surveyed.[14] The best way to minimise corruption in a country like Pakistan is, firstly, by paying officials more; secondly, by reducing human interaction and automating as many systems as possible, as some countries have successfully done. Streamlining procurement procedures and encouraging transparent bidding processes for contracts will also help curtail corruption.

The culture of tax evasion that exists in Pakistan, as well as many other developing countries, is a result of punishing rates, proliferation of the number of levies and extensive human contact between the tax collector and the taxpayer.

I decided that we needed to broaden the tax net, reduce the number of taxes, lower their rates and eliminate loopholes –

simplifying the overall system to make it easier for people to pay. We also had to reduce opportunities for discretion at the hands of tax personnel.

As a result, we gradually lowered the top rate of income tax and saw revenues rise. We also decreased import duties to try and combat the issue of smuggling. One initiative was to segment the taxpayers, focusing on those who could pay more tax – namely big companies. We established new, dedicated, large taxpayer units where these companies could come and pay their taxes, in an attempt to create a more professional environment.

We changed the way income tax worked. Previously, there was a system where every area had regional officials, authorised to set the level of tax people were due. This level of human contact created situations where income tax needed to be negotiated, in some cases leading to corruption. We strengthened the system of self-assessment. Nobody would know the tax assessor; they would simply mail their return and get a receipt. Audits were conducted randomly for a sample of returns.[15]

These measures soon showed a positive effect. As economic activity rose when the economy began to recover, businesses grew and people started spending more.

There is more room for improvement today. The tax to GDP ratio has grown but is still not at the level it should be. As GDP growth has slowed in recent years, this has had a negative impact on the total tax take. In the 2006-7 tax year, 1.8 million people out of the 161.2 million population paid direct taxes through filing of tax returns – equivalent to 1.1%. This number fell to 0.85 million people in 2014-15 – just 0.4% of the population.[16] This fiscal problem in Pakistan is hard to correct but must be fixed in time. Continuing to automate the system and reducing human contact will help increase the amounts collected and bring more tax into the net.

Foreign aid

Pakistan relies on large quantities of foreign aid. This tapered to a trickle as a result of the military coup but began to flow again following 9/11, as Pakistan became a vital ally in the War on Terror.

My experience indicated that the UK's Department for International Development (DFID) was the most effective at running aid programmes in Pakistan. The department was founded by Tony Blair when he became prime minister. Clare Short, the Secretary of State for International Development, paid regular visits to Pakistan, pushed the aid programme forward and lobbied hard within the UK and among other donors to make aid available to Pakistan.

The British government designated Pakistan a 'high priority' country for its international development programme and has consistently allocated one of the highest amounts of bilateral expenditure to it. Generally, we found DFID to be speedy, practical and capable of possessing a better understanding of the local situation. The overhead on their aid was lower than some of the other agencies. DFID also focused on putting money into the institutions and concentrating on capacity building – as opposed to smaller individual projects.

Our task was to ensure the transparent and effective distribution of the funds. Clare Short recalled to me, years later: 'We set some commitments and then we [waited to] see how the partnership worked. The reforms were being carried through – including in the taxation system. The money was properly spent, so our confidence increased.'[17]

Today, the UK continues to allocate substantial resources to Pakistan, with an operational plan to spend £324m in the 2015-2016 tax year – up from £203m in 2012-2013. Short, however, is clear that, without a diplomatic effort to ensure peace, development programmes alone will not be enough. She said: 'I feel sad that our combined efforts did not pay off and produce a more hopeful future. The energy for a big reform effort needs to come again. There needs to be progress on Kashmir, which no one in the international system wants to talk about. If a lasting peace was achieved, the scale of military spending in both India and Pakistan could be cut back and money could be spent on the people.'

Exchange rate stability

Prudent monetary policy played a significant role in helping fuel Pakistan's economic turnaround in those years. One of the government and central bank's main initiatives was maintaining exchange rate stability and low interest rates throughout our tenure. Long-term money was available for several years at 2% - 4%, giving a boost to new capital investment.

We encouraged consumer credit, which covered loans for home ownership, transportation and consumer goods. Availability of credit was ensured and borrowing rates fell.

We relied on a floating exchange rate, rather than one pegged by the government. It remained consistently stable at around 60 rupees to the dollar throughout our time in office, which I consider one of our most significant achievements. Today it is back to fluctuating and can reach 100 rupees to the dollar. We stabilised it by building our reserves and through the central bank's prudent monetary policy. This created an air of stability and helped control inflation.

Pakistan's credit rating improved, which allowed ample capital flow in the form of FDI and foreign loan proceeds. The stable exchange rate was something that I believe really made a tangible difference to the people.

Seeing results

Within a year, our regime was marked by one of the strongest growth rates in the country's history. We nearly doubled the country's GDP during our time. Investment was at an all time high, both domestic and foreign, and the stock market was at its highest levels. Reserves grew to the highest levels that Pakistan ever had in its history. Foreign direct investment rocketed to $1.5 billion in 2005 and $3 billion in 2006. The fiscal deficit was down from more than 7% of GDP when we came to power to under 4.3% in 2006-7. Our successes were internationally recognised and Pakistan was included in the Next Eleven – a list of countries identified by the economist Jim O'Neill as having the potential to become, along with the BRICs nations, among the world's largest economies in the twenty-first century.

All this led to a material change in people's quality of life and average household spending rose from $493 a year in 1999 to $561 in 2007.[18] The person who had been riding a bike wanted a motorcycle, the motorcyclist upgraded to a small car and everybody wanted to carry a mobile phone. More airlines started running flights; hotels were regularly full. We built roads, developed water reserves and started the work on a new airport in Islamabad. We completed the construction of the first phase of Gwadar Port and upgraded Port Qasim.

As well as the economic and social benefits we achieved, our increased financial room for manoeuver allowed Pakistan's

178

defence capability to improve – there was money to spend on the army, navy, air force and important strategic programmes. Considering the region Pakistan is located in and the numerous security challenges it faces, upgrading and updating the country's defence capability was essential in protecting its sovereignty and ensuring peace and stability.

Looking ahead

In many ways the challenges Pakistan has faced over the past decade have made it hard for subsequent governments to maintain growth levels, resulting in a return to firefighting where the economy is concerned. The deteriorating security situation, along with the spread of sophisticated terrorist groups, the repercussions of the global financial crisis and a lack of implementation of the necessary next stages of reform, meant the growth rate reduced. Since 2007, when FDI peaked at $6 billion, it has fallen to an average of $2 billion a year.

In 2008, Pakistan once again sought the help of the IMF. As with its previous experiences with the fund, the subsequent years in the programme have not helped.[19] Pakistan's public debt made up 63% of its GDP in 2013,[20] up from 57% in 2007.[21] Such economic woes have serious implications for the country's capacity to function and maintain its security.

When a government changes, reform initiatives tend to lose momentum and truncate. Reform should be a continuous process for any country, developing or developed. In Pakistan, much more should be carried out. For example, its airlines would benefit from the competition that comes with privatisation and deregulation, as would some remaining state-owned banks. We only need to look at airports such as Heathrow in the UK and Brussels Airport in Belgium, which are either wholly or largely owned by foreign companies, to see that outsourcing management to the private sector does not affect security or impact the country's sovereignty. Meanwhile the regulatory role remains with the government – this can apply to railways, telecommunications, ports, post offices and more. In exceptional cases, units which must remain under government control should have their structure corporatised.

I recently spoke to Masood Ahmed, the director of the IMF's Middle East and Central Asia Department which is responsible for the fund's dealings with Pakistan. He shared his observations about what Pakistan can do to improve its economic performance today. 'The fundamental issue with Pakistan's economy is that there are a set of unresolved structural and macroeconomic imbalances,' he said. 'The government does not collect enough money to pay its bills. Tax to GDP ratio is amongst the lowest in the world, around 9-10%. Every few years they borrow to fill the gap.'[22]

'A lot of the relationship between the private sector and government is one based on looking for privileged position. If you look at, for example, natural gas, there are at least half a dozen different prices at which it is sold. So if you buy gas for one reason, you may pay twice as much as somebody else. As a result, people spend all their energy on trying to get a favourable price for the value of natural gas from the government rather than being competitive at the marketplace. Pakistan is a low tax society. So you have to work on the assumption that you will never get more than 15% of GDP. It is not rational for [the government] to then spend a quarter of its income on subsidising public enterprises.'

Ahmed added: 'The real challenge is to build a national economic agenda, so it is not a party political issue. I have talked to pretty much everybody who was a finance minister or central bank governor in Pakistan over the past decade and 95% of what they think needs to be done is the same. There is a national security policy but there is not a consensus on a national economic growth agenda. Formulating such a national economic agenda would be a good way to move the process forward.'

I agree with Masood Ahmed's remarks. There needs to be a continuing programme of broad-based structural reforms. If this is carried out in the same vein as the reforms during my time in office and by subsequent governments, this should reduce Pakistan's reliance on foreign aid. Reforming a country is a long-term process and governments must always reinvent better ways of doing so.

Increased connectivity and interdependency with our neighbouring region is also needed. Intra-Asian investment is still comparatively low and should be encouraged. We should look towards opportunities in Asia and the Middle East, where there is a surplus of wealth. If we create the right environment for investment, then money could flow in from China, the Gulf and the ASEAN countries. Pakistan supports, and is part of, the One Belt, One Road project (initiated by China) to link markets and allow increased trade and travel between countries in the region.

Existing regional bodies, such as the Shanghai Cooperation Organisation, the Economic Cooperation Organisation and the South Asia Association for Regional Cooperation, could also play a more proactive role by broadening their mandates.

Whatever assistance Pakistan gets, however, only a home-grown reform agenda can have a truly transformative effect. The government must be committed to delivering results, even if they are coupled with temporary pain and political cost. There is no reason why Pakistan cannot once again implement a progressive programme, ensuring a return to economic growth and higher living standards.

11

WALL STREET: THE WORLD'S BEST SCHOOL FOR POLITICS

When a ruler from the Gulf visited Karachi, Citibank received a request to provide His Royal Highness with any banking assistance he required during his stay. We were informed that he would be residing in his private palace in the city.

I was still relatively new to the job when Mike Callen, Citibank's country head of Pakistan, asked me to call on the ruler's staff and establish contact. We went to see him to invite His Royal Highness to a Citibank banquet, which we then hosted in his honour.

This is just one example of the exposure to world leaders and the international elite my career at Citibank gave me. It was a truly global institution, which encouraged its executives to be able to deal with officials at the highest levels. In Pakistan, the first time I met Benazir Bhutto was through Citibank – together with our vice chairman, Paul Collins, I went to see her to discuss obtaining a licence for an investment bank. She was serving her first term as prime minister at the time.

The idea was for us not just to be bankers, but to deal closely with governments, regulators and civil society and to be part of a country's economic process. This ethos came from the very top as John Reed, Citibank's chairman, passed on his interest in geopolitics to his colleagues. He took a cerebral, macro view and was able to hold discussions at the highest level with statesmen across the world. I learned a lot from watching John interact with Lee Kuan Yew, the first prime minister of Singapore, Dr Mahathir, the prime minister of Malaysia, and many others.

I tried to reflect this culture in my own work. When I ran Citibank's corporate and investment banking business in Asia, I made it one of my goals to develop the talent we had working in the region. We had an excellent team of country managers, who were good bankers but needed to have their horizons broadened. So every six months, as part of our off-site review meetings, I organised a series of external speakers to give talks. These included academics, former statesmen, economists and opinion makers who would share their views on geopolitics, the economy and leadership, and then interact with the country managers. The initiative was appreciated by John Reed, who encouraged me to take it to a new level. We started to get high profile speakers such as US National Security Advisor Brent Scrowcroft, Prime Minister Lee Kuan Yew and US Secretary of State James Baker to address our major customers and senior staff.

The experience undoubtedly helped me when I joined the government. General Musharraf would invite me along on trips to meet foreign leaders, which was unusual for a finance minister. I accompanied Musharraf to see the emperor of Japan, the king of Saudi Arabia, the president of the UAE, the German chancellor, the British prime minister, the president of China and many others.

This was a far cry from how I initially pictured banking. To me, it was all green eyeshades and cash registers – the ones I knew from my university campus branch in Karachi. When the prospect of doing an internship at Citibank in 1968 came

1 In 2006 Kofi Annan and
   Mark Malloch-Brown
   invited me to co-chair
   a High-level Panel
   on United Nations
   System-wide Coherence.
   The panel investigated
   how UN agencies and
   programmes can develop
   a more efficient and
   cohesive approach.

2 With US Deputy
   Secretary of Defense,
   Paul Wolfowitz.

3 With Mark Malloch-
   Brown, Prime Minister
   Jens Stoltenberg of
   Norway and Prime
   Minister Luisa Diogo of
   Mozambique, co-chairs
   of the UN panel.

4&5 Addressing the United
   Nations in New York.

China has historically been one of Pakistan's closest friends. Under President Xi Jinping and the rolling out of the One Belt, One Road programme, the ties between the two countries will become deeper and closer.

1   With President Xi of China.

2   With the Chinese prime minister, Li Keqiang, in the Great Hall of the People.

3   With Prime Minister Zhu Rongji, discussing the construction of Gwadar Port, a landmark development project in Balochistan. The strategically located deep-water port has the potential to open Pakistan up to the world and turn it into a vital trade route through South Asia.

4   After signing the Gwadar Port agreement with China in the presence of Premier Zhu Rongji in Beijing.

5   Meeting President Jiang Zemin while on a visit China with President Musharraf.

6   With Prime Minister Wen Jiabao, during the welcoming ceremony in the Great Hall of the People.

In the Great Hall of the People, Beijing, with President Xi. Also present are former Australian prime minister, Paul Keating; former British prime minister, Gordon Brown; former Mexican president, Ernesto Zedillo and the former foreign minister of Singapore, George Yeo.

With President Hu Jintao of China, in Prime Minister's house in Islamabad.

With Zheng Bijian, chairman of the China Institute for Innovation and Development Strategy, in Beijing.

With Chinese Vice President Li Yuanchao, in the Great Hall of the People, Beijing.

With former US national security advisor, Henry Kissinger. Pakistan facilitated his first trip to China, which was kept a closely guarded secret and helped re-establish links between the US and Beijing.

With Jack Ma, the head of Alibaba, Hangzhou and one of China's most innovative businessmen.

With Jin Liqun, head of the Asian Infrastructure Investment Bank, Beijing.

1   With His Majesty King Salman bin Abdul Aziz Al Saud of Saudi Arabia when he was Governor of Riyadh. Also presen was Prince Faisal bin Salman, Governor of Madinah.

2   With HRH Sheikh Khalifa bin Zayed Al Nahyan, president of the United Arab Emirates.

3   With HRH Sheikh Sabah Al-Ahmad Al-Jaber Al-Sabah, Emir of Kuwait, at Islamabad Airport.

4   With His Majesty King Hamad bin Isa Al Khalifa at the Bahrain Grand Prix.

5   With HRH Sheikh Mohamed bin Zayed Al Nahyan, Crown Prince of Abu Dhabi at Prime Minister's House, Islamabad.

6   In Islamabad with HRH Sheikh Mohammed Bin Rashid Al Maktoum, prime minister of UAE and ruler of Dubai in Islamabad.

7   With HRH Prince Salman bin Hamad bin Isa Al-Khalifa, The Crown Prince of Bahrain in Islamabad.

With the Russian president, Vladimir Putin, in Moscow.

With President Islam Karimov of Uzbekistan in Islamabad.

In Astana, Kazakhstan with President Nursultan Nazarbayev of Kazakhstan and President Emomali Rahmon of Tajikistan.

In Beijing with the Chinese foreign minister, Wang Yi, along with Foreign Secretary Riaz Khokhar, and Zafar Mahmood.

With Ilham Aliyev, president of Azerbaijan.

I have always felt the British had a unique approach and understanding when dealing with Pakistan, in part due to their history in the region.

1   I met Queen Elizabeth II at the Commonwealth Summit in Malta and attended a private lunch with Her Majesty held for about a dozen guests. Commonwealth Secretary Don McKinnon looks on as I arrive at the Queen's banquet in Valletta.

2   Prince Charles and the Duchess of Cornwall came on their first visit to Pakistan while I was prime minster. The Aga Khan came especially to accompany them on a visit to our northern areas, which is nature at its best.

3   With former British chancellor, Lord Norman Lamont. Pictured with the chairman of the Arab Bankers Association, George Kanaan, at the ABA's annual dinner in London.

4   The Global Rally Organisation arranged a trip for twenty cars from London to Sydney through Europe, Turkey, Iran, Pakistan, China, Laos, Malaysia and Singapore, where cars where shipped to Darwin and driven to Sydney. I hosted the entire group for tea at Prime Minister's House and reminisced about my days as a member of the Royal Automobile Club in London.

1 As prime minister I had the opportunity to meet with Ayatollah Ali Khamenei, the Supreme Leader of Iran.

2 With His Majesty Sultan Qaboos in Oman at his desert camp.

3 With Iranian President Mohammad Khatami, at a meeting to discuss Afghanistan and regional issues.

4 In Jeddah with HRH Prince Saud bin Abdul Mohsin bin Abdul Aziz, governor of Hail province, Saudi Arabia, as well as Mohammed Alireza and Khalid Alireza.

5 With Josette Sheeran, president of the Asia Society. During the earthquake, Sheeran, then head of the World Food Programme, responded immediately to provide food to the affected.

6 Asim Abdullah, a successful entrepreneur from Silicon Valley.

Never have I felt my abilities more tested than during the earthquake, which devastated vast parts of Pakistan on 8 October 2005.

1   Doctors, nurses and other volunteers flew in from all across the world to help in the relief effort. High profile figures, including Angelina Jolie, helped raise awareness and boost aid. She was also actively involved in helping relief efforts for Afghan refugees.

2   Visiting an earthquake relief camp near Muzaffarabad with Rukhsana.

3   Meeting Abdul Sattar Edhi, the founder of the Edhi Foundation, which helped with humanitarian relief.

4   We held a donor's conference in Islamabad to galvanise funds for the relief effort. It raised $6.5 billion and the UN hailed it as one of the most successful global fundraising initiatives it had ever seen. Kofi Annan's presence in Islamabad made a significant difference.

1   As a banker, I had taken an interest in Pakistan's economy. I was part of a group of expats who would advise Prime Minister Nawaz Sharif. L-R: Tariq Malik, Sajjad Rizvi (head of Citibank Pakistan), Zubaid Ahmed, Ali Naqvi, Junaid Rabbani, Yawar Shah, Alman Aslam and Moeen Afzal and Farhan Sharaf.

2   Japan's prime minister, Junichiro Koizumi, initiated bold structural reforms, at personal political cost.

3   I introduced microfinance with the help of Asian Development Bank in Pakistan, which allowed millions of people access to loans for the first time. Pictured at the Microfinance Summit in Halifax, Canada with Nobel Peace Prize winner and microfinance founder Dr Muhammad Yunus along with Queen Sofia of Spain; the Honduran president, Manuel Zelaya; and the Uruguan vice president, Rodolfo Nin Novoa.

1 IMF managing director Rodrigo De Rato Figaredo meeting the finance team including Dr Salman Shah, finance advisor; Wajid Rarna; Dr Ishrat Hussain, governor of the State bank; Naweed Ahsan, Finance Secretary and Dr Ashfaq Hussan Khan, economic advisor.

2 On a official visit to Kuala Lumpur, my delegation and I visited the Islamic University which has emerged as a centre of learning and harmony.

3 With Jim Wolfensohn, president of the World Bank, who did a lot to reform the bank and promote development.

4 Receiving the Euromoney Finance Minister of the year award from Peter Lee, editor of *Euromoney* magazine, at a ceremony in Karachi.

1   With former Prime Minister Zafarullah Jamali, my predecessor and an experienced political leader.

2   With Chaudhry Shujaat, head of the PML-Q, the ruling party, and Chaudhry Amir Hussain, speaker of the national assembly.

3   With TV anchor PJ Mir, Foreign Minister Khurshid Kasuri and Chico Jahangir in London.

4   At Davos with Citi bankers Bill Rhodes, Chuck Prince and Stanley Fischer.

5   In Los Angeles with the overseas Pakistani community including Hasan Shirazi, Najeeb Ghauri, Shoaib Kothawala and friends.

1 With President Musharraf, his wife Sehba and Rukhsana.

2 Exchanging greetings with the late Makhdoom Amin Fahim, a veteran political leader of the Pakistan's People's Party.

3 With Rukhsana, my children and my father on the QE2.

4 In parliament, I kept in touch with members of the opposition as well. Talking to leaders of Jamaat Islami, PPP and PML(N) parties.

5 With the Amir of Jamaat Islami, Qazi Hussain Ahmed, a prominent opposition leader.

6 With Arif Naqvi, Chairman of Abraaj Capital, a Dubai based private equity group.

7 With Syed Babar Ali, a leading businessman, who set up LUMS, a model of excellence in higher education.

With Rukhsana, after performing
Umrah and praying inside the Kaaba
in the Holy City of Mecca.
An overwhelming spiritual experience.

Coming out of the Prophet's tomb in
Medina, after offering our prayers.

With my family, Maha, Lubna, Abid
and Rukhsana.

In 2007 I invited the Imam of the
Grand Mosque in Mecca, Abdul Rahman
Ibn Abdul Aziz al-Sudais to Islamabad,
where he led one of the largest Friday
prayer congregations in Islamabad's
history.

With Jane McMillan, who put together
the picture section of the book, and
Richard Thoburn, my good friend who
encouraged me to write my memoirs.

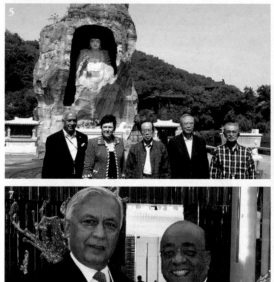

1   After I left office, President Susilo Yudhoyono of Indonesia invited me to address his cabinet, permanent secretaries and heads of government corporations, to describe my experience of turning Pakistan's economy around. It was a productive and interactive session.

2   With Romano Prodi, former prime minister of Italy and Dominique de Villepin, former prime minister of France, at a conference in China.

3   With fellow Atlantic Council members Fred Kempe, Baha Hariri, Brent Scowcroft and General James Jones.

4   With Prime Minister Kostas Karamanlis upon arrival in Athens, Greece, where I lived while at Citibank.

5   At the Boao Forum for Asia, with board members: New Zealand's prime minister Jenny Shipley; Japanese prime minister, Yasuo Fukuda; Chinese vice premier, Zeng Peiyan and Malaysian prime minister Abdullah Badawi.

6   With President Rajapaksa of Sri Lanka during my visit to Columbo.

7   With Mo Ibrahim, founder of the Ibrahim Leadership Fellowship, who has helped improve governance around the world.

8   In London, with Mian Mansha.

Asian Peace and Reconciliation Council board members with Her Royal Highness Princess Maha Chakri Sirindhorn and council chairman, H.E. Professor Dr Surakiart Sathirathai.

With Adel Al Mandil at my daughter Lubna's wedding in Karachi.

With Abdul Rahman bin Mahfouz, flying from Jeddah to London.

With Eisa Al Eisa, chairman of SAMBA in Riyadh, where I served as managing director in my early banking career.

With the Pakistan cricket team, including Dr Naseem Ashraf. I have always loved cricket – I grew up in the Garden Road complex in Karachi, which was also home to many cricketers.

My children Abid, Lubna and Maha.

With friends including Nicolas Berggruen, founder of the Berggruen Institute (1); former Citibanker Shahzad Hussain – better known as Sherry (2); the late Dr Bunyad Haider & Imran Khan (3); Ibrar Mumtaz (4); childhood friend, Farooq Sheikh (5); Ghouse Akbar (6); Asif Mahmood (7); classmates from Gordon College, Rawalpindi and the IBA Business School in Karachi (8) and Raza Jafar (9).

up, it did not fill me with enthusiasm. The placement office at my business school had lined up an interview, which I had every intention to miss.

One day, as I was walking out of class, my economics professor, A. L. Spencer, called out to me: 'Aren't you going for your interview today?'

I told him I wasn't sure.

'You must be joking,' he said. 'This is a good company, Citibank is well known! You have to go.' The professor looked me up and down. 'Your clothes are too casual,' he said. 'You need to be wearing a suit and a crisp, white shirt.'

'I don't have one spare at the moment, and the interview is in two hours,' I told him.

Undeterred, Professor Spencer drove me in his white Morris Minor to Fashion Arcade, a clothing store on Zaibunnisa Street in downtown Karachi. He sat outside while I ran in and bought a white shirt and a red tie. I changed in his car while he drove me to the interview at the First National City Bank. We got there in the nick of time. After I was offered a two-month internship, I called my father to tell him the news. He said: 'I've never heard of this bank. Is it bigger than Grindlays?' As it turned out, it was.

From the start, the placement exceeded my expectations. One of my first tasks that summer was to fix a giant decorative project with Ismail Gulgee, the renowned Pakistani artist. He had created a map of the world made out of copper relief, which was meant to hang in the bank's lobby. The map had to be finished before a New York executive was due to visit the bank, so I would stay with him until the early hours of the morning, supervising the work. At one point we realised Tasmania had been accidentally left off, so the whole relief was taken down and amended.

I developed a passion for the job that summer and, after completing my MBA a year later, returned as a management trainee. My first big position in Citibank came a couple of years later. It was a lucky break – the head of the bank's Lahore branch was asked to attend a management course, so I was sent to fill in for him for three months. This became a permanent position and, soon enough, I had my own office with a private secretary and a staff of about fifty people at the age of only 25.

When Ed Hoffman became the new head of Citibank's Middle East business, he visited Lahore along with the Vice Chairman, Al Costanzo. It was 1975 and the first time a senior executive had visited the city; the bank did not have a proper car to drive them around in, so asked our customers for help. Nasim Saigol leant us his Mercedes in Lahore, where we hosted a reception at the Punjab Club. Nawaz Sharif let us use his brand new S Class Mercedes in Islamabad, which we had sent from Lahore.

As part of their visit, I experienced my first ride in the bank's corporate jet while accompanying Hoffman and Costanzo, as well as Citibank's country head Walter Johnson, from Lahore to Islamabad to meet the finance minister and other government officials. During this trip, the Citibank executives decided to relocate me overseas, as I was later told by Ed Hoffman. He had mentioned the idea of moving me out of Pakistan because he thought I would benefit from gaining international exposure. I had already worked in the Philippines, and now I was being sent to the bank's regional headquarters in Athens, Greece. It was the beginning of a global career – I went on to run Citibank's business in Jordan, Malaysia and Saudi Arabia. I then moved to London to be the head of the Middle East. By this time I had joined the ranks of the bank's senior management, reporting to the chairman, John Reed, and then moved to Singapore to be head of Asia Pacific.

Over the course of thirty years, I lived in nine countries and served as the corporate and investment bank's CEO for Asia-Pacific, the CEO for the Middle East, Central and Eastern Europe and Africa and finally CEO for Citibank's Global Wealth Management Business. I worked on the corporate and investment side of the business throughout.

All this gave me valuable cross-cultural exposure. It felt like quite a contrast to look back at our life in Manila, the Philippines; our first child, Lubna, was born there while Ferdinand Marcos had declared martial law. The same goes for my time commuting daily on the train from Connecticut into Manhattan, surrounded by bankers in their grey Brooks Brothers suits. These experiences undoubtedly expanded my worldview.

The defining moment in my career came on the day I was promoted to executive vice president, joining the policy committee of the bank. The likelihood is I would not have been able to rise through the ranks as quickly in any other American bank at the time. My entire education had been in Pakistan – first Corks Private School, then St Patrick's, a school run by Catholic missionaries in Karachi, and a year at boarding school in Abbottabad. I used to travel in from Karachi on the Awami Express, a low-cost train, up to Rawalpindi, before hopping on the Pindi-Hazara Transport Co bus to Abbottabad.

I got my bachelor's degree at Gordon College, Rawalpindi, majoring in physics and chemistry, and later joined the Institute of Business Administration in Karachi. I had no foreign diplomas and did not travel abroad until my early twenties, aside from a trip to Italy as an infant. Despite this, I went on to become a senior executive at one of the world's leading banks.

Promoting local talent across the world was a unique part of Citibank's culture. This went back to the history of the bank and its foundations. Its precursor, the First National City Bank, was founded in 1812 by a group of New York merchants looking to finance international trade. Following the Great Depression in the 1930s, laws were passed which restricted how banks could do business. As a result, Citibank was only allowed to operate in the five boroughs of New York – even nearby Long Island was off-limits. There was more energy and appetite than there was space, so Citibank's managers decided that they wanted to have an international presence. However, at the time American banks were not allowed by law to have foreign operations. Instead there was the International Banking Corporation (IBC), which was incorporated in Connecticut and founded to cater for American businesses, particularly those seeking to develop a presence in Asia. It had branches throughout Southeast Asia. As soon as the law changed in 1914, permitting American banks to have overseas branches, Citibank absorbed the IBC.

This was how Citibank became the first American bank to establish operations in Asia. It still has the most extensive presence there of any financial institution, with thousands of branches and offices across twenty-six countries. It became the largest issuer of credit cards in the world and one of the biggest American employers in the region, with a staff of more than 15,000.

George S Moore, who was president between 1959 and 1967, led the overseas expansion of Citibank. During the Second World War, many of the bank's staff members were drafted into the military. George Moore wrote to them and said, if you are in the military and you meet people who are unusually capable, hire them. John Reed told me: 'He started this idea that talent is everything. Before that, like all banks, Citibank hired people from the right schools and the right families.'

Walter Wriston, who succeeded George Moore as CEO in 1967 – two years before I started my internship in Karachi – continued to build the bank's global presence. Wriston had studied foreign relations and served in the Philippines during the war. His father had been a distinguished academic and a close friend of President Eisenhower. When Wriston took the top job, he said: 'Let's hire from all the best schools around the world because, given our international character, we should not just have American expats running the business'. So the bank started to recruit actively overseas.

As Reed told me: 'The success or failure of a bank depends on the quality of its people inside and the quality of the customers you choose to deal with.' This was part of the ethos behind Citibank in those days.

Wriston developed the tradition of travelling overseas with the board, taking its members all over the world. As Reed recalled: 'It used to cost us a couple of million dollars to organise these trips. We had to rent private planes, and you couldn't put all the board on the same plane. The people in the region being visited wouldn't work for six months before, in preparation.'

When he became CEO, Reed considered stopping the trips to save on the expense, but the board told him: 'We know it costs you a lot of money, but it is the way we get to know the management directly and to form opinions.' Once a year they would travel to one region, meeting with country heads, bank management and regulators. It was a way to get to know the company and its people. Every two years, they had these board trips. My wife and I went on one to Argentina, meeting the country managers from the region and their customers. It was a useful exercise and helped broaden our minds and understand the business better.

It was John Reed who made it a conscious policy to make the senior management of the bank global in his years as CEO of Citibank. In total, eight out of fifteen senior executives were non-US citizens, including me.

The biggest-ever merger

I was still working in New York when Citibank went through what was then the biggest merger in history. In 1998 we joined forces with Travelers Group, which was run by Sandy Weill, a veteran banker who had built it up into a giant conglomerate. One of the unintended consequences of the merger was that the Citibank culture, its great strength, was diluted. Like many of my colleagues, I only realised its full impact with hindsight.

At the time the merger was announced, it felt groundbreaking. Until then, the regulatory environment would not have permitted it – the Glass-Steagall Act limited what a commercial bank could be engaged in. It had to be repealed before such a merger with Travelers Group, which included insurance and investment banking businesses, could take place.

Travelers was not the first company Citibank considered merging with. First it was approached by American Express and the discussions progressed to an advanced stage. John Reed later told me: 'That would have been a great merger, I wish we'd done it. And it went well, until all of a sudden the person running Amex changed his mind.'[1]

Meanwhile, Sandy Weill had been in discussions with JP Morgan about joining forces, and these talks had progressed far. He and the chairman of JP Morgan, Sandy Warner, had visited the Federal Reserve and the Treasury and spoken to members of Congress to see if merging the two would be permitted. John Reed said: 'That is why Sandy Weill was so confident that it would be allowed with us, because he'd already had that talk with the Fed and with people in Congress.'

Two reasons prevented that deal from going ahead, Sandy Weill told me later: 'One was what Sandy Warner thought it was worth and two – he felt that if we bought JP Morgan, we could destroy the bank's culture. He used the word culture so much, I thought they were in the yogurt business rather then banking,' Weill joked.[2]

'He thought that his seventeen direct reports should be higher than every one of my direct reports. So it fizzled out, but we did have those conversations. I went to see Alan Greenspan and talked about doing it,' Sandy said. 'The only thing that we had a major problem on was that we couldn't have insurance underwriting. And we got that to go away so we could stay an insurance business.'

The atmosphere was already ripe to repeal Glass-Steagall. Weill said: 'We got the insurance people being supportive of it, and Merrill Lynch and Morgan Stanley was supportive of the act going away. It was a law that in some respects made the financial industry not competitive.'

At the time, Bob Rubin was the Secretary of the Treasury and Alan Greenspan was the chairman of the Federal Reserve. Weill recalled: 'Rubin and Greenspan had entirely different positions. They were very good friends, but Rubin came from the political side, and Greenspan came from the independent side. I think Greenspan felt that bank holding companies should be regulated by the Federal Reserve, which is independent of the political spectrum. And I'm guessing Bob Rubin thought, how can a president get re-elected if he can't have influence on the economy through banking policy. He [Rubin] would be fine with getting rid of the act if the Treasury were to become the regulator of bank holding companies. If Rubin had stayed in the Treasury, the Glass-Steagall Act might still be there.'

Then in 1999 Rubin left and Larry Summers took over as Secretary of the Treasury. Weill said: 'This issue was not at the top of Larry Summer's playbook. Within six months of Larry becoming Secretary of the Treasury, he worked out a compromise with the Federal Reserve over how they split up the regulations. So the argument that was stopping Glass-Steagall from going away was no longer there.' In 1999, Congress ruled to overturn the act.

Meanwhile, the Wall Street giants continued to consider possible mergers. After his talks with JP Morgan fell apart, Weill attended a fundraiser with John Reed. Over a couple of glasses of wine, they floated the idea of working together.

What went wrong?

On paper, there was so little overlap between Citibank and Travelers that, when I found out about the merger, it seemed like a perfect fit. Here were two strong, successful companies operating in different fields, which meant there was no need for large redundancies on either side. However, it later became clear they functioned in markedly different ways.

On the day after the merger, I was working in my office when my secretary Pamela knocked on my door and said: 'Sir, there's a Mr Jamie Dimon here to see you.'

The two companies had not yet been brought together under the same roof. I was surprised and replied: 'Jamie Dimon?'

I walked out of my office and there he was in 399 Park Avenue.

Jamie was Sandy Weill's number two in Travelers, his protégé of many years and widely regarded as a potential successor. When Jamie finished his Harvard MBA, having graduated with high distinction, Weill offered him a job – as did several leading banks. Jamie chose to go with Sandy, and stuck with him for years before they began to build up Travelers.

As soon as the merger took place, Jamie decided to come down to Citibank and informally meet the relevant people and executives, talking to them and trying to get to know their business. We had a productive conversation – all in all, it seemed like a positive start.

Weill and Dimon's relationship soon started to sour, however. After the merger, the company's senior management travelled to Bermuda to decide who was going to run what. They agreed that Jamie Dimon should run the investment banking business, which was dominated by Salomon Brothers, and some of the Citibank corporate business. Jamie was there on the trip and knew the decision.

After they came back to New York, Sandy called John Reed and said: 'John, we can't go forward with our plans.'

Reed was amazed. 'Why not?' he asked.

Sandy replied: 'Well I talked to the other people in the business, and they aren't happy with the reporting lines we had planned. Some of them may quit if we go through with it. I don't want to lose them.'

John said: 'Sandy, if we think Jamie's the right guy, tell them to quit.'

But in the end the decision was reversed. Jamie was made co-head of investment banking.

Reed told me he thinks they should have stuck to the original plan. He said: 'It would have been better had we stuck with the first decision and kept Jamie as head of investment banking. The problems that hurt Citi during the financial crash were mostly coming out of Salomon Brothers. They were trading mortgage backed securities.'[3]

Meanwhile, the matter of who would eventually replace John and Sandy was essentially an open question. Reed told me: 'When we merged, Jamie was clearly Sandy's number two. I had asked Sandy: "Do you have somebody who could take our job when we're leaving?"' Weill was not sure Jamie was necessarily the right person for it.

Initially, they considered several scenarios. Reed recalled: 'Sandy and I had both talked about staying for a while, then stepping down. Sandy suggested we agree in writing that we would stay for no more than three years and that we would step down together. I took it to my board and one of my directors said: "John, you can't enter into some agreement about the future management of the company because that's not your business. We decide who manages the company." Which of course is correct.' Reed and Weill became co-CEOs of the new bank.

Meanwhile, Reed already had a successor in mind. He said: 'What I tried to do, and the board chose not to pursue, was to bring in a new person that was not Sandy's or mine. The person I had in mind was one of our directors. The thought was Sandy and I would put the companies together then find new leadership and go forward. Of course, when the time came to step down he [Sandy] didn't want to. So it didn't work out.'

Reed added: 'If the deal from the beginning had been that Sandy will run it, I would have said no.'

After the merger had gone through, it soon became clear that John and Sandy had very different styles of leadership. Richard Huber, a former Citibank group executive and once my boss, was in Peru the day after the merger was announced. He looked at his phone – it was Sandy Weill calling.

'I want to pick your brain,' Sandy told him. 'I want to talk to you about the people in the bank.'

'That'll cost you Sandy,' Huber joked. There was a silence on the other end of the line. Huber added: 'It's going to cost you a very fine dinner and an outstanding bottle of wine.'

A few weeks later, the pair met for a meal at Sandy's usual table at the Four Seasons in New York. They went through the Citibank senior team person by person. 'I told Sandy that he and John were basically the antithesis of each other,' Huber recalled. 'I said: "You, Sandy, have a cadre, a small group of people who you trust and who you are very loyal to, and who in turn are very loyal to you. You manage through this handful of very trusted lieutenants. John is analytical, he manages by the numbers."'

Sandy paused and said: 'You know, that sort of explains it'.

'What do you mean?' asked Huber.

'After we announced the merger, both John and I agreed that we would go away for a week – we had lots of things to do – and in that time each of us would sketch out how we would organise the combined entities. When we met I had an organisation chart with names on it, mostly Travelers people but some were from Citibank, people I thought would be in certain key positions. And John had this much more elaborate organisation chart, with few names on it.'[4]

Essentially, both had miscalculated their ability to work together. Weill told me: 'I said to [John], listen, we're both in our sixties and have had great success, we should be mature enough to get along with each other. But it turned out we were so, so different.'

Cracks in their partnership soon began to form. As Reed later told me: 'Sandy managed by having sets of friends and confidants around him. I would have chosen some people differently. Travelers were good consolidators, and it was a time when the industry was consolidating. There were many mergers and Sandy and his team were good at getting them put together, but then they had to make another acquisition in order to keep it going. What they weren't good at was running the companies they put together.'

Reed and Weill's leadership arrangement was mirrored in the rest of the senior management team – instead of choosing either a Citibank or Travelers person to run a particular part of the business, a system of joint managers was put in place. In some cases there were even three people overseeing a certain area. Dimon later recalled to me: 'I told Sandy and John from the start – what we're doing is outrageous. We are going to blow up the place. They were both very upset with me, saying, Jamie, we like it. We had tri-heads reporting to co-heads – it was an unmitigated disaster.' Jamie did not stop making his voice heard – it got to the point where the disagreements were in danger of affecting the whole business. Dimon said: 'That was the beginning of the end.'[5]

Some of the subsequent tension between Jamie and Sandy appears to have gone back to when they worked at Travelers. Weill later reflected: 'I thought we were a very good team, but Jamie felt he was ready to run the company – this is before the Citi merger. And I was not ready to give it up.'

Weill added: 'That's the recurring problem with a mentor and a mentee – is the mentee going to be reasonable enough to wait till the mentor retires? To get the position that he knows he's going to get. Or is he going to want it sooner?'

Finally, Jamie was called to the corporate compound in Armonk, New York for a meeting with John and Sandy.[6] Dimon recalled: 'He sat me down and said they wanted me to resign.'

Jamie Dimon went on to run Bank One in Chicago and then head JP Morgan, guiding it through the financial crisis. Reed and Dimon stayed in touch. When Dimon was considering merging Bank One with JP Morgan Chase, Reed wrote him a long letter, a copy of which he still has. He said: 'I wrote to him about what to worry about with mergers, what I had learned, and what kind of role he would have to play. It was a substantive letter.'[7]

Recalling his relationship with Weill, Dimon told me: 'In hindsight I was too tough with Sandy, and I was clouded by my anger. I should have realised a lot sooner, even before the deal, that Sandy and I weren't going to be able to work together.'

Eventually it became clear keeping John and Sandy as co-CEOs was not working either. At first they enlisted a business consultant, Ram Charan, to help them resolve their differences. Over a six-month period, he tried to bring them together and they drew up a plan for how they thought the relationship could function: the business units would all report to Sandy, the financial unit would report to both CEOs and John would have control over the other staff functions.

Finally, John approached Sandy and told him: 'This doesn't work. I think the board should fire both of us and find a new CEO.' John told me he brought the issue of the bank's leadership to the board, which met for about seven hours. Sandy and John watched golf and basketball on TV in the office while the board decided, before choosing Weill as the sole head of the bank.

Even while Citigroup continued to perform, tripling its earnings in the five years after the merger, concerns over its consequences began to emerge. In the process, Citibank lost some of the qualities which distinguished it. Gunther Greiner, one of my old bosses in Citibank, said: 'The new Citi culture was too focused on quarterly earnings and compensation. The bank need[ed] to go back to basics and worry about customers and relationships, not just doing deals.'

In 2014, sitting in his home in Boston, where he served as chairman of the Massachusetts Institute of Technology's governing body, John Reed told me he regrets the merger. He said: 'We were bringing two very different organisations together. From a cultural point of view we were very different. I probably naively said to myself: "Be flexible, if Sandy wants to put some people into jobs that I'm not 100% sure are right, time will tell and we'll correct it later." But I don't think we could have successfully merged with this particular company.'

In 2003 Charles Prince succeeded Sandy Weill as CEO of Citigroup and as chairman in 2006. Weill later recalled the decision: 'Unfortunately what I think happened was that the person who I and the board thought was the right person became a different person when he got that title.'

In four years the bank's balance sheet grew from $1.2 trillion to $2.4 trillion. The number of employees went from 240,000 to 375,000 and earnings did not grow to match this. On top of this, Weill said: 'The industry, including Citigroup, was doing all this off balance sheet stuff. I think if you're not proud of what you're doing and you're not willing to show it on the balance sheet, then you shouldn't be able to do it.'

After Prince resigned in 2007, Weill wanted Timothy Geithner to succeed Prince as the CEO. Geithner had been working at the New York Federal Reserve at the time. He consulted his mentor, Bob Rubin, the former Treasury Secretary and Citigroup's senior executive.[8] Rubin told Geithner that he was backing Vikram Pandit to be CEO instead and encouraged Geithner to stay in his job at the Fed.

Weill said: 'I wanted to bring in Geithner to take Prince's place. I thought I had him all set. And then he said Bob Rubin spoke to him and told him not to do it and that he supported Pandit for that job. So he backed off.' Instead Vikram Pandit was made CEO – until he resigned in 2012.

Pandit, a cerebral executive, had limited experience in commercial banking or of running a global institution of this magnitude. Like others at the time, I initially hoped he would be able to turn the company around, but this was not the case.

It could be argued that Citigroup would have been in better shape to weather the financial crisis, had things been handled differently. Reed told me: 'I don't know whether, if we had done [things] differently, they would have missed the 2008 problems. As it turned out, Citigroup was probably one of the most vulnerable institutions in 2008. And I think it is probably the institution that has done least well in recovering from it.'

One of the problems was the level of exposure Citigroup had to mortgage-backed securities, many of which turned out to be toxic sub-prime assets.

Citigroup was badly hit during the financial crisis and required a $45 billion bailout by the government. In 2012 the bank was ordered by the Justice Department to pay $7 billion over accusations of misdeeds in the run up to the crash. As described in the concluding report of the US government's Financial

Crisis Inquiry Commission: 'Many of these institutions grew aggressively through poorly executed acquisition and integration strategies that made effective management more challenging. The CEO of Citigroup told the Commission that a $40 billion position in highly rated mortgage securities would "not in any way have excited my attention," and the co-head of Citigroup's investment bank said he spent "a small fraction of 1%" of his time on those securities. In this instance, too big to fail meant too big to manage.'[9]

Citibank today

Coming out of the financial crisis, the task ahead for Citi was massive and daunting – and required major change at all levels of the company. Citi's board of directors and senior management team have been almost entirely overhauled since 2008.

One of the first steps the bank took was separating its non-core assets into Citi Holdings and then beginning to sell or wind them down. Through that process Citi Holdings assets, worth over $800 billion at their peak, were worth under $74 billion by the end of 2015, or about 4% of its balance sheet (from 32%). Citi sold over sixty non-core businesses, including insurance, consumer finance and private equity. The bank exited the consumer business in over twenty-five countries and its total headcount was also reduced from a peak of about 375,000 employees to about 230,000 by 2016.[10]

By the end of 2010, Citi was able to repay the TARP funding, with the US government reaping a $12 billion profit on its investment. The regulatory and compliance elements have been bolstered – its staff now make up 12% of the workforce, up from about 14,000 in 2008 to about 27,500 in 2016. The bank, under the leadership of chairman Michael O'Neill and chief executive Michael Corbat, has steadily built a stronger balance sheet with increased capital.

However, challenges remain and the way the post-recession environment has been handled by the regulators has arguably been too heavy-handed. They should focus on talking to banks first, and imposing heavy penalties later, instead of the other way round. Michael O'Neill told me in 2015: 'The regulatory environment continues to impose new constraints on our business, which are only getting more rigorous and expansive. Regulatory balkanisation makes compliance more demanding and constraining. We are seeing consistent scrutiny from elected officials and members of the public which in turn places further pressure on regulators to impose new and tighter constraints on us – it also raises the price tag of various enforcement actions against the large banks.'

Regulators should move to a more collaborative approach to the industry if they wish to encourage growth. Punitive measures and an adversarial stance will only serve to stifle it in the long run.

Bad money

After running its business in various parts of the world, I was moved to New York to head Citibank's global wealth management business. One of my legacies was spearheading the effort to clean up Citibank's private bank. I fundamentally believe that bad money does not deserve a home. I was brought into the job by John Reed to restructure the business with this in mind. He said: 'I think you can fix it.' As part of this, we terminated the bank's relationships with those clients who did not meet its transparency standards. These included public figures and people without clear sources of income.

The process to clean up the bank had started before me and it soon dawned on me that what we were not doing enough, so I approached Transparency International and suggested it join the banks in their fight against bad money. I was keen to highlight that it was not enough to focus on illicit payments on contracts. That was only part of the picture – once such a payment is made, it should not be allowed to enter the banking system at all. The payer is as guilty as the recipient. Many countries have corruption laws where the payer is not blamed but the receiver is. Instead, they should have legislation which makes both sides equally guilty and there should be no escape for these people who have enriched themselves at the expense of their country.

I approached the big American banks – Chase and JP Morgan – and urged them to join us in developing a framework of standards. I remember JP Morgan expressed interest. I then went to the European banks, Credit Suisse and UBS in Switzerland and Barclays in the UK. We had a meeting arranged with them in Switzerland, but I could not attend since I had already been called to serve my country by then.

As head of Citibank's wealth management business, I was invited to appear before the US Senate finance committee, but I had already moved to Islamabad by the time it convened, so John Reed testified in my place.

While I was in government, Paul O'Neill, the US Treasury Secretary at the time, invited me to address the G20 finance ministers' meeting held at the Treasury in Washington DC, which coincided with the annual World Bank and IMF meetings. He asked me to speak to the group about the risks of bad money entering the banking system and how to prevent it. I discussed the ways in which financial institutions and governments should manage the process of cleaning up their banking systems, as well as updating my counterparts from other countries about our structural reform agenda.

The future of banking

We must learn the lessons of the latest global financial shock. There were indications of the 2008 banking crisis long before it happened. Banks should be equipped and ready to face realities – and not turn their eyes away from uncomfortable truths, hoping they will go away.

The nature of markets means there will always be another downturn – it is therefore important to develop a culture that anticipates upcoming crises and is ready to take quick action to correct them. For this, policymakers must shore up public support – because the necessary measures can often be difficult ones.

Regulation must be clear and simple. It must encourage innovation and growth and have the industry's long term viability in mind. Regulators must not just regulate – they must collaborate, working closely with financial institutions. It is not about dictating terms – a two-way dialogue is key.

Today the trading model of banks is changing and we will see more emphasis on meeting consumer and corporate sector needs and a reduced reliance on speculative trading, in part as a consequence of the Volcker rules. This should reduce the level of risk and improve the quality of earnings – even if the amounts made in profits fall.

While positive steps have been made with the banking sector, more work needs to be done. Problems with bad money entering the system continue to this day and more efforts are required to stop this. Only through continued structural reform and clear regulation can banks continue to evolve and develop safeguards against another global crisis. It is time to make our economies leaner, fitter and more competitive. Swollen, inflexible public sectors must be slimmed down, while keeping in mind the social needs of the impoverished and disadvantaged. Coordination by banks, civil society and governments is crucial in order to generate an enabling environment for growth.

12
GROWING CITIBANK IN SAUDI ARABIA

It is no wonder Citibank was keen to establish its presence in Saudi Arabia. The Kingdom's ties with the United States have spanned decades, and can be traced to a historic meeting between King Abdul Aziz and Franklin Delano Roosevelt.

It was February 1945, in the last few months of the Second World War. The American president was on his way to Egypt following the Yalta Conference. In his first time leaving the country since uniting the Kingdom, the Saudi ruler travelled up the Red Sea, while President Roosevelt made a diversion from his trip.

The meeting, shrouded in secrecy, took place on Great Bitter Lake aboard the USS Murphy. A tent was specially erected over the bow of the ship for the king, who was used to sleeping in the open. The deck became a *majlis*, complete with rugs, cushions and a decorative chair for the Saudi ruler.

The two leaders developed a warm personal relationship, exchanging tokens of friendship, and the meeting cemented the efforts of King Abdul Aziz to welcome American oil companies into Saudi Arabia. Soon after, the first significant contract with a US company was signed. This eventually helped establish Saudi Arabia as a leading producer of oil, transforming its future. Crucially, Roosevelt reportedly pledged to consult with Saudi Arabia about any major issues regarding the Middle East, which has remained a cornerstone of foreign policy between the two countries ever since.

My own experience of Saudi Arabia goes back to my Citibank days, when I spent a formative part of my career running the bank's affiliate there. I was appointed managing director of the Saudi American Bank (Samba) in 1986. It was a joint venture, with Citibank having 40% ownership and Saudi shareholders, which included prominent Saudi families, owning 60%. This major subsidiary was facing challenges to its loan portfolio and earnings, so John Reed decided to send me there from my position as head of Citibank Malaysia. I had only visited the Kingdom a few times before, but I did not hesitate to accept the position, knowing Samba was one of Citibank's largest joint ventures, with branches all over the country and offices overseas. The potential that could come from restructuring it and making it profitable was substantial.

I moved with my wife and three children to Riyadh, where the bank was headquartered. We shared a Samba compound with four other executives of the bank and their families. At the time Prince Salman bin Abdul Aziz, the current king, served as the governor of Riyadh and I had the occasion to meet with him in his role as governor and senior member of the royal family. During my years there I developed an affinity for the Kingdom – I always found the Saudis very warm, hospitable and accessible, and the friendships I made there have stood the test of time.

When I first started my job there, the task ahead was far from simple. We were working at a time when the banking system was not yet fully developed. It was sometimes difficult to get back loans as banking in Saudi Arabia was still evolving. SAMA, the central bank, played a key role in transforming it into a viable sector.

I was able to clean up the bank's portfolio, reduce expenses, increase its product offering, collect past due loans (some of which had been on the bank's books for years) and boost the franchise's profitability. By the end of my tenure, we had collected all the main outstanding loans, primarily through applying consistent effort, by treating the customers in question with respect, explaining the situation to them and coming to settlement. These included asset swaps, extended repayment terms and offering incentives for repayment.

My lessons from doing business with Saudis are that they appreciate people who are straight talking, professional and deliver results – if you can show these qualities then you can gain their respect. It is also appreciated when a business links its accomplishments to the success of the country. For example, this can mean reducing the number of expatriate workers, hiring Saudi staff, training them and investing in new technology. I changed several senior management positions and reduced the overall staff count from 1475 to 975. At the same time, I hired new local talent to build the bank's bench strength and prepare it for growth. These changes in personnel reduced the running costs and were among the most successful restructuring exercises undertaken by the bank. Today the chairman of Samba is Eisa Al-Eisa, an experienced world-class Saudi banker, under whose leadership the institution continues to expand its activity and profitability.

Both the finance ministry and the central bank are staffed with highly qualified people. I found SAMA, the Saudi central bank, professional and open to new ideas. It was keen to return the banking system to health and introduce state-of-the-art products, giving us space to innovate and compete.

My time in Saudi Arabia turned out to be a turning point in my career. As a result of successfully restructuring Samba,

I was promoted to head Citibank's Middle East business and moved to London. I remained on the board of Samba, as Citibank was a major shareholder.

Paul Collins, Citibank's vice chairman, worked with me on the partial sale of Samba following the need for capital by its parent company, Citibank. We sold 20% of the stock in two stages to a state pension fund. It was unusual for a bank to do this, but it turned out to be a success. We were fully supported by the regulators and the government in handling this sale.

Several years after I had left Citibank, it decided to exit Saudi Arabia. It was a hasty move, which was neither well thought out, nor well-received by the government. Since then, Citi has been trying to get back into the Kingdom, with little or no success.

Going back

Because of my history of living in Saudi Arabia, when I joined the government, I would meet regularly with the Saudi leadership to reinforce our already strong relationship with the Kingdom.

Since my time working there, I have seen Saudi Arabia change substantially. The banking sector has developed into a modern and reformed business. King Fahd bin Abdul Aziz Al Saud oversaw the transition and economic growth of the kingdom in the 1990s. The country's infrastructure was developed substantially and two newly-built cities, Jubail and Yanbu, became models of industrial growth for the world. Several industrial complexes were set up to process hydrocarbons, and the leadership encouraged joint ventures with a range of countries.

I had the opportunity to meet with King Fahd on several occasions while visiting as prime minister. By this time, he was not in good health, but still gave us his time. I always found King Fahd to be a great friend of Pakistan, with a special appreciation for our country and a strong desire to see Pakistan grow and prosper.

Under King Fahd, there was a focus on improving education as well as encouraging the influx of leading technology and expertise from around the world into Saudi Arabia. He was development-orientated and wanted to see an educated society emerge in Saudi Arabia. The king realised education is the only way for the Kingdom to move forward and reach its potential.

King Fahd also spearheaded the expansion of the two Holy Mosques in Mecca and Medina, a valuable contribution to the Muslim *ummah*. The rate of expansion of Mecca and Medina was uninterrupted because King Fahd felt it was his moral duty to keep the work going. It is one of the largest construction projects in history. Work on Mecca and Medina carried on under his successor, King Abdullah bin Abdul Aziz Al Saud, and continues today under King Salman bin Abdul Aziz Al Saud.

The two holy sites are now a feat of logistics, with a high-speed rail link and ambitious infrastructure under construction which will allow them to accommodate 2 million people for several weeks a year. By comparison, I remember the bumper-to-bumper traffic and the basic facilities when I went there with President Musharraf and his delegation. On subsequent visits, the Kaaba door was opened for us and we were allowed to go in and pray. We went to Medina, where the Prophet is buried. We were allowed to access the area where the Prophet used to pray, as well as his tomb. I was overwhelmed at the significance of being in such a revered place.

The presence of Mecca and Medina makes Saudi Arabia one of the most significant countries in the Islamic world.

Pakistanis, and many Muslims in general, have a special reverence for the Kingdom and its leadership. A large number of Pakistanis visit every year for pilgrimage and other religious activities. Saudi Arabia is also one of the biggest employers of Pakistani expatriates – there are more than a million Pakistanis living and working there. They are engaged in all sectors and at all levels, from management positions to construction workers. For example, the first governor of the Kingdom's central bank, Anwar Ali, was a Pakistani. He played a significant part in initially developing the country's banking system.

For decades, Pakistan and Saudi Arabia have enjoyed a strong and close relationship. On the economic side, the Saudis are important donors to Pakistan, giving us cash grants and development loans through the Saudi Fund for Development. Whenever Pakistan has faced challenges, Saudi Arabia has stood by us and helped both financially and diplomatically.

There are also military links between the two countries – Pakistan provides the Saudis with training and advisers; and the army, navy and air force of the two nations collaborate in joint exercises. In the past, Pakistan has had thousands of troops posted in Saudi Arabia and we maintain a small advisory group within the ministry of defence in Riyadh.

By the time he took over, King Abdullah had already gained valuable experience from effectively managing the Kingdom as crown prince for about ten years, while King Fahd's health deteriorated. The first time I met King Abdullah as prime minister, he gave me a very warm welcome, as did Crown Prince Sultan bin Abdul Aziz, Prince Nayef bin Abdul Aziz, the minister of the interior and several other officials, including Dr Ibrahim Al Assaf, minister of finance.

King Abdullah later visited Pakistan, accompanied by Prince Saud al-Faisal, the foreign minister, and other members of the government. When the king arrived in Islamabad, thousands of people lined the streets to greet him. That evening, he gave a speech to a large audience gathered at a convention centre. It was broadcast on television screens across Pakistan and watched by millions. The audience was already hanging on his every word, but, when King Abdullah ended the speech with the words, in Urdu: '*Pakistan Zindabad*!' – which means 'Long Live Pakistan!' – the crowd was thrilled.

During my farewell visit to Saudi Arabia as prime minister, I had a meeting with King Abdullah, who said: 'You will come have dinner at my palace.' He was appreciative of the role I had played in strengthening the relationship between Pakistan and the Kingdom.

I was invited to the king's country residence outside Riyadh, which had stables for his horses, as well as beautiful gardens. When I arrived, I went to meet the king and he walked in with me to the dining room. As we walked alongside the giant buffet full of every type of cuisine you could think of, with two people carrying our plates behind us, the king kept putting more and more food on mine. By the time we were finished, I had a mountain of delicacies to eat. The king was extremely warm and hospitable, which reflected the good relationship between our two countries, as well as my history of living and working in Saudi Arabia with Citibank. He told me on that farewell visit: 'Saudi Arabia is your home.'

After the dinner, the king said: 'You should stay another day and I will show you my horses.'

I wanted to accept the offer, but I knew half my delegation was already waiting for me in the airplane. We were meant to fly out to Medina before returning to Pakistan. I told him I couldn't stay, but requested to visit the section of the Prophet's mosque in Medina, where the Prophet is buried, so we could offer our prayers. The area is usually sealed off and it is a real privilege to go inside. The king immediately authorised it, giving us exclusive access to the holy site.

In recent years, Saudi Arabia has taken steps to improve its infrastructure, expand its education system and gradually move towards having a more open environment while continuing to respect Islamic values and traditions. The country has an active programme for its youth to study both locally and abroad. King Abdullah opened Kaust, the first modern university in Saudi Arabia, attracting professors from abroad. Its first president was from Singapore. I have generally been impressed by the level of education of the people in government in Saudi Arabia, who have often qualified from foreign universities.

After the death of King Abdullah, Prince Salman bin Abdul Aziz took over as king, Prince Mohammad bin Nayef was appointed crown prince and Prince Mohammad bin Salman became deputy crown prince. This marked the beginning of succession in favour of the next generation of Saudi leaders.

Politically, Saudi Arabia is one of the most significant countries in the Middle East, considered by many to be the voice of the Muslim world. It has an important global role to play and has already demonstrated the ability to work with major powers to solve issues and challenges. It hosts the Gulf Cooperation Council (GCC), as well as the headquarters of the Organisation of Islamic Cooperation, which amplifies its importance in the region.

Pakistan has always sought to maintain and develop relationships with all of the GCC countries, which include the UAE, Bahrain, Kuwait, Qatar and Oman. These nations have a large number of Pakistanis working and living there and maintain a close security relationship with Islamabad, which has military advisers in some of them.

The geopolitical role of the United Arab Emirates in the region has been growing and it has become actively involved in issues in the Middle East, including Syria. For example, the UAE air force provided aerial support against rebel forces in Yemen. The UAE has also worked closely with other countries in the GCC to try and maintain peace in the region.

Pakistan has an affinity with the UAE because of historical links between the two countries. Dubai and Abu Dhabi have become hubs for Pakistan, with daily flights to several of its major cities, including Lahore, Karachi and Islamabad. Many Pakistanis choose to work in the UAE, with countless others going there as tourists or using it as a transit stop to travel across the world. The network created by Etihad and Emirates airlines is one example of strong linkages between the two countries. Likewise, UAE investors have been behind several successful projects in Pakistan, including investments in tele-communications, banking and real estate.

Pakistanis have long admired the UAE for how efficiently it is run and its developed infrastructure, as well as its levels of prosperity and security. The UAE government, under the leadership of Sheikh Khalifa Bin Zayed al Nahyan, has encouraged the country's private sector to grow, which has created a favourable environment for Pakistanis to start businesses and buy real estate there. The rulers of the UAE are also regular visitors to Pakistan, which provides an attractive destination for hunting houbara bustard in its desert areas.

As well as its ties with Saudi Arabia and the UAE, Pakistan's dealings with Bahrain, Kuwait, Qatar and Oman are also significant. I was involved in incorporating the first Citibank-run Islamic bank in Bahrain. Since then, the country has developed into a regional financial centre, and Pakistan has retained close defence and security cooperation with Bahrain.

Qatar has been a supplier of natural gas and helped finance various projects in Pakistan. In turn, we have sent a substantial number of construction workers to help with the large-scale infrastructure development taking place there.

Kuwait is a major investor in Pakistan, both in government and private sector entities. Pakistan has joint investment companies with Kuwait, and also Oman, which has helped finance several of our infrastructure projects. Under Sultan Qaboos' leadership, Oman has benefited from impressive levels of growth and development.

Jordan

As head of Citibank in Jordan, I had the opportunity to spend a couple of years living in Amman in the days of King Hussein bin Talal, and I have regularly visited the country ever since. Jordan has always played a significant role in the Levant because of its strategic location next to Israel, Syria, Saudi Arabia and Iraq.

A number of Pakistanis live in Jordan and links between the two countries have historically been strong. As a result of effective diplomacy, and the leadership of the king, the two countries have maintained a strong relationship.

In 2014 I met with King Abdullah II at his palace in Amman. We discussed the latest developments in the Middle East and the implications that the Syrian and Iraqi conflicts could have for the region. We also discussed Jordan's plans to grow its economy, as well as the need for structural reform.

The conflict in Iraq and the civil war in Syria have made Jordan a buffer between these states. Many families have moved to Jordan to escape the hostilities in these war-torn countries, and it has played a positive role in helping those who have been displaced by the trouble in the region – despite Jordan having its own issues to deal with. By the end of 2015, there were more than a million refugees residing in Jordan – the equivalent to a fifth of what Jordan's population was in 2013 – with the majority coming from Syria.[1] Jordan's authorities provided land to build two Syrian refugee camps, Azraq and Zaatari, as well as ensuring their security.

As King Abdullah told me, the influx of refugees from Syria and Iraq has created new challenges for Jordan. At the time of writing, his government has successfully maintained a peaceful border with Iraq and effectively controlled the security environment of the country. As the situation in the Middle East deteriorates, this will have further implications for Jordan. Its disciplined and strong army has so far served as an effective safeguard. Together with King Abdullah's leadership, it should help maintain the stability and growth of the country.

Jordan has strong human capital and the ability to attract local and foreign investment in new projects. In 2015 I attended the launch of the Abdali project in downtown Amman, a new development project which plans to upgrade the city, provide jobs and ensure commercial activity. It was opened by King Abdullah, with Queen Rania, Crown Prince Hussein Bin Abdullah and Bahaa Hariri in attendance. The project is a joint venture between Rafic Hariri's family and the government of Jordan, and will include hotels, apartments, shopping malls and office blocks. It aims to make the city an attractive destination for tourists from the Gulf and Europe, providing the infrastructure to complement its historical sites, natural beauty and Dead Sea resorts.

Focusing on such developments, which create much-needed jobs for both locals and refugees, while continuing to maintain the security situation in the country, is paramount – not only for Jordan, but for the region as a whole.

13

AMERICA'S BACK CHANNELS WITH IRAN

President Bush suddenly turned to me and said: 'Prime minister, what do you think about Iran?' We were having lunch in the White House on my official visit in 2006 with our respective delegations. I said it was a complex situation. Strategically Iran's importance and history requires that its government is engaged. From my experience, if understood and approached correctly, they can be receptive. I said: 'You may want to engage Russia, because they are also close to Iran and could be an interlocutor.'

Nearly a decade later, the deal struck in 2015 between President Obama and President Rouhani, following talks which included Russia, the UK, Germany, France and China, signalled a significant thaw between Washington and Tehran and could prove to be a game-changer for the region, as Iran increases its international reach.

Iran has already shown its capacity to influence beyond its borders with the recent war in Afghanistan. According to several sources who held senior positions at the time of the US invasion, Iran played a key role in helping the transition after the US invasion and the fall of the Taliban. The cooperation even stretched to back channel discussions between Iran and America, long before any official process had started. Kofi Annan told me how diplomats were arranging behind-

216

the-scenes meetings between representatives of Iran and the United States, who officially had nothing to do with each other. 'Conferences would be called in the same city and we knew that, once we got them in the same place, they would meet somehow,' Annan said. Often this involved hushed discussions in coffee rooms, away from prying eyes.[1]

Officially, there were no diplomatic channels open between Iran and America at the time. Kofi Annan described how, in the aftermath of the Taliban's defeat, the two powers secretly coordinated. The former Secretary-General recalled: 'Before the *loya jirga*, we had a meeting of the six plus two – which in a way allowed the United States and Iran to go to the corner of the room and chat. But with deniability – "we don't talk to each other", and then do this.'

I asked Annan for more details of how this initial contact came about. He said: 'Often you just have to open a crack and they take care of it. You just have to have them in proximity and they would deal. For example, if you have a six plus two meeting, all the meetings have coffee rooms or offices somewhere. After the meeting they just withdraw and go there to talk.'

'I think the US came to an understanding on Afghanistan with Pakistan, with Iran, with the Russians, because they needed to use the routes to supply their troops, they needed to keep the Iranian border quiet. The Iranians honoured the accommodation.'

Kofi Annan added that this has caused people who call for engagement between the two countries to argue: 'You made a deal with [Iran] on Afghanistan and they honoured it. Why can't you work with them on other issues in the Middle East? And really come to some understanding. Put 1979 behind you.'

Annan's deputy, Mark Malloch Brown, also recalled Iran's role at the time: 'Briefly, Iran's role was critical. One of

217

the least noticed aspects of this was the logistical support that the Iranians gave the US for mounting a campaign in Afghanistan, both through diplomatic assurances to the Americans and also physical support in terms of moving in heavy equipment.'[2]

I met with Norman Lamont, the former British Chancellor of the Exchequer, shortly after he had returned from a trip to Tehran. Lord Lamont, who closely follows developments in Iran, said: 'After the American invasion of Afghanistan, Iran started giving some limited tactical assistance to the Taliban against the Americans. They [also] supported America going into Afghanistan, they supported America getting into Iraq, but they didn't want them to remain for long. And so they are perfectly capable of playing two sides at once. But I think generally Iran's interest is stability, and Iran's reach in Afghanistan would be for stability.'[3] Iran has influence in western Afghanistan, in the city of Herat and nearby areas, and has played a role in maintaining stability in the area.

Soon after the successful engagement with Iran in Afghanistan, however, relations between Tehran and the West collapsed, particularly over Iran's pursuit of a nuclear programme. It remains to be seen whether, following the 2015 agreement, there will be a substantial turnaround in relations.

Iran-Pakistan

Iran and Pakistan share a border, including that of Balochistan, an area where Pakistan faces domestic challenges. Historically, Iran has been a responsible neighbour and the boundary has remained secure, without tensions between the two nations. A fair amount of border trade takes place between the two countries, officially and unofficially.

Iran's isolated history following the 1979 revolution and its, at times adversarial, stance towards the West and its allies makes this a challenge. However, the United States realises the geopolitical importance of Iran and, since President Obama and President Rouhani assumed office, the possibility of working together has improved.

I went to Tehran in the spring of 2002 for the first time, as finance minister. It was for an extraordinary meeting, where we managed to gather the Afghan, Pakistani and Iranian finance ministers to speak together about how we could open up communication and trade.

One of the initiatives I pushed for was the development of a gas pipeline between Iran, Pakistan and India. We had several meetings with Iranian and Indian energy ministers about this matter. On one occasion, during my official visit to Tehran as prime minister, I met with President Khatami, Akbar Hashemi Rafsanjani, the former president, and a host of other ministers and senior officials. We discussed in further detail the possibility of the gas pipeline between Pakistan, Iran and India. It was intended to be a win-win for all, since Iran had a surplus of gas to sell and Pakistan could use the gas for its own needs as well as use the pipeline to supply it to India. However, when we raised it with the United States, its officials expressed reservations.

In 2005, I had the opportunity to meet with Ayatollah Khamenei, the Supreme Leader of Iran. Sitting in his office in Tehran, it struck me that he was the final decision maker of most major policies in Iran. The visit was meant to formalise the outcome of the Iran-Pakistan Joint Economic Commission's meeting, which had initiated discussions on a preferential trade agreement and purchase of electricity from Iran for Southern Baluchistan. I informed him about Pakistan's economic progress and discussed the proposed gas pipeline. Khamenei reciprocated these sentiments and spoke eloquently about the friendship and shared history, values, culture and traditions of our two countries. He emphasised the need to maintain and further expand our economic cooperation.

Regarding foreign policy, we both expressed a common desire to see peace and stability in Afghanistan and its surrounding countries. According to Khamenei, foreign intervention was the main cause of turmoil in the region.

I believe the gas pipeline would have brought a big bonus to South Asia. However, the project could not mature because the United States actively opposed it and it eventually stalled. Norman Lamont recalls speaking to an energy minister in India, who was in favour of the initiative. Lamont said: 'One of the most foolish things that America did was prevent the building of a pipeline. Everybody wants Iran to behave responsibly, to have a stake in the region. It seems a way to encourage it to behave responsibly.' I believe the project is economically viable and, as the relationship between the US and Iran has started to improve, this is something which should be looked at again by all three countries.

The unfolding crisis in the Middle East means the need to bring Iran back into the international fold is greater than ever. The problems the region faces have been increasingly sectarian in nature. One big question which has emerged concerns the future of Shia militias who are currently fighting Sunni non-state actors. Iran has the greatest potential to influence areas where Shias are in large numbers in the region. This particularly applies to Syria, Iraq and Lebanon. It is increasingly clear that in order to have a sustainable peace settlement in the Levant, Iran must play a role, along with Turkey, Saudi Arabia, Jordan, the UAE, Qatar, the EU, Russia and the United States.

14
'THE LION OF CHINA IS AWAKE'

The handwritten note from President Richard Nixon read: 'Chinese Communists: Short range – no change. Long range – we do not want 800,000,000 living in angry isolation. We want contact.'[1]

This was in January 1969, written during meetings held in the first two days of Nixon's presidency. The United States and China had had no diplomatic contact for about twenty years, after relations had collapsed over foreign policy differences. What followed was a complex effort by President Nixon and his national security advisor, Dr Henry Kissinger, to open lines of communications with China. Pakistan played a crucial role in this historic development. It acted as the main facilitator in the first back channel communications between China and the United States. Nixon relied on Pakistan to deliver the message to Beijing that he sought high-level exchanges with Chinese leaders.[2] The US president later passed on communiques to China through President Yahya Khan while the Pakistani leader was visiting the White House. Yahya Khan then met with Chinese Premier Chou En-lai in 1970 and conveyed the messages from the United States.

The back channel process culminated in Kissinger's secret trip to Beijing in 1971, when Pakistan played a vital role in both providing access to China and masking the true nature of the visit. As part of a tour of South Asia, Kissinger arrived in Pakistan under the pretext of conducting high-level discussions with President Yahya Khan. Kissinger's meetings with the Pakistani leadership ended on a Thursday, before he reportedly fell ill and took to his bed to rest, fooling even his own security service. In fact, he boarded a plane to Beijing in the pre-dawn hours of Friday, 9 July 1971. His meetings there with Chou En-lai produced an agreement that Nixon would visit China the following year. This paved the way to a thaw in relations between the United States and China.

Pakistan's willingness to play this historic role was indicative of its desire to maintain relations with all the major world powers – the United States, China, Russia and the European countries. Pakistan realised early on how critical the US-China relationship was for peace in the world. Recalling Pakistan's role many years later, Kissinger said to me: 'Pakistan was in that period our only conduit to China and constituted practically our only real communication with China. We appreciated the way Pakistan did it, which was efficient, thoughtful and very discreet.'

Kissinger added reflectively on his role: 'You're not often lucky enough when you're in government to be in a situation which is a turning point, no matter how good you are. But this turned the international situation around, and Pakistan helped us at every stage. For example, nobody trusted – even then – communications, and so Pakistan sent us every message we got from China by courier. Our return went the same way.'

Since the 1970s, when China's relationship with the United States was a 'blank sheet' as Kissinger described it to me, its connections with the West have grown and matured. He summed up the transition in the relationship over time: 'In those days it was basically anti-Soviet. Now it has to be global, and not anti any particular country.'[3] With this in mind, the United States and China should find new ways to engage each other in a constructive and peaceful way, in response to the changing geopolitical environment. If these countries cooperate and collaborate, I believe both will reap significant strategic and tactical advantages.

China has already emerged – it is a global power and recognised as such by the international community. The growth in its economy has caused incomes to rise and consumption to increase and, as this continues, China could become an even bigger market for the world. As its economic might expands, it is natural that its political influence should also rise. This will undoubtedly alter the existing geopolitical landscape.

For years, Beijing's stated policy has been the pursuit of a 'peaceful rise' and 'peaceful development'. I have found the leadership very keen to emphasise this and its foreign policy has avoided any dramatic moves. Its focus on building a 'harmonious society' and a 'harmonious world' are in the spirit of ancient China – a preference for gradualism and avoidance of open conflict.[4]

So far, China's military presence has been largely confined to Asia. In order to become a truly global force for peace, however, China must extend its mobility beyond the region. As the centrifugal force of the world, China needs a strong and credible defence to match. A strong global defence capability is therefore essential to the country's peaceful rise. It must have the capacity to protect its interests and those in the region if necessary. Peace with strength will be a true global safeguard.

China is already expanding its military capacity, investing in up-to-date military hardware, especially aircraft and naval equipment, and building the strength of the People's Liberation

Army since the turn of the millennium, upgrading its training and technology. It is the world's largest standing army and the government has been boosting the PLA's operations in line with modern security and warfare developments.

A strong defence should not be a source of worry for the world. China's military spending stands at about 2% of its GDP, according to Beijing's declarations. This amounts to less than half of what the United States spends and is primarily intended to correct the imbalance between China's defence and its economic strength. It should not be viewed as confrontational. As Kissinger has said: 'We have to understand that China will get stronger, and must stop interpreting its every move as an act of aggression.'

When it comes to these examples of China asserting itself, I side with the view of Lee Kuan Yew, the late prime minister of Singapore, who said: 'China is acting purely in its own national interests. It is not interested in changing the world.'

Much has been said of the Thucydides Trap, which warns of the risks of conflict posed by rising powers. President Xi Jinping addressed this head on during a gathering of about twenty former heads of state and government, organised by the Nicolas Berggruen Institute in late 2015. Meeting in the Great Hall of the People in Beijing, President Xi eloquently spoke to us extempore. He began his speech by saying: 'I am the Secretary General of the Communist party and the president of China.' I noted that he mentioned the party first. President Xi continued: 'When I recently visited the US and Britain, I said to Barack Obama and David Cameron – I want to avoid the Thucydides Trap. Many are worried about the impact of China. Napoleon said: "China is a sleeping lion." The lion of China is awake. But remember, the Chinese lion is peaceful. We do not believe in hegemony or expansionism – it is not in our DNA.' President Xi added that, most of all, he wanted to 'avoid the middle income trap.'

He showed a good grasp of nineteenth-century Western foreign policy, saying: 'Countries should not follow the Monroe Doctrine. We cannot close our doors to the world.'

Still, it must be recognised that whenever the global power balance changes, challenges are created. Many countries are not comfortable with China's ascendance. Some have adopted what can only be called containment policies toward China, based on the suspicion that its leadership's stated pursuit of a 'peaceful rise' is but a smokescreen for territorial designs. These concerns were articulated by Hillary Clinton, who said, while serving as the US Secretary of State: 'History teaches that the rise of new powers often ushers in periods of conflict and uncertainty. Indeed, on both sides of the Pacific, we do see some trepidation about the rise of China and about the future of the US-China relationship.'

Washington's decision to 'pivot', in the words of Hillary Clinton, its defence priorities towards Asia, were an indication of this. Trying to counter China in the region has been part of the United States' foreign policy for some time. Nicholas Burns, the former US Under Secretary of State for Political Affairs, described America's approach to China to me: 'I would never use the word containment because it would be grossly inaccurate. You can't contain China. But you can build up the political and military friendship among the democratic countries, so that China would have to be mindful of it, and share the space. That was the big impetus.'5

However, we are nevertheless seeing 'growing pains', as the established powers struggle to know how to react to the changing world order. As a result, global affairs now operate under two parallel paradigms: firstly, the traditional paradigm of power and rivalry; and secondly, the emerging paradigm of interdependence and common interest. At the present stage of history, both paradigms coexist uneasily, as is evident in the seemingly contradictory behaviour of states – competing and cooperating simultaneously.

Obviously, old habits die hard. The power and rivalry paradigm remains dominant in the policy establishments of the United States, China, Russia and other countries. It manifests itself in today's increasingly challenging Asian security environment. The impulses of hegemony and power politics continue to display themselves in various sub-regions of Asia. The string of alliances being built by the United States in Asia and the shift of America's naval power from the Atlantic to the Pacific, as part of Washington's declared 'pivot' to Asia, have been seen as a response to China's growth. Meanwhile, China has been building and developing its relationships with Russia, the Middle East, Central Asia, Latin America and Africa; as well as consolidating old relationships, such as with Pakistan. In the Pacific, China has declared its intention to build and deploy a blue-water navy, capable of operations across oceans.

The interdependence paradigm is now gaining grass-roots support in most major powers – within civil society, business, the media, academia and in international organisations. Given the growing evidence of global challenges, and the compulsion to cooperate for survival and stability, it is possible that the twenty-first century may witness a shift from strategic competition towards cooperation, collaboration and connectivity. However, this will only work when coupled with strong and effective leadership. The present challenge for all global leaders is how to manage the current transition while smoothing over potential fault lines. I believe this can be achieved without any major conflict, but the focus must be on developing lasting economic ties between countries, so that they can act as a safeguard and guarantor for peace for years to come.

China-Pakistan relations

Chuck Hagel started animatedly pointing at a newspaper on his desk as soon as he saw me walk in through his door. I was in Washington for some meetings and decided to pay him a visit at his private office in Virginia. About two months had passed since he had stepped down as United States Secretary of Defense.

I had barely walked through the door when the former Pentagon official asked me what I thought of the latest news from China. Beijing had just announced a $46 billion investment package in Pakistan as part of its expansive One Belt, One Road initiative. I said this could be a game changer for Pakistan.

Days before, President Xi had flown into Islamabad on board an Air China Boeing 747-400. He was escorted by eight JF-17 Thunder fighter jets, which had been built as a joint project between China and Pakistan.[6] They were a fitting symbol of cooperation between the two countries, setting the tone for President Xi's historic visit. He used it to announce the development of a monumental economic corridor, stretching 3,000 km from Gwadar to Xinjiang. As the article on Hagel's desk pointed out, the deal made the aid provided by the United States Kerry-Lugar Bill, which totalled $7.5 billion over five years, look small by comparison.[7]

China's $46 billion investment is undoubtedly a game-changer for Pakistan and has the potential to genuinely shift the landscape of the country. It will bring jobs, development and new industry. The opening up of sea access through

Pakistan, using the Gwadar Port, could have a transformational effect by reducing the distance between China and the Gulf and providing an important new trade route. As part of the total investment, up to $37 billion would be spent on developing Pakistan's electrical system.[8] Of that, about $28 billion worth of new infrastructure projects, from electrical plants and pipelines to roads and railways, were ready to roll out, and it would take three to five years to start the rest. Together with Prime Minister Nawaz Sharif, President Xi witnessed the signing of fifty-one deals and unveiled plaques of eight projects to be undertaken in Pakistan with Chinese assistance. Before arriving in Islamabad, President Xi wrote a column published in the Pakistan media saying: 'We need to form a cooperation structure with the Economic Corridor at the centre and with the Gwadar Port, energy, infrastructure and industrial cooperation being the four key areas to drive development across Pakistan and deliver tangible benefits to its people.'

The deal is part of a wider strategy being pursued by Beijing, which aims to build greater connectivity between China and the wider world. The One Belt, One Road policy, launched by President Xi in 2014, is a $1.6 trillion initiative which includes the Silk Road Economic Belt and Maritime Silk Road plans: an ambitious network of roads, rails and ports designed to link China to Europe through Central Asia and Russia.[9] Planned 'digital highways' will boost connectivity in the region. By 2020, China is expected to be linked in multiple ways to the mouth of the Gulf.[10] Beijing aims to build connections along the old trade routes between Central Asia, China, Russia and northern Europe. At the Boao Forum in 2015, President Xi said the One Belt, One Road policy is intended to 'answer the call of our time for regional and global cooperation.'

For Pakistan, the $46 billion programme is a sign the relationship between the two countries is developing into a greater tactical and strategic alliance. During his visit President Xi highlighted Pakistan's help in combating terrorism. This has been a challenge in Xinjiang, the far western region of China, which has a large Muslim population. China has been keen to seek Islamabad's help in combating separatist groups, which may have linkages to external extremist groups. China also has an interest in supporting a stable and secure Pakistan, to prevent any issues next to China's border.

The scale of the agreement's potential was reflected in the unity it created across political parties in Pakistan. Shortly after President Xi's visit, the government in Pakistan convened an all-party meeting, chaired by Prime Minister Nawaz Sharif, to build ownership and establish consensus over how the development should proceed. The federal and provincial governments have agreed on a broad framework while promising to work together and spread the investment's benefits equitably across the country. The challenge will be implementation, and levels of transparency and quality will need to be ensured.

Pakistan considers its relationship with China, which has now spanned more than six decades, as one of its most important. Pakistan was one of the first countries to recognise the People's Republic of China, establishing formal diplomatic relations in 1951. In 1964 PIA, Pakistan's national airline, became the first in the non-Communist world to fly to China. In the 1950s and 1960s, when China faced difficulties from Western blockades, Pakistan gave it access to an air corridor.[11] In 1963 the two countries signed their first formal trade pact. Pakistan has consistently stood by the People's Republic, supporting the 'One China' policy throughout.

It is an all-weather and time-tested friendship, rooted in history, mutual trust and understanding. Relations between the two nations go back to antiquity, when the Silk Road served as a conduit not only for trade but also for ideas and knowledge. Historically, China has been instrumental in helping Pakistan find its feet. In the 1970s, China built the Karakoram highway, which connects the two countries through the Khunjerab Pass and which is an artery for Pakistan. Positioned at a height of 4,850 metres, it is a marvel of engineering and reflects the desire of the two nations to be connected, even through difficult terrain.

In recent decades, the relationship has matured into a strategic multifaceted partnership and now encompasses links through trade, finance, security, defence and diplomacy. China is seen by many in Pakistan as a trusted and dependable ally.

My own interactions with the leadership in Beijing began in my early days in government, when I was appointed minister in waiting to Chinese Prime Minister Zhu Rongji on his visit to Pakistan in 2001. Accompanied by his wife Lao An, the premier made a historic trip to mark fifty years since diplomatic relations were established between the People's Republic of China and Pakistan. I travelled with him in his Boeing 747 from Islamabad to Lahore, where he attended a citizens' reception at the Shalimar Gardens. Despite it being a hot and humid day, he took time to enjoy the serene setting of the terraced gardens, built by the Mughal Emperor in the seventeenth century. In the evening the governor of Punjab held a banquet in his honour. During my interactions with the Chinese prime minister, he struck me as a thinker and intellectual. It was clear to me that he viewed China's relationship with Pakistan as an important one, and wanted to initiate long-term projects which would benefit Pakistan's future.

We discussed the idea of building the Gwadar Port, a strategically located deep-water port on the Gulf. This has the potential to open Pakistan up to the world and turn it into a vital trade route through South Asia. Providing an alternative to Karachi Port, Gwadar could become a source of uplift for Baluchistan and the country as a whole, creating jobs and boosting economic growth. After we discussed this with President Musharraf, Zhu Rongji told me to come back to Beijing to go over the points we had raised.

Three months later, I was in Beijing. Prime Minister Zhu Rongji chaired the meeting in the Great Hall of the People, gathering all the relevant ministers with him. This sent a serious message about China's willingness to engage with Pakistan and showed that Prime Minister Zhu Rongji was a man of action, keen to build on the momentum of his visit to Islamabad. It was refreshing to deal with him and I was impressed by his sense of commitment, seriousness and engagement. I was accompanied by Lieutenant General Javed Ashraf Qazi, minister of communications. During the meeting with Zhu Rongji, we finalised all matters relating to Gwadar Port and developed a detailed agenda for substantially increasing cooperation. It was evident that the Chinese prime minister firmly believed that developing Pakistan's infrastructure would help its economic growth.

We began building Gwadar Port, with critical assistance from China. President Musharraf and I were there for the opening of the port on 20 March 2007. The problem was a lack of infrastructure for the routes to the port, including the necessary world-class highways, railways and an international airport. Some contracts had been given to build roads, but they were not enough for the port to become functional. The deterioration of the country's security situation, coupled with

231

the political challenges the government faced, diverted our attention.

Today, Gwadar Port will be one of the major focuses of the One Belt, One Road initiative and could bring substantial benefit to both countries. A new economic route through Gwadar would give China an alternative trade route to Europe, the Middle East and Africa, which would be valuable both politically and economically.

While I was in office, I aimed to institutionalise the longstanding relationship between the two countries and develop the architecture for cooperation between them. In all my meetings with Chinese leaders, not once did we discuss our relationship in respect to other countries. Our dealings have always been based on bilateral issues, not aimed at countering a third party. The leadership on both sides has treated the other with consistency, focusing on converging interests and avoiding interference in internal affairs. In my experience both in and out of government, I have witnessed this to be the case.

During my first few years as finance minister, I set up and led the Joint Economic Commission, which provided a platform for government and business communities on both sides to work together. I felt Pakistan was under-represented in China in terms of diplomatic missions. There was only one embassy in Beijing, so I approved the opening of consulates in Shanghai, Chengdu and Guangzhou.

Once I was elected prime minister, I began to push for a free trade agreement with China. In November 2006, President Hu Jintao paid a landmark visit to Pakistan and we finalised the terms of a bilateral free trade agreement during his trip. We also created special trade zones on the China-Pakistan border to encourage local exchange of goods. As a result, trade volumes between the two countries grew and the balance between imports and exports improved. In 2007, we established a target to achieve $5 billion in trade in five years. China is now one of the top five sources of imports for Pakistan. Bilateral trade reached $12 billion in 2014.

During President Hu Jintao's visit we also signed the Joint Five Year Programme for Trade and Economic Cooperation, which was completed in 2011. The second began in 2012 and features plans for thirty-six projects, totalling investment of about $14 billion. We established a joint China-Pakistan investment company, a financial development institution which invests in projects across Pakistan. This became a milestone in our economic relations and a model for cooperation and development. It opened offices in Islamabad, had joint Chinese and Pakistani management and considered investing in projects relating to the two countries. We had signed similar treaties with Saudi Arabia, Kuwait, Iran, Libya, Oman and Brunei.

Meanwhile, the Shanghai and Karachi stock exchanges signed cooperation agreements and the Bank of China, along with the Industrial and Commercial Bank of China, was invited to open branches in Pakistan. We also welcomed Chinese investment in our existing institutions. In 2002 the Chinese company Haier, a major producer of electronic and household goods, jointly invested (with a private sector company from Pakistan) in a production plant outside Lahore. President Hu Jintao and I opened the facility, which became a symbol of Chinese private sector investment. There was also increased cooperation in mining projects.

China continued to provide aid to Pakistan, partly through supplier credits, including commercial loans. China has also given valuable assistance in economic development projects in Pakistan, including the reconstruction efforts following the 2005 earthquake.

The two countries have developed deep military-to-military relations. China has provided Pakistan with naval frigates, aircraft, helicopters, assisted its army's artillery and infantry and helped build several nuclear reactors for electricity generation.[12] In my time in government we also worked together to encourage transfer of technology for our defence services. This included the joint production of a light fighter aircraft, the JF-17 Thunder, as well as tanks and missile technology. The two countries also increasingly share intelligence in their anti-terrorism cooperation. Pakistan is negotiating the acquisition of submarines from China, which would be a significant strategic development. The reported $5 billion purchase was approved by a parliamentary committee in Islamabad in 2015.[13]

In order to maintain the strength of their ties in years to come, the two countries should work together to address some of the challenges they face; including security, terrorism and China's concerns with its Muslim communities and their links to groups within Pakistan. The key is to focus on continuing to build linkages and connectivity between the two countries, to grow the relationship.

There is much more potential for China to invest in Pakistan, particularly in areas where it can provide machinery and expertise, such as power generation, infrastructure and dam construction. Such projects would contribute to a more stable Pakistan on China's border and reinforce the strong historic relationship between the two countries. Pakistan needs significant infrastructure investment and this is an area where China can be encouraged to help. As well as Chinese companies bidding to take part in developing new projects, existing infrastructure, such as the symbolic Karakoram Highway, can be expanded and modernised. The two nations could also work on establishing rail links and developing fiber-optic connectivity and pipelines, if viable.

Today, the relationship between China and Pakistan is set to change in order to adapt to the new geopolitical landscape. As China continues to emerge as a world power, Pakistan will need to recognise that China's focus will shift to become more global as well. Pakistan will need to position itself accordingly to reflect this, while continuing to stand by China. If this can be done, it will build on the historic ties between the two countries and help them move the relationship forward.

What next for China?

From the start of his time at the helm in 1989 to leaving office in 2003, President Jiang Zemin steered China to become the fastest-growing economy in the world through continued economic reform and creating a stable, enabling environment for growth. Together with Prime Minister Zhu Rongji, he negotiated China's entry into the World Trade Organisation in 2001, integrating it into the global economy.

His successor, President Hu Jintao, and Premier Wen Jiabao were the first generation of top officials without personal experience of the 1949 revolution and ushered in a new phase in China's economic history. They successfully managed the country's economic rise as it continued to emerge as a global powerhouse.[14]

Today China, under the strong leadership of President Xi Jinping and Premier Li Keqiang, is going through a process of reform and improved governance that will take it to the next level. It has already largely opened up its economy to the world and has come miles since the days when foreigners had to get special coupons to buy goods in 'friendship stores', as did I during my trips to China in the 1980s.

235

Numerous multinational companies rely on China for their manufacturing facilities and supplies. On the back of a real estate boom and stronger growth, living standards have improved and millions of jobs have been created. The number of people living in extreme poverty – or on less than $1.25 a day – has halved since 1990, according to the latest report from the World Bank. However, the challenge for Beijing's leadership is to create equitable growth, spread more evenly throughout different sectors of society, as well as geographically. This will help guide the country thorough its transition while maintaining stability. Addressing social needs and encouraging human development programmes, while pursuing a structural reform agenda based on deregulation and liberalisation, can help move this process along.

The private sector must be encouraged to increase its role, through incentives and policy measures. There should be room for both the private sector and public/private partnerships to encourage growth and productivity, as has already been done successfully in the Chinese real estate sector. Initiatives such as the Shanghai Free Trade Zone could be accelerated and replicated across the country to allow both local and foreign investment.

As economies mature, they increasingly need to change and deregulate in order to sustain their rate of growth. China's focus should now be on innovation, improving its productivity and continuing to add value. It needs to progress from producing components or goods that are sold under another company's name to developing its own internationally recognised brands, thus moving away from being an 'original equipment manufacturer' to an 'original design manufacturer'. This involves focusing more on Research and Development (R&D) to develop high-tech products. At present there are too few globally recognisable brands originating in China, which is still perceived as a low-cost manufacturing base. More private and public sector companies born in China should be going global. Some, such as Baidu and Alibaba, have succeeded in raising money internationally in financial markets. In my recent group visit to Alibaba's headquarters, its chairman Jack Ma talked our group through his company's potential and ability to reach millions of customers through its vast distribution network. The Internet giant, which is responsible for a growing share of commerce in China, was listed on the New York stock exchange in 2014 at 38% above its initial asking price – bringing in substantial foreign investment.

China's manufacturing companies are also growing, as seen through a range of brands including Huawei, the telecommunications firm, and Haier Group, the consumer appliances company. In 2015 I visited the factories of Huawei, which is based in Shenzhen, and met with its management. The R&D there had progressed to world-class standards. As the private sector gradually increases its role in China, this will only encourage further innovation, while the public sector continues to play a main role in strategic industries.

With increased industrialisation comes a greater need to focus on how it damages the environment. China is conscious about the need to achieve a more sustainable growth. Environmental degradation is something which needs to be addressed by all developing countries. Asia must become conscious of the threats of climate change and global warming, and should work to create a more sustainable environment. While the COP21 agreement in Paris in 2015 was a positive step forward, more will need to be done to encourage global implementation and commitment to addressing climate change.

Overall, as China develops, it will increase its share of high technology and value added goods, which will in turn require greater skill sets. The country already has the human capital to grow and improve the quality and quantity of its industrial production. Whether or not the continuous need for structural reform is addressed will determine the speed of China's economic growth.

China's place in the world

China is expected to be the largest global economy in about a decade. The leadership in Beijing also actively seeks to expand its economic relationships, with a focus on several major countries. The future economic order will therefore be influenced by China, and will pose a challenge to existing stakeholders. How all sides adapt to this changing environment will be of critical importance in preserving peace and stability in the world.

While there are differing policies pursued by China and the United States relating to territory in the South China Sea, the situation is unlikely to reach the stage where it tips over into physical conflict. A more realistic medium-term scenario involves continued contrasting economic approaches, encompassing access to natural resources and attempts to increase influence in global economic and financial institutions. That said, efforts are still needed to diffuse existing tension over disputed territory, as well as focusing on areas where diplomacy and dialogue could help establish a working relationship.

In my interactions with the Chinese leadership, both in and out of office, I did not see any evidence that China has territorial designs. I believe this mistaken attitude stems from a historic misunderstanding of Chinese diplomacy, which contrasts sharply with the more aggressive Western approach. Henry Kissinger fittingly uses the metaphor of chess to make the distinction – in the West the endgame in chess is a battle resulting in total victory; whereas Chinese chess, or *wei qi*, is about long-term gain and relative advantage.[15]

I believe there is room for China to play a major role alongside the United States, which has had additional clout since the collapse of the Soviet Union. A multipolar world order is better than a unipolar one, and the emergence of more than one global centre of power will provide balance and act as a source of strength.

China has already shown welcome willingness to participate in global peacekeeping. It is now the biggest contributor to the United Nations Security Council's peacekeeping missions. The UN Secretary-General Ban Ki-moon recognised China's role by appointing a Chinese military official to head a peacekeeping force for the first time. As well as working with the UN, the People's Liberation Army has carried out dozens of international humanitarian aid missions since 2002, and has provided assistance to developing countries in Asia, Africa and Latin America.

China's track record has been to smooth over relations with adversaries through dialogue, prudent economic policy and cooperation. Since its economic reforms in the 1970s, it has shown flexibility in conducting its international relations.[16] China's historic rival, Japan, is its biggest trading partner. Taiwan is China's third largest overseas investor. China's trade with India has also been growing considerably.[17] China has the largest dollar reserves in the world and the United States is also its largest export market. Japan, Taiwan and the United States are three of the five biggest sources of foreign direct investment in China.

However, some multilateral initiatives have not extended their welcome to China in the way that, for example, the World Trade Organisation has. The Trans-Pacific Partnership (TTP) is a twenty-first century multilateral trade agreement being spearheaded by the United States, which so far has failed to make room for China. The world should embrace and accept China and initiatives such as TTP should be inclusive.

Linkages and interdependencies are the true drivers of lasting peace, something China has been quick to recognise. It has emerged as a significant source of investment in both developing and developed countries, not only in the fields of resource extraction, but also in real estate, industry and infrastructure. The recent visits made by President Xi to the UK, United States and Vietnam highlight Beijing's focus on enhancing bilateral relations.

The Asian Infrastructure and Investment Bank (AIIB) is an opportunity for the region to build a new financial infrastructure and will complement the existing development institutions, such as the Asian Development Bank and the World Bank. The willingness of countries around the world to subscribe to the AIIB, which is headed by the seasoned banker Jin Liqun, shows that there is space for a modern multilateral body to play a role in the world. Unlike the Bretton Woods institutions, the AIIB has the benefit of not being hostage to history nor tied by longstanding rules. Lessons must be learned from past experience and a new structure of governance should be devised. The AIIB provides an opportunity to redress an inequitable and outdated economic global infrastructure. It should run on four key principles – meritocracy, transparency, a level playing field for all stakeholders and high standards of governance. Primarily, there is no need for permanent resident boards of directors and senior management should be empowered instead. In its appointments, the AIIB should aim to be a truly meritocratic institution, recruiting and promoting on the basis of talent, not nationality.

China should have a stronger voice in the World Bank, IMF and other global institutions. Until that is achieved, the AIIB is an opportunity to bring in a new player and set new standards; it also highlights the urgency to reform the Bretton Woods structures. Other countries should recognise that they do not need to control every institution. China has been very conscious about exerting too much influence in the AIIB in this regard. It already has the China Exim Bank and the China Development Bank.

One way to encourage cooperation and peace is through joint initiatives – for example through increased interaction between armed forces. Joint military exercises should be encouraged, regionally and globally, including in natural disaster relief efforts. These military links should be supported by sound diplomacy. In areas of potential conflict, such as the South China Sea, the method of communication should be institutionalised, with hotlines created between key players and frequent contact and meetings to prevent issues escalating through misunderstanding. Initiatives such as joint production for exploiting undersea hydrocarbons in the contested areas could also help smooth over tension.

15
BENAZIR'S RETURN

After leaving office, Benazir Bhutto grew increasingly withdrawn as she settled into her new life in Dubai, vowing never to return to politics – and yet her heart remained in Pakistan. The charismatic daughter of Zulfikar Ali Bhutto could rally mass crowds with her passion for her country. Her experiences in office were less successful – both her terms as prime minister had been tarnished by complaints over her government's record and effectiveness.

Norman Lamont became friends with Benazir Bhutto after a chance encounter in a Nice airport. The former British Chancellor, who had dealt with her on an official level, was struck by her down-to-earth manner when they bumped into each other waiting for a flight home. Lord Lamont noticed Bhutto browsing the Duty Free store, unescorted, and approached her.

Over the years they became close friends, and Benazir even asked him to accompany her to Pakistan for her fateful return in 2007. Lord Lamont recalled: 'She had invited me to go on the plane with her and I wasn't able to go, something I felt rather guilty about. Years ago, when she was very depressed, I kept saying to her: "One day you'll go back. I believe in political cycles." One day I added, jokingly: "I'd like to come with you when you do." I had forgotten everything about it and then she rang me up and said: "Well, you were right, and I'd like you to come with me."'[1]

242

However, during the early days of Benazir's life in exile, even the thought of a comeback seemed unlikely. Lord Lamont described his conversations with her at the time: 'She had said she was resigning from politics and would never, ever return. Her ambition, if any, was just to be speaker of the Parliament. She said she did not want to be prime minister ever again.'

After less than a decade, events started to turn in her favour. Lamont said: 'She started going to the congressional prayer meetings in Washington, meeting congressmen and senators and working on the British Foreign Office. I noticed how her rhetoric became much more pro-Western.'

Benazir Bhutto's lobbying was not an immediate success: 'There was a period here when people in the Foreign Office wouldn't see her, except at a very junior level,' said Lamont. 'They thought she was finished.'

It was the same in Washington, a confidant of Benazir Bhutto there told me. When General Musharraf took over, her access was limited.[2] A US State Department official who met with her in 2002 described how, at the time, 'Benazir never had any traction in Washington. She couldn't see anyone senior.'[3]

Over the course of eight or nine years, however, Benazir managed to turn this around. She would come to Washington three to four times a year, meet with congressmen, attend events and give lectures. On one trip, she met over 100 members of Congress.[4] Ray Mahmood, a wealthy and well-connected Pakistani businessman in Washington, was one of her closest allies in the US. Together they would drive around the capital in his car and he introduced her to his contacts in DC, such as Virginia Congressman Jim Moran. When Asif Ali Zardari became president following Bhutto's death, Mahmood was appointed Pakistan's ambassador-at-large to the US. Benazir Bhutto also had the unwavering support of her close friend and lobbyist in the US, Mark Siegel.

I was later told that her pitch to the officials she met with was usually that a return to democracy was needed in Pakistan. If the military government could go, she indicated that she would be a reasonable leader for them to deal with.

The effort was a success. As soon as Benazir Bhutto's return became more of a possibility, her fortunes changed and the same doors that had been closed before began to open. Lamont said: 'Suddenly she was going up the hierarchy, and then ministers were asking to see her, even though she was living in Dubai. It was quite funny to watch.'

The change in the political tide was triggered by Pakistan's unravelling domestic situation. By 2007 President Musharraf was affected by several crises. After the suspension of the chief justice in March that year, the lawyers' movement took hold and there were mass demonstrations all over Pakistan. This coincided with changes within the Bush administration, as Condoleezza Rice took over as Secretary of State from Colin Powell. She began to push for a greater focus on pursuing the 'freedom agenda', with its stated aim of spreading democracy around the world. She did not have the personal connection to General Musharraf that Powell had, and she had little patience when the general declared martial law. In her memoir, Rice described her response after he first threatened to call a state of emergency: 'It was clear … that Musharraf was on borrowed time in Pakistan. I thought he'd run out of his string of luck, a view not widely shared within the administration. The question was how to use the time we'd bought to create better conditions for the upcoming elections. The answer, we believed, lay in forging an alliance between the two strongest political forces in the country: Musharraf and former Prime Minister Benazir Bhutto.'⁵

The United States put pressure on President Musharraf, saying he needed to hold free and fair elections in Pakistan that met international benchmarks. At the same time, it also urged him to relinquish his role as army chief and participate without his military uniform. In his memoir, President Bush described how he 'strongly suggested' to Musharraf that he 'set a date for free elections, resign from the army and lift the state of emergency.'⁶ In order to make these elections credible, Musharraf knew the Pakistan People's Party had to participate. Benazir Bhutto was its head and very much in control of its operations. He initially asked American diplomats to reach out to Benazir and ask her to take part in the elections. Thus began the talks between the two party leaders, during which they negotiated a power-sharing arrangement.

Washington warmed to Benazir Bhutto thinking she was more palatable to the West. Officially, they said they were happy with Musharraf too. The idea was that he could stay on as president, which, according to the constitution, is a ceremonial role, while she would become the prime minister and chief executive. But both sides would have known that the arrangement could not last. One of them would have to be the other's political casualty.

The British also came on board, and senior officials from the US and UK actively participated in the process, eventually mediating between the two leaders as they tried to come to an arrangement. When in London, Bhutto would meet with senior British diplomats in her favourite cafe in Harrods. She attended larger gatherings to rally support, including a dinner held for her by the US deputy head of mission to the UK at his residence. The former US ambassador to Pakistan, Ryan Crocker, was closely involved in the process. He told me, years later: 'A military leadership could not have endured forever. We started the effort to bring Benazir back and keep Musharraf as president. It might have worked, had she not been assassinated.'[7]

Would her record in office have been different a third time round? She was convinced so. Norman Lamont recalled that by this time Benazir had become increasingly reflective about her political career: 'I think she knew that she hadn't been a great success as prime minister the first two times. She genuinely wanted to do better the next time.'

After initial messages through intermediaries, emails and phone calls, Musharraf and Benazir Bhutto began to meet in person. The president kept negotiations a secret from his own government and would make diversions through the UAE, where she lived, on his way to other destinations. Their first meeting took place in January 2007 in one of the palaces in Abu Dhabi. Benazir was flown in by helicopter from Dubai.[8] The one-on-one meeting went on for four and a half hours while their respective aides were outside. President Musharraf was keen for the PPP to participate in his presidential election but at the time it was not clear who their candidate would be.

General Kayani, who was the ISI chief at the time, and Tariq Aziz took care of the negotiations from Pakistan's side and met with Benazir Bhutto. Richard Boucher, the Assistant Secretary of State for South and Central Asia, described how he sat down privately with Benazir several times in New York, Dubai, Abu Dhabi and London.

Serious talks were required because Bhutto needed corruption charges against her and her supporters dismissed before she could return to Pakistan. She also required the constitution to be amended to allow her a third term, as she had already served the maximum two as prime minister.

There was another dimension to the negotiations. Neither Benazir Bhutto nor General Musharraf wanted the third influential political figure in Pakistan, Nawaz Sharif, to be on the scene. Boucher told me: 'One of the goals for them working out a deal was to keep Nawaz out. I think Musharraf put feelers out to the Saudis and said: "Keep a hold of [him] and don't let him come disrupt the transition."'[9]

However, after the negotiations had already progressed significantly, Musharraf suddenly stalled. Boucher told me: 'Musharraf understood the strategic need to move from military rule to civilian rule, but he failed to really understand how to move from a military ruler to a civilian ruler. And so, every time they would reach kind of a crunch point, where he had to really commit, he couldn't do it. He couldn't let go.'

This created difficulties as Benazir Bhutto would propose an agreement, only to have it rejected, then come back with another option, only to have Musharraf disagree with the changes. 'I think it was just too difficult for him to give up control,' Boucher said.

Boucher had been one of the leading American officials involved in the transition. In October 2007, just at the moment Benazir was finally planning to return, he fell sick with pneumonia and was hospitalised for six weeks. At this point, US Secretary of State Condoleezza Rice became personally involved in the process, dealing with both party leaders directly. 'Rice picked it up personally and talked about it with them,' Boucher recalled. 'She said to Musharraf – basically, let her [Benazir] come back, even without an understanding. If you facilitate a return, you can both find a way to cooperate.'

Eventually, Musharraf passed a law in accordance with what they had been discussing – the National Reconciliation Ordinance (NRO). It was drafted along the lines of Desmond

Tutu's Truth and Reconciliation Commission in South Africa and exonerated Benazir Bhutto and her supporters of political charges.

The next key meeting between General Musharraf and Benazir Bhutto took place in July 2007 at the Plaza Hotel in New York, this time with Asif Zardari present.[10] The details of the transition were discussed – Benazir Bhutto was clear she wanted the NRO to be issued before she returned and the cases against her and her supporters withdrawn. She also needed the constitutional amendment that limited prime ministers to serving two terms in office removed.

The NRO was agreed upon only a day before the presidential election. About 8,000 people were pardoned, including those involved in criminal cases. In return, Bhutto agreed to put forward a Pakistan People's Party candidate to stand against Musharraf in the presidential election, thus lending it credibility.[11]

In late September 2007, Tariq Aziz and Hamid Javed, President Musharraf's chief of staff, flew to London to meet with Benazir Bhutto. Despite the considerable back channel effort on all sides, there was still a lot of uncertainty about the issues being negotiated. A close confidant of Benazir Bhutto recalled that late on the night of 3 October 2007, she received a phone call from Condoleezza Rice.[12] The call lasted about two hours and Rice told her no significant progress had been made in the negotiations and her requests had still not been granted. The confidant said Rice played a key role in ironing out the differences between Musharraf and Benazir Bhutto.

The power-sharing deal was announced on 4 October and Benazir began preparing to leave for Pakistan. In her memoir, Rice said that Bhutto felt she had a 'US guarantee' that Musharraf would follow through.[13]

However, there was still confusion about the arrangements for Benazir's return. The original agreement was that she would not come until after the election. Only there was apparently a misunderstanding – she said 'elections' meaning the election of the president, on 6 October, whereas he had meant the general election, which was months away. Boucher told me: 'I think they almost got there, but, in the end, it was [a case of] changing circumstances and therefore changing positions.' Even though some issues had been ironed out, ultimately the two leaders were not on the same page. General Musharraf was only reluctantly going along with the process.

Lord Lamont recalled Bhutto's apprehension about her return and specifically about the security she was being provided with. 'Several times she said to me, "I don't know what will happen to me,"' he said. But the pull of serving her nation proved stronger. Benazir Bhutto stuck to her interpretation of the agreement and returned to Pakistan on 18 October. She landed in Karachi with a plane full of supporters, greeted by a crowd of hundreds of thousands. The world's media heralded the triumphant return of 'BB'.

Boucher said: 'She knew the risks. She knew the threats against her, extremist threats. She knew she couldn't trust everybody to provide the kind of security she wanted, and she knew that no matter how much security she got, she would be out campaigning and that was taking a risk. She just felt it was her destiny to go.'

It was as she travelled on a truck from the airport that two bombs struck, killing 134 people and wounding 400. Benazir Bhutto was shaken but not hurt. When the attack happened, I was sitting with Musharraf in my residence. He had come over for dinner and, as usual, the television was on in the background. Soon after we saw the attack on the truck

249

broadcast, our phones started ringing as the security agencies reported initial details of what was one of the worst suicide bomb attacks in Pakistan's history.

Tragically, ten weeks later Benazir Bhutto was killed as she stood waving through the sunroof of her Jeep after a political rally in Rawalpindi. It was in the same city that her father had been hanged in 1979. Weeks earlier, I had completed my term as prime minister and was in Karachi when I heard the sad news. Having known Benazir for many years before I had even joined the government, I always considered her remarkably driven, committed to her cause and full of tremendous tenacity and courage. Her father had been a significant influence for her and his death had left deep scars. While she was not as ideological as him, she was passionate and wanted to lead Pakistan.

Three days after Benazir Bhutto's death, her son, Bilawal, read out a note from her to the Pakistan People's Party, saying she wished her husband Asif Ali Zardari to take over its leadership in her absence. The world mourned the loss of one of Pakistan's most high-profile political figures and the first elected female leader of a Muslim country in history.

Condoleezza Rice described Benazir Bhutto's assassination as a 'personal blow', saying that 'it felt as if yet another chance for a democratic and stable Pakistan had died with her.'[14]

The Western powers' efforts in facilitating Pakistan's transition to democracy reflected the foreign interest that exists in the domestic politics of Pakistan, which occasionally encourages changes toward more democratic processes. While the motivation behind such efforts can be noble, they sometimes fail to work within the complexities and context of the domestic situation. In the long run, foreign involvement of even a subtle nature can do more harm than good.

The fact that foreign powers became involved in influencing political succession in Pakistan and mediating in domestic politics demonstrates that its democracy still has a long way to go. In countries where the democratic process is robust, foreign involvement of this sort is not welcome. Pakistan has to move on and get the democratic process standing on its own two feet – foreign facilitation of this kind is not, in the long run, a viable option.

Pakistanis must foster a sense of pride in their political system and resolve matters of governance themselves. Its politicians should work within the democratic process and be mature enough to accept its results when they are not in their favour. When outside powers play a role in domestic politics, and even indirectly influence political change in any country, it undermines the system – even if stakeholders in the country reached out to the mediators themselves. As the former US Deputy Secretary of State Rich Armitage aptly said, regarding foreign involvement of this kind: 'If you put yourself in the middle, it's like trying to be a mediator in a civil war. Sooner or later, you're seen as being on one side or the other.'

Following Benazir's untimely death, President Musharraf's power-sharing arrangements fell through. At the same time, his domestic position began to unravel. While he retained his position as head of the army, he had maintained control. In November 2007, however, Musharraf stepped down as army chief and General Kayani was appointed in his place. As soon as Musharraf took off his uniform and tried to democratise, his grip on power weakened. On 18 August 2008, Musharraf made a television appearance announcing his resignation as president.

16
LESSONS IN GOVERNANCE

Addressing the business and political elite in Kuala Lumpur, Margaret Thatcher began to speak in her deep, confident voice, honed by vocal training as well as years as one of Britain's longest-serving prime ministers. She said: 'It is not necessarily the biggest countries who exert the most influence, it is those with the strongest leadership and the clearest vision.'

We were at a private dinner, hosted for Thatcher by the Malaysian prime minister, Dr Mahathir bin Mohamad, in Kuala Lumpur. Margaret Thatcher's insightful words were bound to have resonance with Dr Mahathir, who had succeeded in transforming Malaysia into one of the region's most thriving economies.

The intimate gathering of about eight people was fittingly held in the Carcosa Hotel. Shrouded in vibrant greenery, the former residence of the British high commissioner had been given to Malaysia by Thatcher as part of a move to resolve a period of significant tension between the two countries. After dinner, I had a rare chance to see these two titans in action. Thatcher and Dr Mahathir talked about the future of Europe, the role of Asia and the emergence of China. As usual, Thatcher led the conversation.

Three years after she had left British politics, Britain's first female prime minister was signed by Citibank to embark on a speaking tour across Asia. She visited Thailand, Singapore, Pakistan, Malaysia and other countries in 1993 and 1996. Since

I was the head of Citibank's Asia Pacific wholesale business at the time, John Reed asked me to accompany her for most of the 1993 tour. We travelled together for about two weeks, flying and driving from place to place to meet with heads of state, ministers and leading figures from civil society. In the evenings Citibank would host banquets for each city's elite, who would come to hear Margaret Thatcher speak.

She would stay up late and get up early, and still be full of energy. While she was staying at the Shangri-La Hotel in Singapore, she invited me up to her suite one evening for a drink. We chatted as she drank her gin and tonic and I enjoyed my orange juice. She asked me what global issues concerned me most.

I said: 'There is a lack of understanding in the Western world about Islam and its values, and this gap must be bridged. The West struggles to embrace the ideas and values of Islamic culture. There is a distance and I think this could lead to more exclusion.'

We discussed the need for interfaith harmony and I said: 'All faiths have to learn to live with each other because their basic values are the same. There is a great need for tolerance and understanding, otherwise we will see prejudices growing, tensions rising and minorities being marginalised, which could result in radicalism and extremism.'

She was aware of this. She was one of the most informed and substantive leaders I have met. Generally my impression is that her grasp of issues was more detailed and broad than many other leaders around the world. I found I could engage Thatcher on any topic – be it the economy, foreign policy, security or the social sector – and she had an informed view. That evening we also talked about the Falklands, the common European currency and about China and its relationship with

253

Hong Kong in the build up to the transfer of sovereignty in 1997.

Years later, Dr Mahathir returned to the high commissioner's residence to write a message in a condolence book, marking the passing of Lady Thatcher. Despite the differences they had while in office – Mahathir's 'Buy British Last' policy was just one example of the tension between the two countries – it was clear the leaders had a great deal of personal respect and admiration for one another.

As part of the same Citibank tour, Thatcher met with Prime Minister Lee Kuan Yew in Singapore, which he had transformed into a global centre of excellence. I noticed during that trip that all three leaders had several characteristics in common – they led from the front, had strong views on various issues and were driven by the desire to make a difference in some way. All three were reformers, who challenged the status quo, had the ability to get buy-in from relevant stakeholders to pursue change for the long-term good of their country, even if that came at political cost.

Citibank also organised a speaking tour with President George H. W. Bush during my time in Asia. It was 1994, a year after he had left office. I received him in Jakarta, Indonesia, where he attended a meeting with President Suharto and addressed the business community there. After this, he travelled to Hong Kong where he was received by its last governor, Chris Patten.

On the day the former president arrived in Singapore on the next leg of his trip, I was meant to see him that evening at the banquet hosted in his honour. I was sitting in my office when my secretary Christine told me President Bush was in the building. I thought she was joking. As it turns out, the bank's security staff had sent a message saying President Bush was already coming up the elevator to my floor. Before I had time to reply, I heard footsteps outside my door and in walked Bush and his wife, Barbara. He stopped and said: 'We had some free time so we thought we'd come and have coffee with you.'

President George H. W. Bush is a truly global figure and foreign policy was always his forte. His years as ambassador to China and the UN gave him sound experience in engaging with countries around the world. But he is also warm, wise, friendly, sincere and down to earth.

We stayed in touch after the trip and he visited me at my residence in Islamabad while I was prime minister and he was on a trip to the Far East. He also took the time to travel to Pakistan in the aftermath of the 2005 earthquake; he visited the affected areas, as well as helping raise funding from across the world.

My early interactions with these global figures taught me valuable lessons in leadership, adding to what I learned through living in nine countries and managing Citibank's business in over forty. Being a banker in these countries exposed me to their management styles and their ways of dealing with complex issues. It also gave me rare access to political, business and civil society leaders.

Effective leaders apply theory within the proper context. As Dr Mahathir told me when I met with him in 2014: 'Market economy and democracy are the best drivers for growth, but you must know your limitations. They must come from within, they cannot be imposed. We must strive towards mature democracy, and understand the limits it can have within each society.'

Today, the world suffers from a leadership deficit and an abundance of career politicians. True leaders worry about the next generation, not the next election. They operate with total integrity and transparency. Introducing and implementing credible structural reforms needs to be an ongoing process and by definition involve short-term pain. It takes skill to convince both the public and other stakeholders that these changes will be in their best interest.

Today the challenge for many countries is to achieve healthy, sustainable and inclusive growth. Structural reforms need to be implemented, covering a broad array of activity. Often necessary economic measures are unpopular, and initiating them comes at high political cost. One example of this was the reform of Japan's huge postal service in 2005. It was the cornerstone of an effort to streamline the Japanese economy and encourage the private sector to play a larger role. However, it was, politically, a highly sensitive initiative. The Japanese Prime Minister Junichiro Koizumi went ahead with it anyway, put his own position on the line and eventually succeeded in doing what many governments before him could not do. He challenged the status quo in doing what was necessary, not what was politically expedient. I remember meeting him the week after he almost lost his position over the unpopular privatisation. With hindsight, the bold move yielded long term results.

Similarly, Chancellor Gerhard Schroeder's economic reforms in Germany were unpopular at the time, but stood Germany in good stead during the global financial crisis. He showed true leadership but his party lost the election in the process.

When restructuring or reforming a country or a company, it is important to learn from others who have done it well. The entire management team of Citibank once spent a day at Disneyworld, Florida, seeing how it handled customer service, customer needs and demands. We were surprised when John Reed suggested it, but ended up learning a great deal from observing such a well-oiled operation. The biggest eye-opener was seeing the back of house operations – an underground world running the whole park, from providing a space for staff to change to controlling the rides and security. I remember learning how the theme park would spray the scent of cinnamon at the children's height level, to make them hungry and encourage their parents to buy them cookies. It was a novel way to create demand. Our own approach and perspective was expanded by observing the logistics, coordination and management of the company.

The effective leaders I have come across are masters of delegation. While I was at Citibank, a major multinational conducted a survey of successful leaders and found that they should ideally have a helicopter-like quality – they should hover over the scene and make sure everything is under control, watch it and if there is a problem, land, fix it and leave immediately, letting the local management deal with the issue.

I have also noticed that farsighted leaders will plan their succession. They have the courage to step down and make room for the next leaders at the appropriate time. I recall paying a visit to the former president of South Africa, F. W. de Klerk, after I left office. I was in Cape Town to watch the football World Cup in 2010 and went to express my appreciation for him and his role in ending apartheid. He stepped down from being president to become vice president, enabling Nelson Mandela to take over and complete the process of ending apartheid in South Africa once and for all – an extremely wise and bold move on de Klerk's part. I had met Nelson Mandela at Davos, while working in the Middle East for Citibank. I paid my respects to the leader who had relentlessly fought for

257

what was right and had a global impact in promoting equality, justice and human rights.

I believe individual leaders have the power to shape the course of their people's destiny. This was certainly the case with Mohammad Ali Jinnah, who fought tirelessly for the creation of Pakistan, guided by a vision that Muslims should be given a home. Jinnah was a visionary, determined to achieve independence from British rule and a fair solution for Muslims in India. Even when the odds were against him, he persevered and eventually succeeded.

True leaders fight for what they believe, even if it ultimately costs them their life. Martin Luther King's campaigning against the racism and lack of rights for African-Americans transformed the plight of oppressed people not only in the United States, but across the world.

Strategic leaders have the ability to unite many different stakeholders and foster political consensus; as was the case for King Abdul Aziz, who created modern-day Saudi Arabia, and King Faisal, who later took significant steps to reform and encourage education in the Kingdom.

In 1978 Deng Xiaoping opened China up to the outside world, moving away from Chairman Mao's economic policies. At the Third Plenum in December 1978 he set out a comprehensive reform of the economic system. Later that month China ordered three Boeing 747s from the United States and Coca-Cola announced it would be opening a plant in Shanghai. It was the beginning of a modern and prosperous China – and Deng Xiaoping had the courage and foresight to guide his country through this step.

True leaders must have a broad outlook and consider the wider world. The longest-serving president in American history, Franklin D. Roosevelt, helped his country emerge from the throes of the Great Depression and redefined US policy at home and abroad. Decades later in Europe, Helmut Kohl showed true leadership in guiding Germany through the difficult process of transition and unification which followed the fall of the Berlin Wall.

I have been fortunate in my life to observe and interact with some of the people whose decisions have shaped our world. I have tried to learn from them, although in reality leadership can only be truly honed in practice. Never have my own skills and abilities been tested as much as during the earthquake which devastated vast parts of Pakistan. Responding to it undoubtedly became the toughest test I faced in my career, both in the public and private sectors.

The day the earth shook

At 8.52 a.m. on 8 October 2005, millions of Pakistanis saw their world turn upside down in a matter of seconds. An earthquake measuring 7.6 on the Richter scale struck the country's northern areas, bringing total destruction and the worst humanitarian disaster in Pakistan's history.

It took seconds for the earthquake to devastate many parts of Pakistan and Kashmir. More than 80,000 people lost their lives and over a hundred thousand were injured. More than 3 million were left without a home. It was one of the worst traumas in the history of Pakistan, which completely changed the nature of the northern parts of the country; it destroyed and displaced families, leaving countless children orphaned, left people paralysed or living as paraplegics or quadriplegics.

Even in Islamabad, which was far from the epicentre, we felt the ground shake. I was sitting in my official residence, reading a newspaper, when the earth moved. The earthquake

259

had disrupted communications so it was initially hard to find out exactly what had happened and understand the extent of the problem. President Musharraf came to my office where we discussed a plan of action. First, we visited an apartment building in Islamabad which had collapsed, where many locals and foreigners had been staying. As we walked through the rubble, I felt strong aftershocks and crashing sounds coming from below. As we were there, new reports emerged about the scale of the tragedy in the northern parts of the country.

The relief effort faced serious logistical problems, since the earthquake had struck Pakistan's mountainous and remote areas. Communications were disrupted and supply lines were cut. Roads were blocked for miles as citizens tried to get relief to the affected areas. In Azad Kashmir the earth had moved, creating a dam and blocking off a river.

I saw these logistical hurdles first-hand. I remember flying by helicopter through a deep ravine to get to the affected zones and, as we were about to make our descent in the designated area, we saw that the road ahead had been cut in two, as if by a knife. I turned to the captain and asked: 'Are you sure this is OK to land in?'

He looked at me and said: 'Inshallah!'

My spine tingled as we made our precarious landing.

There was no agency equipped to handle or respond to this human tragedy. The existing Disaster Management Cell consisted of a few people whose job was mostly running a warehouse of relief goods, without the capacity to do much else. The key element in disaster management is coordination and knowing who to access for information and logistics. It is of little use having doctors and volunteers who wish to help without knowing where they should go in the relief effort and with no clear channel to report to. The scale of the disaster was so great we needed to mobilise everyone we could in the country – and the world.

For the first two days after the earthquake, the army was our only lifeline to the devastated areas. Throughout the relief effort and the later reconstruction work, the armed forces were integral to managing the task at hand in these challenging conditions and handled the situation with professionalism and efficiency.

Overnight, we created the Earthquake Relief Commission (ERC) to manage the relief effort and filled it with the best talent we could find. I recall trying to think who would be best to lead it when Lieutenant General Farooq, a very capable officer on my staff, walked into my office about a completely unrelated matter. It was as if a light bulb had lit up over my head – I knew he was the right man for the job. His organisation successfully coordinated the entire relief effort, including food, medical attention, clothing and tents for temporary living, as well as providing daily press briefings to keep the nation informed.

We sent messages through the media and the foreign office to appeal for help and the relief effort galvanised the whole nation. I witnessed spirit and unity in our people of a kind I had not seen before. Volunteers rushed from all parts of Pakistan to help out. There were giant traffic jams from Karachi to the Khyber Pass as people drove to the affected area and relief camps with supplies. The army, the government, charities and civil society as a whole all mobilised.

I remember visiting a hospital in Bagh, Azad Kashmir, which had been destroyed in the earthquake. The Belgians had swiftly built a temporary hospital nearby, and Doctors Without Borders, the charity, came to treat the injured. While I was walking around the hospital, I came across two female doctors and asked: 'Where are you from?'

'Shikarpur, Sindh province,' they replied.

Shikarpur is a medium-sized city north of Karachi. While we stood and talked these two young Florence Nightingales made me feel proud to be a Pakistani.

The global response was highly encouraging. Volunteers and medical teams flew in from across the world – including the United States, the UK, Saudi Arabia, Jordan, Turkey (which rebuilt part of Muzaffarabad), China, Iran, the UAE, Japan, Germany and other European countries. Trained social workers in uniform came from Malaysia. More than 2,000 medical professionals travelled from Cuba alone – among them an army of doctors sent by President Fidel Castro. Cuba had no embassy at the time in Pakistan, so it opened a temporary one in a hotel in Islamabad.

Often we would fly in the helicopter to drop parcels of dry food and water to people who were stranded. On one such journey, flying north of Garhi Habibullah, I saw a few people standing below and landed in order to give them supplies, thinking they were earthquake victims. They turned out to all be from Doctors Without Borders, which had quickly mobilised a large number of doctors to come to Pakistan to help with the tragedy. Among them was a Brazilian, two Frenchmen and a Belgian. I asked the Brazilian: 'What made you come here?'

He told me: 'I saw the news and wanted to help.'

In another part of the devastated area, ten days after the earthquake, a Korean businessman set up a kitchen, funded everything himself, and brought in local cooks who made curries, kebabs and naan, all of which were supplied to nearby camps. The businessman stood there making chapattis, even though he had no links to Pakistan and did not speak Urdu or English – he simply wanted to help. These are just a few examples of the help we received from across Pakistan and all over the world.

The United States and the UK sent helicopters which were invaluable in the rescue mission. The British were one of the first teams to arrive at the first wreckage site I went to in Islamabad – a BA flight came within forty-eight hours of the tragedy, with experts and sniffer dogs to help clear the rubble and look for survivors trapped in the collapsed building. They had skills and experience we did not possess and they helped save many lives. The World Food Programme, led by Josette Sheeran, also provided invaluable help throughout the relief effort. I regularly called for more supplies, saying: 'We want tents, tents and tents'. The UNHCR (UN Refugee Agency) provided useful advice in managing tent villages. In one of my earliest visits to a makeshift tent village, we saw there were no toilets on site, and that people had to go to the nearby field instead. We said: 'This is not good enough', and temporary facilities were set up.

Sheeran, who now runs the Asia Society in New York, recalled being in Afghanistan with Secretary of State Condoleezza Rice on the day of the earthquake: 'The next day we diverted the plane to Pakistan, and the full force of every asset the US had was [deployed]. This is the kind of diplomacy, on the economic and humanitarian front, that really moves things.'

We waived visa requirements for those aid volunteers who had travelled to Pakistan without one. We welcomed the local and global media, which played an effective role in spreading the word around the world and raising awareness of the issue. Lieutenant General Farooq negotiated with IBM and DHL to provide us technical assistance in handling large inflows of aid coming into Pakistan, automating the process. With any donations and the relief effort, we placed the emphasis on transparency, efficacy and correctness of expenditure. We published information online, had parliamentary groups and external auditors overseeing the process. Lieutenant General Farooq deserves credit for directing the relief effort and keeping a cool head during such a critical time.

Some of the affected areas in Azad Kashmir were no-go zones for foreigners. We opened all areas up to aid workers and visitors. This was in my mind one of the most positive side effects of the earthquake. In some cases, entrenched taboos were shattered overnight.

High profile visitors also came, including the Hollywood actor Ben Kingsley, Prince Alwaleed bin Talal bin Abdul Aziz Al Saud, President George H. W. Bush and Ted Turner. Angelina Jolie turned up with her photographer and uploaded shots of her visiting the refugee camps onto the Internet, instantly raising awareness. Prince Rashid bin Hassan, the son of Prince Hassan bin Talal of Jordan came and stayed for quite a while in Rawalakot in Azad Kashmir. Even a delegation from the Mormon Church from Utah came in a Boeing 747, loaded with relief goods. Several heads of state and government, including those of China, Turkey, the US, the UK and Australia, visited the affected areas.

As well as encouraging aid and organising the relief effort, it was important for the government to lead from the front and to be a visible presence throughout the process. Almost every day I would put on my bulletproof vest, climb aboard the helicopter and fly to affected areas, temporary shelters and hospitals. I would typically take the route through Mansehra toward the Kaghan valley and Balakot. This continued for months. I also covered Azad Kashmir, visiting those affected in several towns and villages.

My wife Rukhsana accompanied me on many trips. We went to Abbottabad, Mansehra and Rawalakot, as well as many other affected areas, and to the furthermost hospitals. President Musharraf made several public visits to the earthquake areas and personally became involved in the relief effort. It was important for the government to be on the front lines, to show a bias for action and care for those affected. For the next three months my main focus was entirely shifted on the relief effort, earthquake management and raising and allocating resources.

Some areas were too dangerous to visit. I remember landing in Alai, a village up on a hill, in my helicopter. As I was about to get out, we got word that it may not be advisable to visit the local village as it had not been cleared from a security point of view. The helicopter captain turned to me and said: 'We'd better survey the area from the sky instead.' This only indicated the scale of the effort required by those who went into these areas to help with the relief effort.

President Musharraf and I realised the scale of the disaster meant we were in urgent need of extra funds. Rescuing people from the rubble, relocating them and providing food and shelter all required resources and our initial flash appeals were not bringing in enough. There was a risk that humanitarian and rescue flights would be grounded if a fresh stream of funding did not come in time.

In November we held a donors' conference in Islamabad – I asked Kofi Annan, the UN Secretary-General, to have the main meeting in Pakistan in order to draw more support and provide an opportunity for delegates to see the damage. Annan came personally to the meeting, which made a big difference. He co-chaired it with President Musharraf and me. With the help of the World Bank, the Asian Development Bank, the

Islamic Development Bank and the UN, we had estimated that Pakistan needed $5.2 billion for the reconstruction effort.

We decided to make the pledging an open process – that way the seventy-six represented countries would see how much the others were giving and be encouraged to match it. However, days before the conference, I heard that the amount the United States was planning to pledge was very low. I knew that if this happened, the other countries would instantly reduce their contributions. While we were discussing our approach, it was decided that President Musharraf would call President Bush directly, who was in South Korea at the time, and explain the importance of American aid.

The US Assistant Secretary of State for South and Central Asian Affairs, Christina Rocca, who was in Pakistan after the earthquake, recalled: 'When we got the final number, there were those of us who said: "That's not going to cut it." It was small for this kind of deal. And I remember that President Musharraf's call to President Bush is what pushed the amount up. President Musharraf said: "It is important that you have a big number because others will follow suit." And President Bush said: "How much do you need?" He said: "$500 million", and President Bush said: "Fine, not a problem".'

The donor conference was a resounding success. In the end we raised $6.5 billion, $4 billion of which was as debt and $2.5 billion as cash grants. The UN hailed it as one of the most successful global fundraising initiatives it had ever seen. Kofi Annan's presence and commitment made a big difference in securing this result.

As well as giving medical assistance, food and shelter, we also needed to help those traumatised by the destruction. Setting up temporary schools in rescue areas was an important way to keep people occupied, give them some sense of normality and daily routine through taking their children to school. In this, USAID provided helpful assistance. I recall inaugurating some of the schools in the affected areas with the US ambassador to Pakistan, Ryan Crocker, and being impressed by American reconstruction efforts.

It was important not only to handle the immediate relief effort, but to put in place a clear strategy for the years ahead. We provided compensation to those who had lost a family member or a home. As well as rescuing people from the rubble and moving them to tents, a plan was developed to give them temporary accommodation and then a permanent home. We set up temporary vocational training schools to provide more skilled labourers, needed for rebuilding homes, and to give people the skill sets they needed to work overseas.

New economic activity had to be financed and people had to be given the ability to make a living. In the earthquake, thousands of children were orphaned, and many survivors suffered from life-altering disabilities. These people required permanent support and there needed to be adequate state provisions set aside for this. In my trips around the affected disaster zones I also noticed that we had no facilities for psychiatric treatment to help those with trauma and stress suffered as a result of the earthquake. We encouraged volunteer groups, as well as psychology university students, to come to the affected areas.

The rebuilding of homes, services, infrastructure and public buildings also had to be handled correctly. Initially, we commissioned experts to quickly design makeshift homes and started handing out building material for roofs. We then developed new building codes and better construction practices in vulnerable seismic zones, to minimise the potential damage of a similar catastrophe. All of this required planning

267

and funding. We set up the Earthquake Rehabilitation and Reconstruction Authority (ERRA) to manage the long-term effort; it was headed by Lieutenant General Zubair. We received help from China to carry out seismic surveys of the earthquake areas, find future possible fault lines and select new areas for reconstruction.

I also felt that a permanent organisation with the expertise and capacity to handle natural disasters, with formally trained staff, was needed. We set up a National Disaster Management Agency to create a core competency in dealing with such unexpected crises at both the federal and provincial levels; the agency was also led by Lieutenant General Farooq. Each province was encouraged to establish a disaster management agency to deal with natural calamities and pool necessary skills.

The final death toll of the earthquake was estimated at over 80,000, with over a hundred thousand injured – a major human tragedy, and one which should not be forgotten.

The United Nations – 'We don't do buffalos'

The United Nations and its agencies played an important role in managing the aftermath of the earthquake and in galvanising global support. However, our experience also highlighted some areas in which our multilateral approach to disaster management needed improvement.

In an earthquake, time is of the essence – minutes can make the difference between life and death. It is impractical not to have relief money set aside and rely on a flash fundraising process every time calamities occur. There must be global contingency funds that can be immediately tapped. It would help to create a disaster management fund, which has contributions from all nations and can be used for immediate initial relief in disasters around the world. This is something the UN could coordinate.

Similarly, we should encourage greater sharing of best practice between countries when it comes to natural disasters. Those that are leaders in the field could help with training and identifying possible fault lines. There should be an institutionalised way of sharing expertise – we must create an organisation to do this on a global level, under the auspices of the UN.

Following the end of the Second World War, the United Nations was created with the purpose of maintaining peace and security across the globe. However, over the years its structure, bureaucracy and slowness to adapt to the changing world have hampered its effectiveness. In an attempt to address this, in 2006 Kofi Annan and Mark Malloch Brown invited me to co-chair the High-level Panel on UN System-wide Coherence, along with Prime Minister Jens Stoltenberg of Norway and Prime Minister Luisa Diogo of Mozambique. The idea was to bring together serving public figures, as well as former leaders and technical experts, and investigate how all UN agencies and programmes can develop a more efficient approach. The panel included the former presidents of Chile and Uganda, the British Prime Minister Gordon Brown and several former heads of state and government.

The report we prepared listed the reasons why the United Nations had become fragmented and weak: from a lack of buy-in and mixed messages from member states; to a proliferation of agencies, mandates and offices, creating duplication and dulling the focus on outcomes; to moribund entities never being discontinued.[1]

United Nations development at the country level is overly splintered and driven by what can be supplied, not what is needed on the ground. Even when their mandates intersect, United Nations entities tend to operate alone and with little coordination. At the time of the report's publication, the UN system encompassed seventeen specialised agencies and related organisations, fourteen funds and programmes, seventeen departments and offices of the UN Secretariat, five regional commissions, five research and training institutes and a plethora of regional and country-level structures. The panel concluded that the loss of cohesion between these prevents the UN from being more than the sum of its parts.

More than one-third of UN country teams had ten or more UN agencies on the ground at any one time, the report found. Several teams included twenty or more. This led to incoherent programme interventions and excessive administrative costs. It also burdened the capacity of developing countries to deal with multiple agencies. Mark Malloch Brown, Deputy Secretary-General who was actively involved in the One UN project, told me: 'Because of the cost going into maintaining the overheads of different offices, I had almost nothing left to actually spend on real development.'

It is important for all these efforts to be brought under the effective leadership of an empowered resident country coordinator – someone who is selected on the basis of merit and competition demonstrably open to candidates outside the United Nations Development Programme (UNDP) and the UN system.

The panel found there was no central management authority in the UN to implement common rules and practices. As a result, individual organisations pursue various initiatives, without incentives to harmonise their activities for the benefit of the UN system as a whole. One recommendation was to establish a system of One UN at country level – having one leader, one programme, one budgetary framework and, where appropriate, one office. The idea was to encourage everybody to fall behind a single country-authored plan for development priorities, which the UN would support in a coherent, cost-effective way. We recommended trying a pilot system along these lines in five countries.

Significant changes need to be made to the way donor funding is managed. Current UN funding patterns are highly fragmented, unpredictable and constrained by too much earmarking, which has encouraged duplication and inefficiency.

Funding should be linked to performance to improve outcomes. Programme countries and donors should be able to see and compare the true overhead costs of delivery through the introduction and publication of administration and back office costs.

The report also analysed how gender equality could be better addressed by the UN. It found that while the organisation remains a key actor in supporting countries to achieve gender equality and female empowerment, there is a strong sense that the UN system's contribution has been incoherent, under-resourced and fragmented. For reasons of both human rights and development effectiveness, the UN needs to pursue these objectives far more vigorously.

The international community has a duty to ensure the UN is fit for purpose, reinvigorated and strengthened to meet global challenges. Bold reforms are needed to improve the effectiveness of the UN in delivering its mandate.

Reform recommendations included establishing evaluation mechanisms to boost transparency and accountability. Human resource policies and practices should be updated and harmonised. Executives should be selected according to clear criteria and for limited periods – capped at two terms of four or five years.

At present, the UN is staffed with dedicated people with an abundance of goodwill, but they could be deployed more efficiently. As it stands, this situation can result in the incorrect allocation of resources and a lack of out-of-the-box thinking.

Josette Sheeran, who ran the UN's World Food Programme (WFP) and participated in the panel, recalled visiting Jabori, a village in Pakistan that had been destroyed by the 2005 earthquake. 'The UN had built a pharmaceutical hut with every kind of medicine,' she said. 'I brought all the women together and asked, if you had a magic wand, what would you want?'

They told her: 'We want our buffalo – our buffalo was killed during this earthquake, and nobody will get us one. We don't know what any of these medicines are, we need the buffalo.'

Sheeran sat down with the UN and said to them: 'All this village wants is a buffalo.' And UNDP said: 'We don't do buffalos', and the World Food Programme said: 'We don't do buffalos', and the UN's Food and Agriculture Organisation said: 'We don't do buffalos.' In the end, Sheeran said it fell to private donations to raise money in that particular case, which illustrated the lack of flexibility of disaster relief efforts. She added: 'We are all shooting way too high for the problems of people.'

There has been some effort to take on the suggestions we made for improving the United Nations. Secretary-General Kofi Annan presented the report to the UN General Assembly, and announced he was taking on board the first recommendation to establish five pilot One Country Programmes by 2007. As a result of Annan's initiative, some of the panel's recommendations have been implemented, such as the streamlining of country-level organisation. However, with the departure of Annan as Secretary-General shortly after the panel presented its results, his reform drive's momentum slowed. Today, much more needs to be done for the UN to be an effective institution.

Reform of the Security Council, which has no permanent seat for South America, Africa or any Asian country aside from China, is also overdue. Kofi Annan told me in 2014: 'I pushed very hard to reform the UN from various angles, not only administrative and managerial, but I also pushed the member states to reform the Security Council, with solid proposals on the table. We did not succeed, because the member states were not ready.' He added: 'The problem was not always the developed country, sometimes [it was] the developing countries themselves.' Existing tensions between member states make it difficult to agree on changes if they may mean that one, but not the other, will get representation and greater influence.

Annan stressed that the need to adapt to the modern world is greater than ever today: 'Either the UN reforms and those who have privileges sit back and discuss very seriously how much power they are going to give away to seek cooperation and make it workable, or they keep their privileges and that will lead to constant tension and a situation where the other countries may balk at council decisions.'

Conflicts remain the biggest threat to human development, with fragile and conflict-affected countries typically experiencing the highest poverty rates.

Gender inequality persists, even though more girls are now in school and women have gained ground in parliamentary representation in nearly 90% of the 174 countries surveyed over the past twenty years. However, women continue to face

discrimination in access to work, economic assets and partici-
pation in private and public decision-making.

About 800 million people still live in extreme poverty
and suffer from hunger. In countries affected by conflict, the
proportion of out-of-school children increased from 30% in
1999 to 36% in 2012. More work needs to be done. The UN
Secretary-General Ban Ki-moon has outlined a vision for the
post-2015 sustainable development agenda. The Sustainable
Development Goals aim to continue the work to eradicate
global poverty and improve the lives of people across the
world.

Climate change threatens the entire planet. Major carbon
emitting countries, such as the US, China, the European
states and India, must take joint action to reduce emissions
and build a world economy based on green energy. China's
emissions are high and require a comprehensive strategy to
achieve environmentally sustainable growth. The future of
all of us is at stake – creating a sustainable environment is a
global task.

In order to be able to address these global challenges, the
United Nations must be reformed to better reflect the realities
of our current world. Its failure to do so limits its scope and
reach in many countries. As Mark Malloch Brown told me:
'In some ways the UN has become an almost Europe-Africa
institution. It is enormously strong in Africa and Europe, but
not widely respected always in Asia and almost irrelevant in
Latin America.'

Malloch Brown recalled the difficulties he and Kofi Annan
had in finding a successor to the Secretary-General: 'Kofi
and I strongly felt that it was Asia's turn. Asia was strangely
disengaged and disinterested in producing one of its best to
be Secretary-General. It became a competition of foreign

ministers, which Kofi and I both felt was wrong. Our view was it would be better served by someone who had been a national leader, to do justice to the development side, the security side. I was trying to encourage some Asians with bigger boots to get into it.'

However, there are many interests within the P5 which do not want a strong personality running the UN. Malloch Brown told me in 2014: 'There's a folklore that certain P5 members want somebody who is more secretary than general, particularly if it comes after a strong Secretary-General.'

Meanwhile, there are more and more opportunities for the UN to play an important part. Today there appears to be an unwillingness between the major powers of the day to work together, more so than I ever witnessed during my dealings with them when in government. Arguably this leaves space for the United Nations to take up a bigger global role and be a force for good. Reforming its structure and encouraging cohesion and cooperation would be a step towards achieving this objective.

17
PAKISTAN: THE WAY FORWARD

Today Pakistan arguably faces more challenges than ever. The existential threat of terrorism risks undermining the fabric of our society. The squeeze the economy and infrastructure faces from our rapidly growing population, as well as the need to modernise and introduce new technology to keep up with the rest of the world, present a monumental task for any government. However, I firmly believe Pakistan can be put on the path of a thriving, mature democracy, which is necessary to fulfil its potential. It is the drive for excellence which can get the best out of a nation. I believe this is attainable, but it will require a significant improvement in the quality of governance. We need to rise to the occasion and show we can move away from quick-fix, incrementalist approaches to a world-class level.

In order to guard Pakistan against any abuses of power and guide it on to the path of healthier, responsible governance, it is imperative that its political institutions are strengthened and improved – and that a more robust system of trusted checks and balances by Parliament, independent bodies and the judiciary is put in place.

With poor governance, the whole fabric of the state becomes fragile. That is when other actors may come in to fill the void. As we have seen in the aftermath of the Arab Spring, democracy does not come about after regime change or revolution. It takes time to become ingrained in the culture of the country. Simply holding elections is not enough – political institutions must have credibility. The role of the Parliament as a legislator as well as providing oversight of the government is important for a well-functioning system. There should be a strong judiciary acting as a check and balance on those in power and enforcing the rule of law.

Pakistan inherited a Westminster-style parliamentary system following its independence in 1947. While, in theory, this could have been a strength, in reality it was not suited to Pakistan's complexities and idiosyncrasies. Partition paved the way for years of political turnover, triggered either by weak coalition governments or military coups. As a result, no civilian government had completed its full tenure until the 2013 general election finally marked such a transition.

Frequent premature government changeovers and interruptions of the democratic process, coupled with a lack of balance between different centres of power in Pakistan, have impacted the country's standing both internationally and domestically. They have impaired the performance and quality of governance, reduced the government's credibility, both with its electorate and across the world, and impacted on the economy and investment as policies often lack continuity.

Having observed both presidential and parliamentary systems around the world up close, I have come to the considered view that Pakistan should move to a presidential form of government. This would better suit its needs and state of development, allowing it to progress to new heights.

At present, the president of Pakistan has limited authority and a largely ceremonial role. The prime minister is the chief executive under the constitution. A directly elected president would be fully accountable to the people of Pakistan, and therefore have greater legitimacy, boosting his or her executive power. There are numerous examples around the world of presidential systems functioning effectively. In Turkey, the president is fully empowered, for example.

Having a directly elected president would make Pakistan's decision-making process clearer and help create unity of command. A strong and empowered chief executive, who would also be the supreme commander of the armed forces, would provide all stakeholders with the room and ability to be able to implement good governance. The president would have their own staff of analysts and experts in their field who could oversee the functioning of the various ministries. This could constitute a 'strategic analysis unit' and function as part of the presidential office. It would review policy initiatives and develop a structural reform agenda. It would have no administrative responsibility and be purely there to offer expertise and consult on various matters.

The role of the prime minister could change to primarily overseeing the legislature and serving as leader of the house. The president could also choose to delegate some powers to the prime minister, such as running key ministries. To use a corporate analogy, the prime minister should effectively be the chief operating officer of the country, while the president would constitute its chief executive.

The Parliament has a responsibility to ensure transparent governance, adequate legislation and continuous improvement in the delivery of services. Under the proposed presidential system, Parliament would have a vital role for oversight through its committees, serving as a check and balance on the president, prime minister and the cabinet. However, for this it must be filled with people who have the relevant expertise to be able to keep the government accountable. Ministries will have their own parliamentary committees, staffed with qualified full-time professionals to analyse the issues, brief MPs and oversee and monitor the chief executive.

It is time for Pakistan to relinquish the system of having interim governments. At present, a new temporary cabinet is assembled before every general election. The interim ministers and the interim prime minister are sworn in for three months and serve to keep the system in a holding pattern before a new government is elected. They do not have the legitimacy, empowerment or time to start anything worthwhile; and this system is disruptive and confusing, paralysing the political process around election time. Our recent successful handovers between democratically elected governments should give us confidence in our electoral processes, eliminating the need for this interim scenario. Instead, an empowered independent electoral commission should be trusted to oversee the process with no need for interim governments. This follows practice, which is common all over the world.

Pakistan could look to and analyse the political systems in countries which follow similar models of governance, such as Chile, Indonesia, Korea, Mexico, Turkey and Brazil. In these countries the Parliament is typically still active, keeps a check and balance on the government and votes on major policy decisions.

Unlocking our human capital

One of the first steps to reforming any institution is to attract the best quality people for public life. In Pakistan it is important to raise the level of discussions and debates in Parliament to make them more substantive and professional. We have a repository of knowledge but, with so many people regularly

279

moving from one ministry to another, it becomes harder to get the right people for the job. At present, the prime minister has to select his or her cabinet from the MPs in Parliament. It is not sufficient to, once a government comes into power, assign cabinet positions and expect these ministers to become experts in their new field overnight. This often leads to a mismatch of skills and needs. For the country to be equipped to meet the numerous challenges it faces, we need to promote people with administrative experience and a deep understanding of their given area of responsibility. They must have prior knowledge of their subject and the ability to design and execute structural reforms. It is not enough to learn on the job – our fast-paced, increasingly globalised and thus competitive world requires us to adapt our management practices.

One of the most important changes under a presidential system would be providing the president with the ability to appoint cabinet members and allowing for greater capacity to hire them based on talent, experience and competence. Members of Parliament would not be eligible for appointment to the cabinet without giving up their seats. This will give the president room to bring in candidates possessing relevant expertise in their field. The health minister, for example, should be an expert on health and already know his or her area when appointed. The minister of education must be an education expert, who can not only manage the existing system but also take it to the next level. The same principle should be applied to any ministry and discipline. The country needs a sea change in the quality of its governance.

While there are some capable ministers in Pakistan, many are there because of political accommodations or coalition needs. Although our government did try to stipulate educational standards, in practice this did not make much difference.

More wide-reaching structural change is needed to raise the quality of debate in government.

The accountability of the cabinet is essential. When I started as prime minister, I initiated carrying out quarterly reviews of goals and priorities for every minister. The secretary and minister would come and report what their objectives were and how they were performing against these targets. The idea was to create an environment in which ministers could clearly see what was expected of them and self-evaluate their performance; and to develop a new culture of accountability and increased levels of ownership. This was the first time this was formally done in the government and the results were mixed. I clearly saw the benefits in some ministries, in particular finance, telecommunications, commerce, health and petroleum. Today this process should be enhanced and a transparent performance review process reintroduced, with clear goals, strategies and timetables. These should be disclosed to the public to encourage transparency.

Opposition political parties should develop the concept of shadow ministers – at least in important fields – and form a shadow cabinet when in opposition, which would be able to constantly monitor and critique the government. This system works successfully in the UK, for example. It would professionalise the opposition's role in Pakistan, allowing it to be taken more seriously.

All parties must also publish their views and have credible policy statements in print – not just manifestos during election time or research conducted for tactical purposes. They should have an active voice, even when out of power. Parties must also develop full-time area-specific think tanks engaged in constant research in all areas – not only in foreign policy and security. As governance becomes more complex, each party must have experts in place who can provide knowledge and help frame policy. Each party should have published positions on specialised fields – be it in foreign policy, the economy, education, agriculture, internal security, defence or health.

Political party structures also require reform. When party leadership candidates are selected, the emphasis should be on merit and competence. There must be credible leadership elections within the parties, held under the supervision of the election commission. At present, there is a greater reliance on having the necessary connections. The nomination process must be transparent and the political environment should not be dominated by the same names. This would lead to a more open democracy in Pakistan, which is necessary for it to reach its full potential. A change in culture does not come overnight, but reforming the way the party process works would be a good first step.

Improving education and literacy across the country is a priority. Existing schools struggle with capacity and not enough new schools are being established to meet the growing population's needs. Boosting education would not only strengthen the intellectual aspect of government, it would also lead to a better-informed electorate. Both public and private sector institutions should be encouraged to set up quality schools, colleges and universities, and create a world-class level of education. Institutions such as the Aga Khan University, LUMS, IBA, NUST, Beacon House, SZABIST and several others need to be replicated across the country; as well as those established by missionaries, including Forman Christian College in Lahore and my own alma mater, St Patrick's School in Karachi.

The country also needs to improve opportunities for women, giving them equal access to opportunities. As well as providing them with their due human rights, such efforts will also unlock what remains an untapped resource for the country, which could boost growth and development. As Mohammad Ali Jinnah said in 1940: 'I have always maintained that no nation can ever be worthy of its existence that cannot take its women along with the men. No struggle can ever succeed without women participating side by side with men.'[1]

An effort must be made to rebuild Pakistan's brand, to remind people of its beauty. The country's unique landscape once attracted tourists from all over world, among them Robert De Niro. The legendary actor was a fan of holidaying in Chitral, in the northernmost part of Pakistan, near the Afghan border. It is a luscious oasis surrounded by snow-topped mountains, known for its vibrant colours.

I had an opportunity to mention this to De Niro while on a visit to New York as prime minister. While I was having dinner in Nobu with friends, the head of my security detail came over and said: 'Sir, Mr Robert De Niro would like to come and say hello.'

Initially taken aback, I told him: 'Prime ministers come and go, but there is only one Robert De Niro – I will go to him!' and made my way over. The restaurant was packed. It was a veritable who's who of New York society. The CNN anchor Wolf Blitzer greeted me as I passed his table and reminded me we had an interview scheduled the following day.

De Niro was having dinner with his fellow *Mean Streets* star and friend, Harvey Keitel. I brought up the subject of Chitral and De Niro fondly recalled his holidays in Pakistan's northern steppes, adding that he had ceased going there on account of the deteriorating security situation.

A demographic tidal wave

One of the biggest challenges for Pakistan this century will be how to handle its population boom. A demographic tidal wave is coming. Since I left office, Pakistan's population has grown from about 160 million to 190 million and is set to increase to 210 million by 2020. The economy must be fit to absorb these people – new jobs will need to be created, infrastructure and social services will have to adapt to their requirements. While we tried to expand infrastructure fast enough to meet the needs of the growing population, this did not grow at the rate that was needed, particularly the availability of electricity. That said, some initiatives, notably the construction of Gwadar Port, are bound to eventually play a key role in developing the country and creating new trade routes – particularly following the Chinese One Belt, One Road investment, in the case of Gwadar.

As the population continues to expand, broad-based educational reforms are needed. At present, young people joining the labour force often do not have the required skill sets, which limits the number of opportunities open to them. As a result we run the risk of having an alienated generation which feels no sense of investment and ownership in society. If left unattended, the potential growth in youth unemployment could be a serious problem for Pakistan, with their dissatisfaction and disengagement pushing young men and women into the hands of extremists. Conversely, unlocking the potential talent and capacity to work in these young people could be huge boost for Pakistan.

With growth comes the problem of inequality. The economist Thomas Picketty argues that inequality is a systemic feature of capitalism because capital accumulates wealth faster than labour and economic growth generate it, and that the rate of return

284

from capital is higher than from labour and growth by a ratio of about five to one. This means extra resources should be set aside to manage the problems created by inequality, with wide-ranging social sector reform being implemented.

The country's rapidly changing demographics have serious implications for the way its local government functions. The boundaries of Pakistan's provinces were drawn up while their population numbered about 30 million. Punjab alone is now home to over 100 million – greater than the population of Germany. And yet Pakistan has maintained the same four-province structure since independence. They are vast in geographical scale, making it incredibly difficult to realistically manage as one entity. The representatives of a province are too removed and inaccessible to a large majority of their people. The growing population numbers make it even harder to effectively implement policy.

Since Punjab was split in 1947 between Pakistan and India, the Indian part has been divided into three provinces. In Pakistan it has stayed as one, and managing it has become a Herculean task. Instead, the existing 'divisions' should be converted into provinces. This will make the provinces more manageable and also better equipped to respond to people's needs. The tribal areas and Baluchistan should also be fully integrated into the national system.

We must be able to devolve power and make the heads of the provinces more accessible to the people they govern. People must be able to have access to their provincial capital, to be able to redress their grievances. With the size and geographic scale of Pakistan's four provinces, this is not realistically possible for millions. Each province should have a reasonable span of supervision because the issues it handles relate to the everyday needs of the people.

There are issues of unclear property titles, which can become a nightmare for people when they try to sell their home or get a mortgage. They also leave people open to land grabbing. These need to be resolved as a priority and automating the system will be essential to meet this challenge. While at the National Reconstruction Bureau, Daniyal Aziz developed several ideas to streamline land titles – it is worth updating and implementing these.

Institutions of government

Soon after joining the government, I learned that Pakistan has many centres of power, which can all pull in different directions. This can cause gridlock and make it harder to implement policies as the executive, the judiciary and the military do not always work in unison.

From the days of independence, Pakistan inherited a military from the British that was strong and effective, and many of its officers received high quality training abroad. The military became distinguished by its discipline, efficiency and structure, and perceived as a respected career path which treats its soldiers well post-retirement.

The military – consisting of the army, the air force, the navy and the intelligence agencies – has since developed into one of the strongest and most effective institutions in Pakistan. The country's geopolitical position means the military will always have an important role. As a result of India's hostile and militant attitude towards the very existence of Pakistan in the decades following Partition, the strategic importance of Pakistan's military grew. Many of the country's resources have historically been directed at building up its defence. Aggression from India and the lack

286

of resolution of disputes has thus historically influenced much of Pakistan's policy.

Pakistan's military views itself as the keeper of the country's sovereignty and territorial integrity. Political instability and weak, rapidly alternating governments tend to create a power vacuum. In the past, when the political process has been stuck in gridlock and government performance was inadequate, the military has intervened.

Understandably, the military has an interest in many areas of policy, when these interact with security issues. This gives them input into issues beyond military matters. It includes foreign policy, in particular Pakistan's strategic relationships with countries such as China, the United States, India and Afghanistan.

The military has a professional meritocratic system for hiring and promoting officers. I witnessed this first hand when President Musharraf invited me, as prime minister, to attend the army's promotion board. Even coming from the corporate world and seeing internal human resources processes in many leading private companies, I was impressed. The army's system of promotion is professional, transparent and merit-driven. Every proposed case was discussed in various independent committees and there was a frank debate about each candidate. The military also has a rigorous system of managed attrition, operating on a strict pyramid structure, where at each level people are let go instead of automatically progressing. Reviewing the human resources and personnel processes in civilian institutions would be useful and relevant aspects of the military's process could be adapted.

I was actively involved in funding and supporting the military – during my years as finance minister the joint chief of staff put together a five to ten year strategic plan for its future needs. With the advent of new technology and the introduction of new weaponry in the region, it was important for Pakistan to develop adequate defences and enough capability to deter any aggressive designs against its sovereignty. It is important to continue these efforts – a wide-ranging upgrading programme is needed. The air force needs stealth technology and state-of-the-art ammunition. Steps should be taken to reduce the military's teeth-to-tail ratio, which refers to the correlation between its operational component and the administrative and logistic detail. The existing administrative set-up can be made more efficient through automation, outsourcing and modern management techniques.

Because of budget constraints and, at times, sanctions, we would buy whatever was available from friendly countries on the open market. Our military hardware needs involved dealing with the US, Europe, China and Russia. Sometimes we bought used equipment and all three services of the military had the ability to re-engineer, upgrade and overhaul it, extending its life; all at a much lower cost than buying new products. All three services needed to have the required capability and they always received my complete support. For the navy, whose surface fleet was depleting fast, we added new frigates and continued to improve our sub-surface capability. We also enhanced our aerial surveillance capacity and maritime surveillance. Various restrictions in selling weapons to Pakistan meant we usually had to move fast if we had a willing seller, before any new restrictions could come in. We had to be nimble and ready with the funds when opportunities emerged. This budgetary support should continue, although diplomatic efforts to settle our disputes must be renewed.

In the long run, it is in Pakistan's interest to have a strong elected political leadership, which can govern effectively. While Pakistan has seen many challenges, the democratic process should be given room to work and each pillar of government should be allowed to conduct its own activities.

It is crucial that Pakistan finds a way to move to a mature democracy phase, which not only involves having a democratically-elected government but an improved quality of governance. Other countries in Asia, Latin America and the Middle East have achieved this, and there is no reason why Pakistan cannot do the same.

The increased freedom given to the media in our time also played a role in highlighting areas where the system was not transparent and in increasing accountability. The media needs to be made even freer but with tougher libel laws. The press should be self-regulating and focus on reporting in the public interest, therefore fulfilling a role as a vital check and balance on the government.

The civil service

When I joined the government I saw the civil service had an abundance of talent but not enough relevant training or exposure to the world. I started an initiative to train middle management civil servants by sending them to the John F. Kennedy School of Government at Harvard University. The two-month tailor-made course was intended to open their minds and expose them to the wider world. I would meet every group before they left for Cambridge, Massachusetts, and once again when they came back, to motivate them. Many had never crossed the Atlantic before. About two-thirds were usually positive about the prospect of going, and the rest were negative or cynical. By the end, a few of the cynics had usually changed their mind and I was pleased the majority of participants said they found the process useful.

The idea of the course was to encourage the capacity to reform, change and improve efficiency and delivery of services. The programme gave a bird's-eye view of new planning and execution techniques, and an awareness of what was happening in the rest of the world. Our bureaucrats are capable and hard working, but we need to invest more in them. Many countries, including China, have undertaken similar initiatives with their civil service.

With the implementation of any credible structural reforms, if the bureaucracy is not part of this process, the initiatives will not work. Crucial steps must be taken to push through the next stage of reforms in the country, covering all major parts of governance, including the civil service, the judiciary, the police, education, the economy and much more. The National Reconstruction Bureau initiated some positive measures, although not all could be implemented due to existing vested interests and an inability to create ownership. Structural reform agendas only succeed when there is absorptive capacity for them and when they are accepted by most stakeholders.

We started a process of promotion to improve the effectiveness of the civil service, developing specialised courses and academies for advanced training in foreign affairs, finance, health, education and women's issues. Promotions could not happen until the person had completed the required courses.

Today, the civil service would benefit from having more area experts and fewer generalists. There is also a lack of adequate human resource planning and development. We must send the civil service to the best quality schools around the world. Pakistan should analyse what other counties, which are leaders in specific fields, have done – such as Malaysia and Argentina for agriculture, the United Arab Emirates for urban planning, logistics and automation, Hong Kong for telecommunications and Singapore for developing infrastructure such as world-class airports and ports.

One necessary reform would be to consider raising the mandatory retirement age of the civil service to 65, from the previous 60. The way the promotion process works, someone could be made a top official and then have to retire shortly afterwards, which means the system is not making the most of valuable expertise and potential. In addition, there should be a process of fast-tracking the most talented civil servants to being promoted. We must not rely on seniority alone. A fast-tracked system will ensure they have more years on the senior positions before they retire, thus helping bridge the skills gap.

Pakistan's power structures

Like all countries, there are many centres of power in Pakistan, which need to coordinate effectively to ensure good governance and security.

The military in Pakistan has always played a crucial role in ensuring the internal and external security of the country and protecting its sovereignty. The intelligence community also has a vital role, particularly considering the region Pakistan is in, its neighbouring countries and the security threats it faces. Moreover, its importance has increased since the growth of terrorist threats within Pakistan.

In a presidential system, final decision-making would lie with the directly elected president, who as chief executive of the country would see all elements of power in Pakistan report to him or her. The country's politicians, military and security services must all work in tandem to ensure effective governance. For this, we need to create a more formal reporting line with the president at the top of the chain, without diminishing any stakeholder's importance. This should pave the way for faster reforms, better governance and more effective implementation. The security, civilian and military establishments would therefore ultimately report to the president. Pakistan should avoid having separate decision makers and multiple lines of authority, or a lack of communication between them – otherwise they inevitably end up crossing over on some issues.

An empowered full-time national security council is needed to bring together all the main stakeholders before the chief executive can make final decisions. The council should be under the president's office with analysts who have the ability to filter what comes in from all parts of the government. It should focus on defence, foreign, interior, security and economic policies. This is necessary to boost the policy-making side in Pakistan's political system, which is currently too individual-oriented and not institutional enough in focus. There needs to be a stronger approach to government planning and strategy. The planning commission should not just be concerned with approving projects, but should look at policy, developing strategic vision, providing a valuable input on how to prioritise reform and improve governance. It should have a global perspective on key issues and be staffed accordingly with the requisite talent.

In addition to ministries and the government, the president's office should also be staffed with specialists who have no administrative role and who would function as experienced advisers. They will ideally be experts in their field and specialise in developing and planning new initiatives, such as structural reforms – whereas ministers will focus on improving and analysing existing policies.

Any change to the political system would require a constitutional amendment as well as buy-in from the public and all the important stakeholders. Broad-based support will lend the reforms much-needed legitimacy and increase their potential effectiveness. The country has to decide whether it is time to jump the curve, raise the quality and standard of governance and progress towards excellence.

Security challenges

Since 9/11, the role of the intelligence service in Pakistan and the world as a whole has changed dramatically. In Pakistan, the security services are made up of the Inter-Services Intelligence (ISI), the Intelligence Bureau (IB) and the Military Intelligence (MI), as well as naval and air force intelligence and special branch in the provinces.

The ISI is essentially a military unit, reporting to the prime minister but with close links with the army. It has a separate budget and is typically better funded and equipped. The IB handles civil intelligence and reports to the prime minister on internal security. Though substantially under-resourced compared with the ISI, the IB also plays a useful role in information gathering and is more focused on domestic security. Because the intelligence agencies have an extensive network within Pakistan, they pick up intelligence in other areas including the political, economic and social sectors. As a result, the realm of the security service has increasingly

293

expanded into domestic matters. There is close interaction with the domestic security infrastructure because of the nature of external and internal threats to Pakistan today. The country's security agencies must work in unison to effectively counter the challenges facing the nation.

Traditionally, the threats Pakistan's intelligence agencies had to face were external. Now non-state actors have spread their influence across the country, attacking government buildings and army, air and naval bases. As these threats to Pakistan's security multiply, the security services have an increasingly critical role to play. Pakistan's government must make sure they have the latest techniques for intelligence gathering and requisite funding to be able to deal with these challenges.

Reforming the economy

Deregulation was one of the main pillars of our structural reform programme. Government intervention gives opportunity for corruption and delays. If done properly, liberalisation, privatisation and deregulation can help minimise corruption. This does not mean abdication by the state and it must be accompanied by strong regulatory regimes. The regulators must be ahead of the curve in terms of knowledge of the industry. In many countries this is not the case and the company being regulated tends to be better informed than the regulator.

When people bring matters to the government there is usually a risk of delays, corruption and rule bending; this is endemic and present at every level. One initiative we undertook was setting up the Public Procurement Regulatory Authority. We worked with the World Bank to devise rules to minimise corruption and make the bidding process for contracts more transparent. This involved creating a change in the way bids were received and evaluated. It ensured that those who could influence the bids would not benefit from the contracts. These new rules helped reduce corruption, but did not eliminate it. What is needed is a culture, which starts from the very top and makes it clear we will run a meritocratic system and that no one will be allowed to personally benefit. Pakistan is in need of a better system of checks and balances, and government processes should be backed up by transparency and oversight by Parliament. Leaders have a responsibility to curtail corruption during their time in power and set a good example. Government employees should be paid higher wages, to curb the need to resort to other methods of making money.

In terms of transparency, our system, while improved, is not where it ought to be. The tender process of bids for projects and contracts must be made totally transparent. Local and foreign suppliers must disclose whether they have paid any consultancy fees, commissions or other fees either in Pakistan or abroad. If it is later discovered that payments were made that were undeclared, this should be a criminal offence – applying to all sectors of government procurement. While it is common practice for foreign companies to hire representation or consultants to acquire contracts, their details should be disclosed and declared to a central authority in order to minimise underhand payments. The National Accountability Bureau plays an important role in addressing corruption and does much more. Its focus should be on the preventative side, so that opportunities for misuse are minimised.

The role of the media has been critical in highlighting corruption, and press freedom should be encouraged. During my time in government we invited Transparency International to come and look at our procedures, to see how corruption could be addressed. I dealt with Peter Eigen, who was the head of Transparency International and set up a chapter in Pakistan. While they were helpful, they must do more in focusing on systemic corruption issues, improving the level of disclosure of contracts and making it illegal to make or receive illicit payments. There is a need to look at the processes and procedures and improve them, making them more transparent and imposing strict penalties if illicit payments, in cash or in kind, are made. Pakistan's laws should be amended to make it illegal to both receive or give monetary payments to procure a deal or secure a contract. All local and foreign suppliers must, under law, provide an indemnity that no such payments have been made. Moreover, under no circumstances should a country allow such payments to be tax-deductible, as is the case in parts of the world. Auditors have a crucial role to play to ensure accounts with irregular payments are not approved. Expanding automation and continued investment in biometric technology will also help minimise corruption throughout the system.

Agriculture is the biggest sector in Pakistan's economy, providing a livelihood to millions. Investment and reform is needed to bring it into the twenty-first century, raising productivity and profitability. The technology used in agriculture must be modernised, new types of seeds, pesticides and fertiliser must be provided, and the irrigation system improved. The availability of agricultural credit should be streamlined and available from commercial banks as well as specialised institutions.

Pakistan's judiciary

The judiciary in Pakistan, particularly in the higher courts, has come a long way and plays an increasingly active role.

However, as the population grows to nearly 200 million, the judicial system has not been adapted to match this. The number and complexity of cases is growing and court capacity must be expanded. At present, there is a problem in Pakistan with delays in access to justice. A large number of cases take too much time to resolve and end up staying in court for many years. There are too many people languishing in jail awaiting trial – some end up living and dying in custody. This must be addressed – justice delayed is justice denied.

While the Supreme Court and high courts do tend to move major cases along in an expedient way, the lower courts are overwhelmed by cases and struggle to meet capacity and act without delays. Several governments in Pakistan have tried to address the problem of the backlog of cases, but I believe the area is in need of further reform. The recent decision to get military courts to deal with cases of terrorism further reflects the need to have speedy justice when it comes to serious crimes – provided they get an open and fair trial.

Even cases which do come to court often fall down at the evidence stage, because the process of evidence gathering and case building is weak. Criminals end up being acquitted, which in turn scares off potential witnesses – people become less likely to come forward and testify. Crime scene management techniques, including forensics, are not up to global standards. After a bomb explosion or terrorist attack, objects are often picked up by hand. The process of collecting DNA and other evidence, as well as the analytical and investigation parts, are not adequate.

The prosecution service in Pakistan needs improvement, as well as analytical and technical support. Like all government employees, those in the prosecution and investigation service are not paid enough, making it difficult to attract the necessary talent for the job. There must be more investment into adapting the process to the modern world and bringing in world-class practices. We cannot have antiquated prosecution techniques. More training, modern technology, technical assistance are needed. We can also learn from other developing countries that have adapted their systems.

With the help of the Asian Development Bank (ADB) we started an Access to Justice programme to improve our systems. However, this area requires much more funding and reform. More resources need to be provided at the local and provincial level in particular: to speed up the justice process, improve evidence gathering and prosecution techniques and provide relevant intensive training. With the increase in terrorist activity across Pakistan, this area requires serious attention. We need to jump the curve when it comes to justice and reform, taking help and guidance from countries which lead the way.

Overall, the priorities facing Pakistan's leaders today are the need to control terrorism, foster political stability, boost its defence and grow the economy. Pakistan must find a way to manage the expectations of its rapidly growing population. With these challenges in mind, the country must decide – is it content with being mediocre, or does it want to pursue excellence? Economic sovereignty, the smooth functioning of the political process, good governance, internal security, social sector development, a credible defence and effective diplomacy – these are the seven elements of statecraft which can transform a nation like Pakistan.

It is time for Pakistan to get on track to becoming a developed, progressive, tolerant and enlightened Islamic state. A Pakistan that provides peace, prosperity and security to its people. A Pakistan where children have access to quality education, where there is social justice, rule of law and opportunities for its citizens to reach their full potential.

Pakistan requires leaders who believe in the country's future and are willing to take the necessary steps to set it on a path of growth, even if it comes at personal political cost. The country's founder, Mohammad Ali Jinnah, had a vision to create a home for Muslims. It could have been described as idealistic but ultimately changed the lives of millions, offering a new sense of hope and a brighter future for people like my parents. In 1947, Mohammad Ali Jinnah addressed the newly-formed constituent assembly with the words: 'I can look forward to Pakistan becoming one of the greatest nations of the world.' The following year, on the first anniversary of independence, Jinnah said: 'The foundations of your state have been laid and it is now for you to build as quickly and as well as you can.' It is his sense of belief in the country's potential, and his ability to break with the status quo, which Pakistan needs to replicate today.

ACKNOWLEDGEMENTS

After I left office as the prime minister of Pakistan, many people suggested I write my memoirs and share how I transitioned from the private sector to the government, as well as how I handled dealing with political issues, parliament, local and world leaders. This would have not been possible without the support of my family, staff, colleagues and well-wishers.

Let me start by acknowledging the contribution of my wife Rukhsana, whose support, judgement, maturity, simplicity and prayers were major assets for me. During my eight years in government, she had no appetite for pomp and ceremony and was very popular with all the staff at Prime Minister's House, a huge compound comprising the official residence, offices and staff quarters in Islamabad.

My children, Lubna, Abid and Maha were very supportive but very concerned for my security after two suicide bombers attacked my car during an election campaign.

Mohammed Hassan, my private secretary stayed with me for the eight years I was in government. He was an important member of my team, dependable, smart and always thinking ahead.

Anna Mikhailova, as my co-author, was a key player in the entire project – without her tireless efforts this book would not have been possible. She spent long hours contributing to the content and design of the book and was the major driver in planning, writing and completing it.

Many generously gave their time during interviews or discussions related to the book, including Josette Sheeran, Vuk Jeremii, Kevin Rudd, General Colin Powell, Paul Wolfowitz, Kofi Annan, Mark Malloch Brown, Herman Van Rompuy, Mike O'Neill, Donald Rumsfeld, Dr Mahathir Mohamad, Abdullah Badawi, Gerhard Schroeder, Stanley Wolpert, General James Jones, General David Petraeus, Ryan Crocker, Mark Lyall Grant, Zalmay Khalilzad, Khalid Alireza, Brent Scowcroft, Steve Hadley, Lakhdar Brahimi, Dominique de Villepin, Bahaa Hariri, Shuja Nawaz, Eisa Al-Eisa, Mohammed Al Shrooghi, Mir Shakil-ur-Rehman, Adil Mandil, Abdulrahman Bin Mahfouz, Christina Rocca, Sheikh Nahyan bin Mubarak Al Nahyan, Ray Mahmood, Zheng Bijan, Lord Norman Lamont, Ian Scott, Mir Ibrahim Rehman, Mohsin Baig, Jack Straw, Farhan Sharaff, Tariq Malik, Zubaid Ahmed, George Kanaan, Bashir Ahmad, Dr Ashraf Chohan, Richard Huber, Brigadier Irfan Azam, Lt. General Nadeem Taj, Arif Naqvi, Raza Jaffer, and many others from all over the world.

I started thinking about writing a book recounting my experiences as soon as I left office. I wanted to share with the rest of the world what I went through, what we achieved, the challenges we faced and to share with the world insights on Pakistan. It was a momentous task which was much more challenging and complex than I had imagined. However, it was a great learning experience and gave me the opportunity to reflect and get my thoughts together.

My good friend Richard Thoburn helped me formulate a plan. I consulted many others, including Fred Kempe at the Atlantic Council, Stephen P. Cohen at Brookings, Shahzad Husain, Tariq Azeem, Lt General Nazir Butt, Major General Dr Azhar Kiani, Riaz Khokar, Riaz Mohammed Khan,

Munir Akram, Zamir Akram, Wajid Rana, Khalid Saeed, Tanwir Ali Agha, Abdullah Yusuf, Naweed Ahsan, Zafar Mahmood, Malik Mushtaq, Dr Ashfaque Hasan Khan, Dr Salman Shah, Tariq Malik, Farhan Sharaff, Zubaid Ahmed and many more.

Several people were encouraging and helpful: Asif Mahmood, Zafar Malik, Chico Jehanghir, Hasan Shirazi, Asim Abdullah, Dr. Nasim Ashraf, General Ehsan Ul Haq, Wajid Shamshul Hasan, Shuaib Ahmed, Ghouse Akbar, Sultan Allana, Raza Jaffar, Imran Khan, Shujaat Azeem, Sir Anwar Pervez, Arif Naqvi, Jimmy Engineer, and Farooq Shaikh.

My daughter Maha helped with the editing and advised me on the content and layout. Anna Stothard did a great job putting the book in shape and Naim Attallah, the chairman of Quartet, provided us all with the encouragement to keep going. Jane McMillan, my private secretary, worked very hard to get all the photographs together and coordinate their layout. Jane has been deeply involved in the on-going logistics, meetings and travel to meet with various world leaders related to the book. She has been a key player from start to finish.

After growing up in Garden Road, Karachi, followed by Rawalpindi, I had just one employer – Citibank – for thirty years before joining the government of Pakistan. I have lived in ten countries and travelled to over a hundred, giving me a global perspective, which I have tried to share with the reader.

This book is dedicated to the people of Pakistan, my parents, my wife Rukhsana and my children, Lubna, Abid and Maha.

CHAPTER NOTES

INTRODUCTION: THE PHONE CALL

1. Population Census Organisation & Planning Commission, 1999 population census

A TALE OF TWO COUPS

1. Riaz M. Khan, *Afghanistan and Pakistan: Conflict, Extremism and Resistance to Modernity* (Johns Hopkins University Press, 2011), 305-6
2. Ibid. 317
3. Benazir Bhutto, *Daughter of Destiny* (Harper Perennial, 2008), 122-3
4. *Handbook of South Asian Politics* (Routledge, 2010)
5. Khan, *Afghanistan and Pakistan*, 304
6. Ibid. 312
7. Ibid. 309

UNDER ATTACK

1. Population Census Organisation & Planning Commission
2. Khan, *Afghanistan and Pakistan*, 210
3. Interview with Mark Lyall Grant in London, 2013
4. Khan, *Afghanistan and Pakistan*, 310
5. Ibid. 236
6. Off-the-record interview with former Pakistan intelligence officer, 2015
7. Interview with General Petraeus in New York, 2014
8. Pakistan demographics profile, *Index Mundi* (June 2015)

9. UNESCO Education for All Global Monitoring Report (2012)
10. Umair Khalil, *The Madrasa Conundrum — The state of religious education in Pakistan* (HIVE, 2015)

BIN LADEN: WHO KNEW WHAT?

1. Interview with General Jones in Washington, December 2013. Previous reports had claimed the discovery was made in August 2010 while the United States was helping in the 2010 flood relief effort.
2. Interview with General Jones in Washington, December 2013.
3. Interview with General Petraeus in New York, 2014
4. 'American Held in Pakistan Worked with CIA', *The New York Times* (21 February 2011)
5. 'President Asif Ali Zardari and President Hamid Karzai visited Washington', *The New York Times* (5 May 2009)
6. 'Academy distance was 1km "in a straight line"', in *The Abbottabad Commission Report* (2013)
7. *The Abbottabad Commission Report*
8. Children count according to Carlotta Gall, *The Wrong Enemy* (Houghton Mifflin, 2014)
9. *The Abbottabad Commission Report*
10. Ibid.
11. Ibid.
12. Interview with General Petraeus in New York, 2014
13. *The Abbottabad Commission Report*
14. India was 'in effect considered the only major threat to Pakistan's security, according to *The Abbottabad Commission Report*
15. Interview with former senior Pakistan Intelligence Officer, 2015
16. Nicholas Schmidle, 'Getting Bin Laden', *The New Yorker* (8 August 2011)
17. *The Abbottabad Commission Report*
18. Ibid.
19. Schmidle, 'Getting Bin Laden'
20. *The Abbottabad Commission Report*
21. Interview with Christina Rocca in Washington, 2014
22. Interview with Brent Scowcroft in Washington, 2014

23. 'Pakistan Military Asks US to Cut Number of CIA Operatives', *DAWN* (11 April 2011)

AMERICA'S TRANSACTIONAL RELATIONSHIP

1. Khan, *Afghanistan and Pakistan*, 82
2. Interview with Richard Armitage in Washington, 2014
3. Ibid.
4. Pervez Musharraf, *In the Line of Fire* (Free Press, 2006) 206
5. Conversation with Christina Rocca, 2014
6. Ahmed Rashid, *Descent into Chaos* (Non Basic Stock Line, 2009) 86
7. NSA archives, quoted in Daniel Markey, *No Exit From Pakistan* (Cambridge, 2013) 112
8. UN: www.un.org/millenniumgoals/
9. John B. Taylor, *Global Financial Warriors: The Untold Story of International Finance in the Post 9/11 World* (W. W. Norton & Company, 2007) 17
10. Interviews with Christina Rocca in 2013 and Rich Armitage in 2014
11. Taylor, *Global Financial Warriors*, 32
12. US Government Accountability Office, gao.gov
13. Interview with Steve Hadley in Washington, 2013
14. Interview with Richard Armitage in Washington, 2014
15. United Nations Refugee Agency, 2015 Pakistan country profile
16. SIPRI Arms Transfer Database, sipri.org
17. Interview with Nicholas Burns in Boston, 2014
18. '"Will I be Next?" US Drone Strikes in Pakistan', Amnesty International Publications, 2013
19. Khan, *Afghanistan and Pakistan*, 159

FIGHTING OUR ALLIES IN AFGHANISTAN

1. Interview with Mark Malloch Brown in London, 2013
2. Ibid.
3. Off the record interview with former senior UN official, 2013
4. Interview with General Jones in Washington, December 2013
5. Khan, *Afghanistan and Pakistan*, 56

6. Ibid. 57
7. Interview with Lakhdar Brahimi in Paris, 2014
8. Conversation with Ryan Crocker, August 2014
9. Interview with Donald Rumsfeld, 2014
10. Christina Lamb, *Farewell Kabul*, (William Collins, 2015) 8-9
11. Shaukat Aziz speech to peace *jirga*, 2007
12. Interview with Lakhdar Brahimi in Paris, 2014
13. World Bank, latest available data, from 2014
14. World Bank, latest available data, from 2011
15. Conversation with Ashraf Ghani, 2014
16. United Nations Refugee Agency, 2015 Pakistan country profile
17. 'Pakistani Taliban "No 2" Captured in Afghanistan', *DAWN*, 11 October 2013
18. Interview with Zalmay Khalilzad in Washington, 2014
19. Anatol Lievin, 'Afghanistan: the war after the war', *New York Review of Books* (July 2013)
20. United Nations Refugee Agency, 2015 Pakistan country profile
21. Interview with Ashraf Ghani, London, 2014

GADDAFI'S SURPRISE

1. Interview with Kofi Annan, Geneva, 2014
2. Transcripts published by the House of Commons Select Committee, 7 January 2016
3. Interview with Dominique de Villepin in Paris, 2014
4. Interview with Alain Minc in Paris, 2014

THE COLD WAR ON TERROR

1. Interview with Donald Rumsfeld, 2014
2. Interview with Tony Blair in London, 2014
3. www.britishpakistanfoundation.com
4. Off the record interview with former US State Department official, Washington DC, 2014
5. 'The Islamic State', *Council on Foreign Relations Backgrounders*, 3 March 2016

6. United Nations Refugee Agency, 2015 Pakistan country profile
7. Interview with Herman van Rompuy in Brussels, 2015
8. The International Centre for the Study of Radicalisation and Political Violence, icsr.info, 26 January 2015
9. As reported in *Die Welt* in February 2016
10. Dr Evin Marie Saltman and Charlie Winter, *Islamic State: The Changing Face of Modern Jihadism* (Quilliam Foundation, November 2014)
11. Interview with Dr Mahathir in Kuala Lumpur, 2014
12. Interview with Kofi Annan in Geneva, 2014
13. Ibid.
14. Interview with Jack Straw in London, 2014
15. Saltman and Winter, *Islamic State: The Changing Face of Modern Jihadism*

NUCLEAR PEACE WITH INDIA

1. 'PM Modi's "nuisance" remarks in Bangladesh "unfortunate", Pakistan says', *Times of India*, 9 June 2015
2. Khan, *Afghanistan and Pakistan*, 160
3. Off-the-record interview with senior British diplomat, 2014
4. 'Pakistan expresses concern over Manohar Parrikar's remarks on terrorism', *The Indian Express* (23 May 2015)
5. Shashank Joshi, 'Pakistan's Tactical Nuclear Nightmare: Deja Vu?' *The Washington Quarterly* (Summer 2013)
6. Colonel Ali Ahmed (Retd.), 'Cold Start and the Sehjra Option', The Institute for Defence Studies and Analyses (October 2010)
7. Wikileaks
8. Arms Transfer Database, Stockholm International Peace Research Institute, sipri.org
9. Joshi, 'Pakistan's Tactical Nuclear Nightmare: Deja Vu?'
10. General Khalid Kidwai speech at the Carnegie Endowment For International Peace, 2015
11. Ibid.
12. Jack Straw, *Last Man Standing* (Macmillan, 2012), 354
13. Former Indian army officials quoted in Nayak and Krepon, *US Crisis Management in South Asia's Twin Peaks Crisis* (The Henry L Stimson Center, September 2006)

14. '12 Million Could Die at Once in an India-Pakistan Nuclear War', *The New York Times*, 27 May 2002

15. Off-the-record interview with US State Department official, 2014

16. Interview with Steve Hadley in Washington, December 2013

17. 'US Exploring Deal to Limit Pakistan's Nuclear Arsenal', *The New York Times*, 15 October 2015

18. Stephen P Cohen, *Shooting for a Century* (Brookings Institution, 2013), 4

19. Shaukat Aziz speech to AJK council, February 2007

20. World Bank Regional Integration in South Asia, 3 October 2015

21. Interview with Tony Blair in London, 2014

22. Interview with Jack Straw in London, 2014

23. Interview with Clare Short in London, 2015

TURNING THE ECONOMY AROUND

1. The World Bank databank

2. Pakistan's Economy1999/2000 – 2007/2008, Institute of Business Administration

3. Off-the-record interview with former IMF board member, 2014

4. Interview with James Wolfensohn, 2015

5. Pakistan's Economy1999/2000 – 2007/2008, Institute of Business Administration

6. Interview with Jill Dauchy in London, 2014

7. IMF website – List of Countries That Have Qualified for, are Eligible or Potentially Eligible and May Wish to Receive HIPC Initiative Assistance (as of September 2014)

8. Interview with Jill Dauchy in London, 2014. The team was headed by Derrill Allatt, who went on to form New State Partners which continues to advise governments.

9. Ibid.

10. Pakistan's Economy 1999/2000 – 2007/2008, Institute of Business Administration

11. Interview with Jill Dauchy in London, 2014

12. International Monetary Fund country report, 2007

13. Pakistan Economic Survey 2006-2007, Ministry of Finance

14. Transparency International, Corruption by Country Index, January 2016
15. Shaukat Aziz speech at Credit Suisse conference, 2007
16. First Quarterly Report of the State Bank of Pakistan for the year 2015-16
17. Interview with Clare Short in London, 2015
18. Household final consumption expenditure per capita (constant 2005 US$), World Bank
19. Interview with Masood Ahmed in Washington, December 2013
20. State Bank of Pakistan data
21. Pakistan's Economy 1999/2000 – 2007/2008, Institute of Business Administration
22. Interview with Masood Ahmed in Washington, December 2013

WALL STREET: THE WORLD'S BEST SCHOOL FOR POLITICS

1. Interview with John Reed in Boston, 2014
2. Interview with Sandy Weill in New York, 2014
3. Interview with John Reed in Boston, 2014
4. Interview with Richard Huber in New York, 2014
5. Interview with Jamie Dimon in New York, 2014
6. Andrew Ross Sorkin, *Too Big to Fail* (Penguin, 2010), 75
7. Interview with John Reed in Boston, 2014
8. Sorkin, *Too Big to Fail*
9. Financial Crisis Inquiry Commission Report, January 2011, p xix
10. Memorandum from Michael O'Neill, February 2016

GROWING CITIBANK IN SAUDI ARABIA

1. United Nations Refugee Agency, 2015 UNHCR country profile for Jordan

AMERICA'S BACK CHANNEL WITH IRAN

1. Interview with Kofi Annan in Geneva, 2014
2. Interview with Mark Malloch Brown in London, 2013
3. Interview with Norman Lamont in London, 2014

'THE LION OF CHINA IS AWAKE'

1. US Department of State archives
2. Henry Kissinger, *On China* (Penguin, 2011), 23
3. Interview with Henry Kissinger in New York, 2014
4. Kissinger, *On China*, 500
5. Interview with Nicholas Burns in Boston, 2014
6. Pepe Escobar, 'Pakistan enters the New Silk Road', *Asia Times* (April 2015)
7. Jane Perlez, 'Xi Jinping Heads to Pakistan, Bearing Billions in Infrastructure Aid', *The New York Times*, April 2015
8. Statement by Ahsan Iqbal, Pakistan's minister for planning and development
9. Perlez, 'Xi Jinping Heads to Pakistan'
10. Escobar, 'Pakistan enters the New Silk Road'
11. Mohan Guruswamy, 'The China Factor'. In Stephen P Cohen (ed.) *The Future of Pakistan* (Brookings Institution, November 2011)
12. 'Corridor of Power', *The Economist* (April 2015)
13. Perlez, 'Xi Jinping Heads to Pakistan'
14. Kissinger, *On China*, 488-9
15. Ibid. 23
16. Guruswamy, 'The China Factor'
17. Ibid.

BENAZIR'S RETURN

1. Interview with Norman Lamont in London, 2013
2. Meeting with Ray Mahmood in Washington, 2013
3. Off-the-record interview with former US State Department official, 2013

4. Ibid.
5. Condoleezza Rice, *No Higher Honor* (Broadway Books, 2011), 608
6. George W. Bush, *Decision Points* (Virgin, 2010), 216
7. Conversation with Ryan Crocker, 2014
8. Interview with senior Pakistani official, 2015
9. Conversation with Richard Boucher in 2014
10. Interview with senior Pakistani official, 2015
11. Interview with Mark Lyall Grant in New York, 2013
12. Interview with senior Pakistani official, 2015
13. Rice, *No Higher Honor*
14. Ibid. 624

LESSONS IN GOVERNANCE

1. 'Delivering as One' UN report (2006)

THE WAY FORWARD

1. Speech at Islamic College for Women, 25 March 1940

INDEX

INDEX

INDEX

INDEX